WORSHIP THE FIRST-CENTURY WAY

One of a Two-Book Series

WANDERING SOUL, ENTITLED HEART, AND THE SIDE-TRACKED CHURCH

By K. M. Haddad

Other Books by the Author

CHRISTIAN LIFE
Applied Christianity: Handbook 500 Good Works
You Can Be a Hero Alone
Worship Changes Since 1st Century + Worship 1sr Century Way
The Best of Alexander Campbell's Millennial Harbinger
Inside the Hearts of Bible Women-Reader+Audio+Leader
The Lord's Supper: 52 Readings with Prayers

BIBLE TEXTS
Revelation: A Love Letter From God
The Holy Spirit: 592 Verses Examined
Was Jesus God? (Why Evil)
365 Life-Changing Scriptures Day by Date
Love Letters of Jesus & His Bride, Ecclesia (Song of Solomon)
Christianity or Islam? The Contrast
The Road to Heaven

FUN BOOKS
Bible Puzzles, Bible Song Book, Bible Numbers

TOUCHING GOD SERIES
365 Golden Bible Thoughts: God's Heart to Yours
365 Pearls of Wisdom: God's Soul to Yours
365 Silver-Winged Prayers: Your Spirit to God's

SURVEY SERIES: EASY BIBLE WORKBOOKS
→Old Testament & New Testament Surveys
→Questions You Have Asked-Part I & II

HISTORICAL RESEARCH BIBLE
for Novel, Screenwriter, Documentary & Thesis Writers

HISTORICAL NOVELS & STORYBOOKS
Series of 8: They Met Jesus
Ongoing Series of 8: Intrepid Men of God
Mysteries of the Empire with Klaudius & Hektor
Christmas: They Rocked the Cradle that Rocked the World
Series of 8: A Child's Life of Christ
Series of 10: A Child's Bible Heroes
Series of 8: A Child's Bible Kids
Series of 10: A Child's Bible Ladies

GENEALOGY: Climb Your Family Tree w/o Falling Out
Volume I & 2: Beginner-Intermediate & Colonial-Medieval

Copyright ⓢ 2014 Katheryn Maddox Haddad
ISBN-978-1-948462-98-3
NORTHERN LIGHTS PUBLISHING HOUSE

Printed in the United States

In Praise Of
WORSHIP THE FIRST-CENTURY WAY

* * * * * JEWEL TAYLOR. Great Read.

* * * * JUSTIN SPEER. Haddad's book "Worship the First Century Way" is well timed in the context of significant confusion within the Christian religion. Confusion of focus and practice have crept into the assembly, and Haddad works to "uncover the mask" of the motives at play. Even an outside observer can see that the religious confusion has led to much unnecessary division throughout the centuries. The author points out that this friction has led many to question the relevance of worship and Christianity in their lives. Elaborating on what the inspired Word of God presents concerning Christian worship, Haddad weaves this into a story that gently corrects religious worship practices that have no basis in the traditions handed down from Christ to the apostles to us in the Bible. Many may be surprised to learn that worship practices that they assumed had always been in place are actually quite recent in their invention (and often contradict what was authorized by the Bible). She also goes well beyond the perfunctory elements of worship to explore the reasons and, perhaps more importantly, the foundation of such practice in the Bible.

Haddad also provides historical accounts of how second generation Christians worshipped, providing yet another template for us to examine since many of these individuals literally walked with the men and women who walked with Jesus (including the apostles).

Haddad's book drives home why we go to church, but also stresses that Christianity isn't an inactive, passive state of being. She rightly points out that our neighbors view Christianity as boring. They see Christians 1. Going to a building; 2. Listening, 3. Talking, 4. Going home. If this is all Christians do, then it is boring.

Her work incorporates very practical, loving ideas to promote a more intimate relationship with neighbors in the community, with Christians in fellowship and with God. This is perhaps the greatest contribution the author makes in exploring this important, relevant subject.

I encourage Christians of all maturities to take the time to read this book

* * * * * AMAZON CUSTOMER. The most important thing I learned from this book is the difference in reforming the church and restoring the church. The Reformation period was an effort to reform the Catholic church, what they should have been striving for restoring the First Century church.

I also learned that many people leave the church out of loneliness. After reading this I will make a greater effort to make contact with visitors and members outside of my circle of friends.

TABLE OF CONTENTS

DEDICATION

Dedicated to all people everywhere who want to go
FORWARD — BACK
to the Bible.
If we all did that, we would once again have
Christianity unity.

1. DARE-TO-CARE WORSHIP

Pride goes before destruction,
A haughty spirit before a fall.
Proverbs 16:18

In 2010, a Harris Poll revealed only 26% of Americans attend religious services every week. Which countries are worse than the US? Canada listed 20%, Austria 18%. Belgium 7%, France 12%, Hungary 12%, Latvia 7%, United Kingdom 12% attending religious services every week.[1]

What if church attendance was required? During the reigns of Edward VI and Elizabeth I in England, church attendance was required. But religious leaders often complained about the rudeness of congregations during worship "whilst those that did not attend would go to public houses or be watching cockfighting [or other games]." This was a regular occurrence despite the fact that non-attendance was punished with a shilling fine per week.[2]

According to *Open Doors* (an organization that helps get Bibles to restricted countries and helps persecuted congregations) today, whereas western nations used to send missionaries to South America, Africa, and Asia, now they are beginning to send missionaries to western nations where they are planting churches. These are nations whose people have experienced hardships unknown in western nations. But they grew and western congregations did not.

No Atheists in Foxholes

We can learn indirectly that, during World War I, church attendance was fairly high. That's because the *Literary Digest* reported "Male Church Attendance Dropped in the Twenties." By 1929, only one male out of every nine attended Sunday services with any regularity.[3]

Then it rose again during World War II as reported in 1942. "Two years ago, most churches were considered fortunate if forty-five people attended the morning services; today devout worshipers fill the pews morning and night."[4]

In 1991, the *Los Angeles Times* reported that church attendance grew during the Gulf War.[5]

Jason Hansman, Director of Member Services with Iraq and Afghanistan Veterans of America said that veterans frequently turn to faith-based communities as a bridge between combat and civilian life. In fact, a 2011 Pew Forum survey found that faith increases the chances of a veteran readjusting more easily.[6]

How long-lasting is the devotion of veterans to their Christianity? In 2013, Professor John S. Dyson of Cornel University, and Craig Wansink, Professor at Virginia Wesleyan College, revealed results of their survey of 1,123 veterans of World War II. Prayer during combat rose from 42% to 72% on average. Those who remained or became religious after returning to civilian life were those who had experienced heavy combat and disliked war.

Fifty years after combat, many of these same veterans were still loyal to and participating actively with the church. This loyalty to the church was attributed to the powerful commitment between comrades in their units that carried through in civilian life.[7]

As shown in the other book of this series, *Worship Changes Since the First Century*, the persecuted church standing up for right has always had much in common with "persecuted" individuals standing up for right. Their Christianity always grew. When hardships and persecutions ceased to exist, entire congregations gradually ceased to exist or became rather "worldly" as they tried to attract the less spiritually-minded.

What type of Christianity do both men and women prefer? *Christian Century* reported that those serious about their Christianity tend to prefer organizations that are demanding on their personal life for change and growth. One man interviewed said he was "sick of bourgeois, feel-good American Christianity."[8]

Lord, God. Give us the stout-hearted. The truth defenders. The self-sacrificers. Jesus, help us be like You.

Demanding God's Gifts in an Age of Entitlement

I will ascend above the tops of the clouds.
I will make myself like the Most High
Isaiah 14:14 (NKJV)

Has our present society lifted itself up above God to the degree that everyone is sure of invading heaven and even being welcomed into heaven, despite never having had much time for God in this life here on earth? Has our society lifted itself up above God to the degree that we are now telling God what to do? Are people basically saying, "God, you'd better take me into heaven, or I will deny you exist, because God is supposed to be good"?

Because you say, 'I am a god, I sit in the seat of gods...'
Yet you are a man, and not a god.
Ezekiel 28:2b (NKJV)

Does this present society even want God? Well, probably. But the more it makes itself god, the more it creates its own gods. This present society is head-over-heels in love with its media superheroes — men in capes and other-world aliens — gods they can control to do what they want.

Although those born and raised during the 1980s and 1990s are often called the Entitlement Generation, we must also include parents. This younger generation didn't raise itself. It seems that most generations in our society today feel entitled. Entitled to things now, entitled to mansions in heaven later.

By your great wisdom in trade
You have increased your riches,
And your heart is lifted up
Because of your riches.
Ezekiel 28:5 (NKJV)

Some of the studies explained below are of young people,

but we cannot claim the youngest part of society originated entitlement.

An Inventory of Narcissistic Personality given to over 14,000 university students reported in 2006 that over 65% of the students fit into the narcissistic category.[9]

A report made public in 2013 by the American Freshman Survey covering roughly nine million students over 50 years revealed that "egotism and a sense of entitlement among college students is at an all-time high, even though their actual abilities as assessed on objective aptitude screenings are on the decline."[10]

More and more at the end of the school year, every player on a team "won" a trophy. Instead of just one "student a month", there were many. Teachers inflated grades so no one would fail, and the "C" became the new "F".

In "Practical Family Living: Entitlement, Money and Families" it found, "Children growing up with few resources can feel deprived and that others owe them things....They may feel the pain of their upbringing justifies their feelings of entitlement. Children growing up with plentiful resources can grow up believing that whatever they want, they deserve. Sometimes this is because they have not had to work for or sacrifice anything in order to receive material things or money. "[11]

What is the attitude of entitlement people toward God? "As long as I don't murder someone, Jesus will feel obligated to save me from hell." "As long as I pray sometimes, God will feel obligated to take me into his home, heaven." "Even though I don't have time for God, he will make time for me." "Even though I don't think God is very important, God must surely think I am important." "Even though I think it's rather boring to adore God at a worship service, God surely does not think I am boring!"

What does all this have to do with loneliness? People who feel they never have enough, never can do enough, never can be handsome or beautiful enough, have centered their lives on themselves. It is a lonely life being centered on oneself.

Dear God, we praise you, adore you, and worship you. Your majesty is all power and all nobility. You wear the universe as your robe, the stars as your crown. You sit on the throne of eternity. We love to sing your praises. It's such an exciting time!

The Neverwents and the Dropouts

Murray dropped out of his denomination as a teenager. Later he went back because of his kids. He chose a congregation that did not have rigid guidelines and wasn't always asking for money.

Would Murray feel comfortable in our congregation? Would he learn that the few rules our loving heavenly Father has for us are just as much to help his holy household as Murray's rules for his own household? Or would he find multitudinous regulations as set forth in the creeds, the synods, and church politics?

Alicia never did go to church; her husband did, but stopped when grown. She basically believes organized religion interferes with people's lives. She has questions about the meaning of life, but forces them into the recesses of her mind.

Would Alicia feel comfortable in our congregation? Would she find services that reflected both interest in and care for what happens to the members in their everyday life and in their hereafter? Or would she find it impersonal with only a few up front doing the officiating and performing?

Dylan says he is Catholic although neither he nor his parents ever attended. He feels the church won't let people do what is best for their own lives and is materialistic. He prays sometimes and is curious about what in the Bible could possibly get some people so interested in it.

Would Dylan feel comfortable in our congregation? Would he find tithing sermons, pledge cards in the pews, fund-raising thermometers on the walls, bake sales in the lobbies? Would he find a church where the Bible is never referred to except an isolated verse here and there from who knows where?

Mary Ann grew up in an active denominational church

family but now only occasionally goes church hopping, searching for a church interested in solving people's problems and in providing her with a deep sense of spirituality she cannot get alone.

Would Mary Ann feel comfortable in our congregation? Are people with needs mentioned in the bulletin, in announcements, in prayers, in sign-up sheets in the lobby? Is the worship full of performances that she is expected to appreciate but which she could never feel qualified to be a part of?

Sam grew up Jewish, and finds church formalistic, narrow and limiting. He considers creeds divisive of the religious world. He longs for the spiritualistic, so searches for it through world religions and time spent alone contemplating what it might be.

Would Sam feel comfortable in our congregation? Are parts of the denomination's creed written in the backs of songbooks or up on the wall? When a particular form of worship is begun, is its inclusion in the service explained intelligently from the Bible only? Would he feel as though he really touched the heart and soul of God, and the love and devotion of the members after visiting just one time?

This survey was related in the book *A Generation of Seekers: The Spiritual Journeys of the Baby Boom Generation* by Wade Clark Roof.[12] Isn't it interesting that in his survey no one complained that the entertainment was not as good as TV or the building was not as grand as an opera house or Madison Square Gardens? They all complained about relationships they were not getting in worship.

Oh, God, we didn't realize. The visitors and dropouts never told us what they were really thinking. Perhaps we never gave them a chance.

Lonely At the Top

It is lonely at the top. As long as we consider ourselves entitled to even things we did not work for, did not struggle for, we will carry our burdens alone, sometimes even hiding them from ourselves.

In *The Narcissism Epidemic: Living in the Age of Entitlement*, Jean M. Twenge and W. Keith Campbell said the sense of entitlement that so many of us has shows itself in bigger houses, increased plastic surgery, out-of-control credit card debt, among other things. [13]

In "Entitlement, Money and Families", it states, **"A rigid sense of entitlement can feed a strong sense of self-centeredness and narcissism. This rigidity can lead to the closing off of the heart and pride. Pride does not promote care, compassion and connection. Pride leads to isolation and intense loneliness.**[14]

Whether or not they admit it, people everywhere feel isolated from others who really care about them. They don't feel as though they belong; and if they did, they're not sure they want to belong. So, they stand aloof with an outward shell of being self-sufficient. But only outwardly. And behind the shell. An unknown author wrote this:

> *There is so much of loneliness*
> *On this uncharted earth*
> *It seems each one's an outcast*
> *Overlooked from birth.*
> *There is such need for union,*
> *Such need for clasping hands,*
> *Yet we deny the brotherhood*
> *The human heart demands.*

Loneliness has always been with us. The first problem of Adam was not disobedience. It was loneliness. Humans have suffered from loneliness since.

Pioneer psychologist Eric Fromm declared the most basic fear of every human is a dread of being separated from other humans. It is first encountered in infancy. It is the source of anxiety until death. Separation and interpersonal loss are at the roots of the human experiences of fear, sadness, and sorrow.

Clarence Macartney, a Presbyterian minister, in a previous generation, described loneliness in a crowded city by saying, "You could lie down on the sidewalk and breathe your last, and not a heart among all those thousands of hearts would beat more rapidly, and not an eye would be suffused with tears."

In *Look Homeward Angel,* Thomas Wolfe says, "Naked and alone we came...into her womb ....from there we have come into the unspeakable and incommunicable...earth ....Which of us is not forever a stranger and alone?"[15]

Possibly the most desolate description of loneliness was given in the book, *How Green Was My Valley* by Richard Llewellyn: "A man is a coward in space, for he is by himself, and if you feel you are lone, with not even yourself, that is fright for you. I wonder where the real You goes to when you are strange like that."[16]

Over one-fourth of American adults reported they had felt extremely lonely at least once within the previous two weeks. This was referred to by Dan McAdams in his book, *Intimacy: The Need to be Close* as reported over thirty years ago.[17]

What is it like now?

In an article entitled "All Alone," in *Ladies Home Journal,* 1991, Margery Rosen quoted Anne Peplau as saying, "At any given time, at least ten percent of the population feels lonely."[18] In 2013, studies revealed people on Facebook feel more lonely after going offline.

Why today? One of the main reasons is because half America's population moves residences within a typical ten-year period.

Vickie Kraft in her book, *The Influential Woman,* said, "Our mobility has made us rootless. It is difficult to sustain intensive friendships when forty million of us move every year. These facts encourage shallow personal relationships. Consequently, there is a pervasive loneliness eating away at the deep inner core of millions of people."[19]

There are still other reasons, reasons of our own making. In the book, *The Day America Told the Truth,* Peter Kim and James Patterson reported that 50% of Americans said they'd never spent an evening with the people next door, 25% said they'd never been in their neighbor's house, and 20% said they didn't even know their name.[20]

We add more and more activities to our day in an effort to alleviate our loneliness. This same survey revealed that adults watch an average of 24 to 41 hours of television every week, more than teens and children. But all we do is get more and more lonely.

God, we know there are lonely people out there. But how are we supposed to know who they are? Help us understand.

Even Within the Church

The book, *Building People Through a Caring Sharing Fellowship* by Donald L. Bubna and Sarah Ricketts, begins with this account of one of their "active members."

"I want to withdraw my membership from the church. I have been living a lie, and I can't continue to hide it....I have discovered I don't believe in Christianity as a valid philosophy of life. Therefore, I can't remain a member of this church. I can't pretend any longer."[21]

James Thompson, in his book, *Our Life Together: A Fresh Look at Christian Fellowship*, explains that a few years ago some congregations allowed themselves to be analyzed by a specialist studying how groups work together. The response? "The great majority of church members had to admit that they knew a very small percentage of the people. Those who gathered for worship on Sunday were an anonymous group of worshipers."

Many go to church as they would go to the movie theater, the author concluded.[22]

Admittedly, in our day everyone seems to be time-poor. We rush, rush everywhere. We don't have time for Christian fellowship. An hour or two on Sunday is all we feel we have time for, and even then, once a month or less.

Some people purposely avoid getting intimate with the members because it only means heartache when they have to move on. Who could fault them for trying to protect their hearts?

Others would like to get intimate, but the worship is not conducive to it. In fact, the only reason many attend church is to make sure they "get saved;" that is, to make sure God feels obligated to take them to heaven when they die. But they would never invite their friends to attend with them. Maybe they would a civic club meeting, but not a meeting of the church. The visitor would be even more bored than the member. Or, if the church offered entertainment, once that was over, their questions about the loneliness of life would remain hidden.

In the first-century Church, "Within the Christian community there was a sense of warmth: Someone was interested in them both here and hereafter. Here the stranger found a place where the people were 'members of one another!' It is no wonder that the church enjoyed such growth. There was no other community quite like it. The fellowship of the church meant far more than inviting one's close friends to a social gathering; it meant providing a little warmth to people who wanted to belong....The church can minister to loneliness and uprootedness."[23]

Although people today feel they do not have time for functions outside the Sunday morning worship, their needs can be met right then. We do not have to wait for a separate period of fellowship to accomplish this.

The first-century church certainly did not flourish because the twelve apostles were an impressive group of leaders with their MBAs or degrees in theology. It did not grow because of their superior organizational skills or the talents of its members.

It grew because of an active sense of family. It started with Jesus and grew like wildfire. One day "he looked at those seated in a circle around him and said, 'Here are my mother and my brothers!'" (Mark 3:34). Indeed, it caught on with the apostles, for one of them announced all believers in Christ were "brothers" (1 Peter 2:17).[24]

Although Jesus' sacrifice and forgiveness was the power, caring for each other was the essential ingredient that kept the Christians together and drew others into them. Jesus said, "By this all men will know that you are my disciples, if you love one another" (John 13:35).

Do we show our love for each other by holding an important position in the church where we're seen a lot? Jesus said to be the most important we must become everyone's servant (Luke 22:24-27). That means that, if one member suffers, we all suffer; and if one member rejoices, we all rejoice (1 Corinthians 12:26). That means bearing one another's burdens (Galatians 6:2). That means receiving our weak brothers (Romans 14:1). That means strengthening each other's feeble arms and weak knees, and helping to make life's paths more level (Hebrews 12:12-13).

How are we to do this if our worship services are full of formalism or emotionalism and people always in charge of other people? Not only have we created a clergy system, but we now have a clergy auxiliary system — all the chairmen and performers. And we will move heaven and earth to protect our system that continually magnifies the leaders, and demands respect by the rest of the congregation — albeit "in the name of the Lord."

Do we claim Christian worship is impossible without all the highly-qualified leaders? That is not necessarily so.

Paul said over and over in 1st Corinthians 14 that what we do in our worship services is to edify each other. This is not an "if we want to" type of thing. This is not an "if we have time" type of thing. This is a command. Is our congregation doing it?

As Thompson explains, "Our Christianity was never meant to be lived alone." The first-century church took its inter-relationships very seriously. They did not view "going to church" as just something to enhance their own relationship with Jesus.

The writer of Hebrews said the purpose of our worship services was to stir up one another. To emotionalism? To legalism? To admiration for people? No. Hebrews said we are to stir up each other to love and good works (Hebrews 10:24-25).

Apparently when this was written, many Christians had quit going to church. Apparently they had gotten bored because the worship was not relative to their lives. Hebrews 13:16 says we are to "not forget to do good and to share with others, for with such sacrifices God is pleased."

If our worship services are designed strictly to "get more faith," maybe we're missing the boat. Jesus' brother in James 2:17-19 said, "In the same way, faith by itself, if it is not accompanied by action, is dead....You believe that there is one God. Good! Even the demons believe that — and shudder."

Thompson concludes, "As long as the church is incapable

of caring for the sufferer, it has not broken through to establish real fellowship."25

Dr. Frederic Flach concluded in his *Secret Strength of Depression* that more and more as each year passes, loneliness is being manifest in our society through casual sex, drive for success, and suicide.

Oh, God. All this time I thought I was helping the church. They said my talents were needed to glorify God. But, if people are truly going away lonely, what am I doing wrong?

Symptoms of Hidden Loneliness

Casual Sex Emphasis

Dr. Flach related, "The growing demand for intimacy and sexual fulfillment in human relationships [over the past several years], both heterosexual and homosexual, arises in part....the demise of family life, with parents, grandparents, and adolescents all inhabiting their own separate worlds.

"In spite of crowdedness, loneliness is epidemic. The average individual feels isolated and alienated, and these feelings reinforce the need for, and challenge of, intimacy.

"....profound depersonalization fostered by this culture.... with millions of people the computer has helped to feel like things....The social scientists aptly describe this as a marketing society...more than a little disquieting to hear people discussed statistically as if they were items for sale or rent. The individual begins to feel like an object....

"Loneliness and a feeling of being alienated have become common ways of experiencing depression. At the same time, many lonely and depressed people turn to sex as a way of relieving that inner emptiness....yet there is usually a sharp return of depression afterward, when the bogus reassurance wears off."26

In *The Day America Told the Truth*, interviews revealed that "this sexual hunger leads us to places and practices where the Bible and many federal and state laws explicitly tell us not to go. We couldn't care less....At a time when greed is celebrated, it is only fitting that sexual greed in the form of the harem should be popular both for men and women."[27]

The Bible says in Ecclesiastes 2:1-2; 8-11, "I thought in my heart, 'Come now, I will test you with pleasure to find out what is good. But that also proved to be meaningless. 'Laughter,' I said, 'is foolish. And what does pleasure accomplish?....I acquired men and women singers, and a harem as well — the delights of the heart of man....I denied myself nothing my eyes desired; I refused my heart no pleasure.... everything was meaningless, a chasing after the wind; nothing was gained under the sun."

But the Bible does not leave us hopeless. Hosea 8:9-10 says, "They have gone up...wandering alone...sold self to lovers....I will now gather them together."

Do members of our congregation feel so alone that, at some time or another, many of them have gotten involved in illicit affairs, just searching for someone who cares about them? Do our members have an opportunity to share their cares with others every time they come, or are they expected to act "decently and in order"?

How are these lonely people supposed to know the Bible addresses their problem if they don't think anyone in the church cares about them, and neither does God?

Those of you who have attended your congregation for a long time, get out some old directories and note those who no longer attend. Make a note of all the people who left because they got involved in a sexual relationship that was not good for them.

Career Emphasis

I have heard female clerks earning minimum wage during a lull at work tell each other they didn't have to work, but they could never stay home because they had no idea what they would do with their time. They had no confidence they could even think of anything.

Elsewhere in his book, Dr. Flach relates what one career

person told him: "There just wasn't anyone I could talk to. At work I had what I would call working friends, but I couldn't open up to them. We had a veneer of camaraderie, but under the surface there was always the jockeying for better position. Besides, in business you're not supposed to have problems. Everybody does — but if you admit it or show it, you get tagged as unstable....

"And having no one to share feelings with, everything became magnified in my mind. I couldn't get rid of things that kept bothering me or get any perspective. I just kept feeling more and more hopeless about things at home, and about my life in general."[28]

Many people today pursue success in the business world to fill the loneliness. Resulting success finally brings a lot of friends, but they are superficial. Some people's marriage is even based on status, and so it too fails.

Then the loneliness comes crashing in. The loneliness can't even be filled by children, for they were never really close either. The loneliness can't be filled by aging parents because they've become separated and distanced through the process of trying to gain success. The final question: Is the cost for success too much?

Ecclesiastes 2:4-11 and 4:8 says, "I undertook great projects: I built houses for myself and planted vineyards. I made gardens and parks and planted all kinds of fruit trees in them....I amassed silver and gold for myself....I became greater by far than anyone....My heart took delight in all my work, and this was the reward for all my labor. Yet when I surveyed all that my hands had done and what I had toiled to achieve....There was a man all alone; he had neither son nor brother. There was no end to his toil, yet his eyes were not content with his wealth."

But the Bible does not leave us hopeless. Luke 10:40-42a relates, "But Martha was distracted by all the preparations that had to be made. She came to him and asked, 'Lord, don't you care that my sister has left me to do the work by myself? Tell her to help me!' 'Martha, Martha,' the Lord answered, 'you are worried and upset about many things, but only one thing is needed.'"

Do members of our congregation only feel religiously successful if they have some kind of title, thus thrusting them in a control atmosphere? Although we don't say it, is importance measured by title—head of this project, leader of that committee, member of the 'See-How-Holy-I-Can-Look movement? Is our congregation so caught up in success that there is always some program for the improvement of the building, a building that everyone claims is, of course, for the glory of God?

How are these lonely people supposed to know the Bible addresses their problem if they don't think anyone in the church cares about them, and neither does God?

Those of you who have attended your congregation for a long time, get out some old membership directories. Make a note of those who no longer attend because of power pulls or arguments or never being a part of anything.

Suicide Emphasis

After "trying everything," some people come to a dead end and see no hope. They see no answers. They feel completely deserted by the world.

In *The Day America Told the Truth*, it was reported that nearly half the people they interviewed knew someone who had committed suicide, usually someone close to them. One-third of those they interviewed said they had seriously contemplated suicide.[29]

Numbers 11:14 tells about the greatest law-giver in history, Moses, and what he went through: "I cannot carry all these people by myself; the burden is too heavy for me. If this is how you are going to treat me, put me to death right now—if I have found favor in your eyes—and do not let me face my own ruin."

Psalm 102:7-8, 11 tells about King David. "I lie awake; I have become like a bird alone on a roof. All day long my enemies taunt me....My days are like the evening shadow; I wither away like grass."

Ecclesiastes 3:1-8 refers so matter-of-factly—so fatalistically—to things that should be important in our lives, as though there was no use fighting fate. "There is a time for everything, and a season for every activity under heaven: a time to

be born and a time to die....a time to kill and a time to heal....a time
to mourn and a time to dance....a time to search and a time to give
up....a time to love and a time to hate."

In fact in verse 18-21 he says outright that he was thinking
fatalistically. "Man's fate is like that of the animals; the same fate
awaits them both: As one dies, so dies the other. all have the same
breath; man has no advantage over the animal. Everything is
meaningless. All go to the same place; all come from dust, and to
dust all return. Who knows if the spirit of man rises upward and if
the spirit of the animal goes down into the earth?"

But the Bible does not leave us hopeless. The writer of
Ecclesiastes ends his hopelessness this way: "Here is the conclusion
of the matter: Fear God and keep his commandments, for this is the
whole of man" (12:13). When Jesus felt deserted, he said, "The one
who sent me is with me; he has not left me alone....You will leave
me all alone. Yet I am not alone, for my Father is with me" (John
8:29; 16:32).

Do members of our congregation feel that meeting with the
other members is not worth fighting for, resulting in a constant
outflux of members? Over the past ten years, have our members
been committing spiritual suicide by just ceasing to attend church
at all?

How are these lonely people supposed to know the Bible
addresses their problem if they don't think anyone in the church
cares about them, and neither does God?

Those of you who have attended your congregation for a
long time, get out some old membership directories. Make a note
of those who no longer attend, and whose lives have gone down
farther and farther since then.

*God, I thought they were just defying the Bible. I thought I should keep
my distance from people like that. We're doing something wrong, God. What is
it?*

Denials and Coverups

It was reported that, when Rupert Brooke, an English poet,

was boarding a ship to travel from Liverpool to New York, he noticed everyone had friends waving farewell to them. But he had no friends. He looked around and eventually spotted a little urchin nearby.

The poet rushed over to the pauper and asked, "What is your name?" "William" was the reply. "Do you want to earn sixpence, William?" Of course he did. "Then wave to me when the boat goes."

The world is full of people trying to buy their way out of loneliness, and their purchases are only artificial.

Why, then, aren't the churches full of those lonely people? They certainly should be. And could be.

Psalm 142:4 reports, "No man cared for my soul." But we can always have a friend in Jesus can't we? Ecclesiastes 3:11 says that God "has also set eternity in the hearts of men."

Samuel Taylor Coleridge wrote nearly two centuries ago, "So lonely 't was, that God himself scarce seemed there to be" (*The Ancient Mariner*, Part vii).

In the play, *Our Town* by Thornton Wilder, a teenage girl who died was allowed to return to see her family one more time and to watch herself in earlier days with them. When she went into the kitchen of her childhood home, she went up to her mother and began talking to her, but her mother did not even look up. She cried out, "Look at me, Mama! Just look at me!" Then she went over to where her father was reading the newspaper and tried to get his attention. She failed there too, though she pled once more, "Look at me, Papa! Just look at me!"

When people come to our worship services, especially the visitors or those whom members do not know very well, is this their plea? "Look at me, Christians! Just look at me!"

What is the church like to outsiders? What is our congregation like to people in the neighborhood of our building? Do they see people go into a building and come out again and that's all? No one is any different from what anyone else can tell?

Do we even care what outsiders think of us? **Are we afraid outsiders will come in and "change everything"?** Are we putting our egos in front of their eternity? We may pay with our own eternity. What kind of defenses does our congregation set up against intrusion by strangers and change?

How many souls are being saved because our congregation exists and because we worship as we do? We must face it. Can we do it? Do we dare make those lists of all the people our congregation has lost through the years? Do we dare look at each name, each one representing a soul, and cry out to God, "Did we try hard enough? Did we try the right things? Did these souls ever know that everyone in our congregation loved them?"

It might be easier to stay in denial and not make those lists. Facing it may cause a frightening depression.

God, I know people in the community aren't attracted to us. But I thought it was just because they didn't love you as much as we do.

Temporary Congregational Depression

The book, *The Secret Strength of Depression*, offers many suggestions for individuals that could be carried out by congregations because congregations are made up of individuals. Below, whenever this book is quoted, a word referring to congregations will be substituted for individuals.

Chapter two states, "Any event or any change in a [congregation's] life that forces [them] to break down some of these defenses, for whatever reason, is going to be painful. To experience acute depression is an opportunity for a [congregation] not just to learn more about [themselves], but to become more whole than [they were]."[30]

The loss of past members and failure to bring in new ones as they move into our neighborhood is good cause for depression. For our congregation, such a loss is like a death. Are these losses being mourned like they should be? If the loss of members, just like the loss of a personal loved one, is not acknowledged, the problem will come out eventually in a disguised form.

"Not only does depression afford a chance for insight," Dr. Flack continues, "but 'falling apart' can accelerate the process of reordering [a congregation's] life after a serious stress — a loss, for example. Becoming depressed is an inevitable concomitant of letting go—of [people, positions, pieces of our identity]."

A congregation falling apart can be symptomized, not only by loss of members, but also by arguing and spatting. Take time to discover the deeper problem such behavior is reflecting. Why do individual members feel frustrated enough to argue or to quit? Is that hard to do? It's as hard as any individual trying to discover their own faults. We can see others' faults, but it is next to impossible to see our own, as hard as we try. But it can be done in an atmosphere of humility.

Jesus' brother said, "What causes fights and quarrels among you? Don't they come from your desires that battle within you? You want something but don't get it. You kill [reputations?] and covet [positions?], but you cannot have what you want. You quarrel and fight...." (James 4:1-2).

Dr. Flach goes on to say, "Depression reduces vitality. The mood makes it difficult, if not impossible, to envision solutions to problems....denial of [members'] emotional needs in order to defend [our own emotional needs] against the possible hurt of another rejection, were the first steps in the building of [the congregation's] trap....Instead of reacting to them appropriately and working the issues through, [a congregation] denies the feelings, shuts them out of consciousness, and conceals them through the formation of mechanisms designed to protect [the long-time members] against future hurt."[31]

God, don't make me face this. I know the only way it seems we can get along is to not try anything new and keep our mouths shut. We're not growing, true, but....

Funeral: From Death to Resurrection

Before a congregation can be resurrected, it must go through a death. That does not mean it literally closes its doors and goes out of existence. We're not talking about a physical death here. We're talking about a spiritual death.

Even though some of the individual members have gone through a spiritual death and resurrection, everyone recognizes that not every member of a congregation is really and truly a Christian.

Repentance is a form of death. The word comes from the Greek *meta-noeo*, *meta* meaning afterward, and *noeo* meaning perception. It contrasts with *pro-noeo* meaning to perceive beforehand.

We must put to death our mindsets, our habits, our egos. Romans 8:6 says, "The mind of sinful [congregations] is death."

Paul told the weak congregation at Corinth in his second letter to them, "We always carry around in our [congregational] body the death of Jesus, so that the life of Jesus may also be revealed in our [congregational] body" (4:10-11).

Here he was talking about persecutions and threats of death to the apostles. But can not this concept be carried into the church? Can not our congregation put its ego to death so that the plain gospel of Jesus Christ—his saving grace made possible by his death and resurrection—can be made obvious to our members and visitors EVERY TIME WE ATTEND?

Jesus was so determined to carry out the things necessary to be done for the salvation of mankind, that he did everything God told him to—all the way to torture and death on the cross. Is our congregation led by Jesus' example? Are we willing to put to death the way we've always done things, so that we may carry out the things necessary to be done for the salvation of our members and our neighborhood?

Was this easy for Jesus? Indeed not. Hebrews 5:7 says that "During the days of Jesus' life on earth, he offered up prayers and petitions with loud cries and tears to the one who could save him from death."

To put our wills, our egos, our identity, our habits—everything we've always done—to death is torture. Jesus did not want to face it. Just what made him go through with it all?

Verse 8 explains, "Although he was a son, he learned obedience from what he suffered." And what was the result? Verse 9 says, "and, once made perfect, he became the source of eternal salvation for all who obey him."

By suffering for a while, our congregation could be perfected and, vicariously through Jesus Christ, become the source of eternal salvation to people in our community.

Obviously, no congregation will be made perfect, except by the blood of Jesus. Still, we have to face each other's faults and our corporate faults each time we come together. But we can at least try to put them to death. Why? So that our congregation can "become the [citadel for] eternal salvation for all who obey him."

What it does mean is for the congregation to come together alone — with no visitors — and allow each person to stand and say something about self, but definitely not about other people: "I have had this attitude which I thought was protecting the church because to me...."; "I have been pushing my pet program because in my mind...."; "I have resented....because I always thought...."; "I have insisted on directing...because I felt...."; "I have been afraid of new people coming into the congregation, because...."

Then, in the spirit of repentance, let the congregation go to God in prayer — perhaps even silent prayer at first — and ask God to forgive all our inabilities to see things the way other members do, see things the way visitors do, and see things the way God does.

Then have your funeral.

Just as imperfect people are not remembered for their imperfections at funerals, we must not either. Just as imperfect people are eulogized for the good they did and for a savior who forgives and offers life anyway, we must do that for our congregation.

Let us not use this as an opportunity to bash the programs our congregation has tried in the past or is now trying, but to no avail; or to bash people who always insist on being in the forefront "lest the congregation go astray" without this person's leadership.

Instead, let us remind ourselves as a congregation that we are now forgiven. And now forgiven, we look to God the Son and once more make Jesus our only leader. Now forgiven, we look to God the Father to raise us from our death unto a marvelous resurrection as a congregation. Now forgiven, we look to God the

Spirit as revealed in the Word (John 14:17 and 17:17) to lead us as we lead others to that same forgiveness.

Let us openly declare at our funeral, "Jesus, we will have no leader besides you, regardless of how religiously important other leaders may seem." "Father, we will base our resurrected congregational life on the way you want us to live." "Spirit, we will follow you, the Word, to the ends of the earth, and we will bow down to no other word besides you."

Forgive us, God. And forgive my specific part in what we have failed to do. I fall at your feet just as unworthy to be saved as everyone else. I fall at your feet in tears. And I whisper, thank you.

The New Regenerated Life

Now that the funeral is over, what? People do not just automatically "snap out of it" after the funeral. Congregations cannot. After the funeral, there is a whole strange new life ahead. A life so completely different that we can hardly fathom it. Life without the way we always were before? Life without all those activities we always had to do together?

It may be that in the days that follow when your congregation assembles, you will reach over and long for that which you miss so much, just like a widow or widower in the night. Oh, to have things back the way they always were.

But a new life means just that: A new life. A life of starting all over again as though we were just born. Just born, like the first congregation in the history of mankind. Is that possible? Could it be? Can any congregation be just like the first congregation of the church of Jesus Christ in history? Can we possibly know what it was like? Is there enough written about the first-century church to know?

Oh, to be like them! Oh, to start over so fresh that everyone in our congregation feels they, too, are newborn with us. So fresh that everyone in our neighborhood feels they can be newborn with us. Oh to have the same form and spirit as they did in the first century so that lonely and frustrated souls can be brought to the Lord every day (Acts 2:47).

God, I'm not sure we can do it. We've been like this since we organized years ago. Change is too frightening. What if we lose control? How can we possibly do it?

God's New Last Will and Testament

What does it take to be like the church was in its infancy back there in Jerusalem?

First, we need to recognize that there have been many changes to the church since then. Some call it growing and maturing. But, if we are going to be like the infant church of the first century, we new-borns must go back to doing things as they did.

Well, didn't Martin Luther accomplish that? After all, he got rid of the priest-laity system, and he got rid of indulgences that "paid" in full the penalty for our sins, and he got rid of the worldly headquarters at Rome. Didn't Martin Luther go all the way back to that first-century church?

We must realize that, by Martin Luther's time, there were hundreds and hundreds of church laws. To work backward and one by one strip away each law is practically, if not actually, impossible. By sifting through them all, eliminating some and keeping the rest until we can figure them out, is not restoring our infancy. It may take us back to an earlier age, but it is not a complete restoration.

Darryl Tippens wrote "Rediscovering Christian Worship" for *21st Century Christian Magazine*. He began his article this way:

"Saul Bellow, the prize-winning American novelist, tells of his visit to an Israeli kibbutz, a small farming community near Herod's Caesarea. Bellow was struck by the fact that Roman ruins lay all about the farm....[While they were plowing] a field one day they turned up an entire Roman street.

"As I read Bellow's description, I couldn't help thinking of the state of today's Christians who seek to renew Christian worship. Just as those modern citizens of Israel carry out their mundane chores on top of a buried classical culture, today's Christian worshipers live atop a rich spiritual past which they only dimly recognize. How these worshipers would be nourished if only they could get in touch with the resources of their past!

"Much of Christian worship today is safe, predictable, and orderly, but it also may be dull, lifeless, and shallow. Does it have to be? Not at all. Christians everywhere are seeking and finding biblical ways to improve their public worship....

"We need archaeologists of the spirit who can sift the past of biblical tradition and restore the rich possibilities for devoting ourselves to our Maker. Fortunately, there are churches today still practicing these lost-forgotten elements of worship, and they have much to teach us, if we will listen and observe."[32]

What would those farmers have if they dug up those classical ruins and incorporated them with the houses and barns they presently have? They certainly would not have a restored first-century.

But that's exactly what we've been doing for centuries to try to recreate first-century worship. We only got rid of what we were doing that we didn't like, and filled it in with first-century worship we happened to like. This is not restoring the original. This is reforming what we presently have with just SOME of the original. Reformation is not Restoration.

Centuries ago there was a grand Reformation Movement. Its purpose was to reform the world-controlling Catholic church by sifting through all its practices and trashing all that we did not agree with.

As a result, we came up with major denominations beginning with the Lutherans, then the Episcopalians, then the Presbyterians, Methodists, Baptists, and so on. People who attend one of the major denominations are part of the Reformation Movement.

Although this was an outstanding movement with God's blessings, they did not go far enough. They did not put completely to death the church as it was in their day and let it start all over again, resurrected as a first-century church in its infancy.

Probably the main thing that has interfered with congregations returning to the way things were in New Testament times is our not understanding that God has taken mankind through three eras, and his rules for one era never applied to actions in the other eras.

Ages of Mankind's Life

The first era could be called the "Father Age." It lasted from the creation to the time of Moses. In those days, there was no organized religion as such. Each family worshipped the way the father led them. The book of Genesis covers this "Father Age."

Romans 1:19-23 explains that "since the creation of the world God's invisible qualities—his eternal power and divine nature—have been clearly seen, being understood from what has been made, so that men are without excuse.

"For although they knew God, they neither glorified him as God nor gave thanks to him....and exchanged the glory of the immortal God for images made to look like mortal man and birds and animals and reptiles."

However, there were a few godly people. Job, for instance, lived in this "Father Age" and whenever his grown children got together for a feast, "Job would send and have them purified. Early in the morning he would sacrifice a burnt offering for each of them, thinking, 'Perhaps my children have sinned and cursed God in their hearts.' This was Job's regular custom" (Job 1:5).

This first era was God's way of showing mankind that we, left on our own with our own imagination, cannot be perfect.

The second era was called the "Mosaic Age." God selected one nation on earth to give his special law to—the Jews. He gave it to them through Moses on Mount Sinai. The books of Exodus, Leviticus, Numbers and Deuteronomy lists all the laws, about six hundred in all. They covered types of worship God wanted from them (such as having a high priest and going to the temple three times a year) and the way they should live day to day (such as not eating pork and not doing any work on Saturdays).

This second era was God's way of showing mankind that we still—even with every conceivable type of law to show us how—can't be perfect. In fact, Romans 3:20 says, "Therefore no one will be declared righteous in his sight by observing the law; rather, through the law we become conscious of sin."

Romans 2:12 says, "All who sin apart from the law will also perish apart from the law, and all who sin under the law will be judged by the law." And later in his explanation, God concludes, "All have sinned and fall short of the glory of God" (Romans 3:23).

The third era is called the "Christian Age." Colossians 2:14 says, "Having canceled the written code, with its regulations, that was against us and that stood opposed to us; he took it away, nailing it to the cross." Ephesians explains this further by saying that Jesus destroyed the old law, "by abolishing in his flesh the law with its commandments and regulations" (2:15).

The book of Hebrews in the New Testament says that Jesus was without sin (4:15); he is the only one who ever kept the laws of the Old Testament perfectly.

There is a reason for calling the first half of the Bible the Old Testament, and the second half the New Testament. Hebrews 9:15 explains that Jesus "is the mediator of the new testament, that by means of death for the redemption of the transgressions that were under the first [old] testament, they which are called might receive the promise of eternal inheritance" (KJV—Hebrews 9:15).

We all know what a last will and testament is. The Bible is God's. He had one last will and testament until Jesus came—the Old Testament. Then he changed his will.

"For where a testament is, there must also of necessity be the death of the testator. For a testament is of force after men are dead: otherwise it is of no strength at all while the testator liveth" (KJV—Hebrews 9:16-17).

The Old Testament was kept in effect by the death of animals.

"Whereupon neither the first [old] testament was dedicated

without blood...according to the law [of Moses], he took the blood of calves and goats...saying, This is the blood of the testament which God hath enjoined unto you" (KJV — Hebrews 9:18-20).

Likewise, the New Testament was put into effect by the death of the Lamb of God (John 1:29).

"So Christ was once offered to bear the sins of many" (KJV — Hebrews 9:28).

What does all this mean? It means that we are not to keep the Old Testament, whether it be from the "Father Age" where individual families were led in worship by their fathers, or from the "Mosaic Age" where people were hounded day in and day out with hundreds of minute laws.

James, the brother of Jesus said, "Whoever keeps the whole law and yet stumbles at just one point is guilty of breaking all of it" (James 2:10). The apostle Paul warned in Galatians 3:10, "All who rely on observing the law are under a curse, for it is written: "Cursed is everyone who does not continue to do EVERYTHING written in the Book of the Law."

Therefore, if on Sundays we use one kind of worship from the Old Testament, we have to use all the other kinds. And that includes animal sacrifices, having a temple, not eating pork, reporting to priests when we recover from illnesses for permission to return to worship, living in tents one week a year, etc.

Paul says it again in Galatians 5:3: "Again I declare to every man who lets himself be circumcised that he is obligated to obey the WHOLE law [of Moses]. You who are trying to be justified by law have been alienated from Christ; you have fallen away from grace."

Pulling things equally out of the Old Testament and the New Testament to guide us in worship is throwing us into confusion. Paul said so himself, by the guidance of the Holy Spirit: "You were running a good race. Who cut in on you and kept you from obeying the truth?...The one who is throwing you into confusion will pay the penalty" (Galatians 5:7, 10).

As stated earlier, what would we have if we mixed the ruins of ancient buildings with buildings that have been built since then? We would not have a restoration of the ancient building. But that is what we have been doing in our worship.

As a result, we are confusing people. And we are missing the real intimacy that simple and true New Testament worship offers us. As a result, people are popping in and out of churches searching for an immediate sense of spirituality among the worshippers and an immediate sense of connectedness with God that they are not getting.

We want that, God. We want to be like the first-century church. But how? How can we know what it was really like? Help us.

Restoring First-Century Worship

Believe it or not, a large part of the way most protestant denominations worship today is a direct influence of the Roman Catholic church, and their influence was the Old Testament. Some readers will throw up their hands in denial at the thought. Follow the pope? Never! But it is true.

Many Catholic additions to and changes in our worship were resurrected from the Old Testament Law of Moses. Most are nearly carbon copies of Jewish worship except for animal sacrifices. There is even a movement among Protestants to rebuild the Temple on its old foundation in Jerusalem. What in the world for?! God destroyed it. How arrogant of us.

Infant baptism was introduced in 187 AD, copying the Jews who circumcised babies. They made it church law in 1457. Sprinkling as a form of baptism was introduced in 250 AD, but was not very well accepted until the twelfth century.

In 451, priests began wearing sacred vestments, copying priests under the law of Moses, and it was made church law in 850 AD.

Also in 451, the Roman church insisted church heads refrain from changing their dress to the more modern styles, saying they must imitate the clothing of our first parents, Adam and Eve. It was also in imitation of the Jewish practice of the priests wearing special vestments for respect. It was made official in 850

AD.

In 666 AD musical instruments were introduced into Christian worship, copying the Jews who had instruments during the daily worship at the temple.

In 1079 candles were introduced into worship, copying the use of candles in the Jewish temple, and it became church law in 1611. Incense was introduced into worship in 1079 copying the use of incense in Jewish worship, and it became church law in 1213.

In 1095, common Christians were told they could take the bread if given by a bishop, but not the cup ever, by copying Old Testament Jewish priests who drank the wine part of the sacrifices.

In 1215, taking the Lord's Supper was declared to be necessary only once a year, copying the Jews who celebrated the Passover Feast once a year, and it became church law that same year.

In 1274, the church announced that presbyters (elders) were the same thing as pastors, and pastors were the same thing as priests. Therefore, priests and pastors could head the local congregations. This was copied from Aaron's descendants in the Old Testament being priests.

In 1495, choirs were introduced, copying the choirs in the Jewish temple. In 1547, the use of choirs became official, and their wearing of vestments like the priests was required. This copied the Jewish use of choirs in the temple and their wearing fine linen vestments.

In 1547, the Catholic church declared ministers and pastors had to be ordained, copying Jewish priests and Levites being ordained in the Law of Moses.

The Old Testament not only proved our sinfulness, but it showed on a literal and material level what Christians are to do on a spiritual level. The Old Testament is a commentary for the more spiritual New Testament. Galatians 3:24-25 says the Old Testament is our schoolmaster. We cannot fully understand or appreciate the benefits of Christianity without studying the Old Testament with its literalness.

For instance, Romans 12:1 says we are to offer our own bodies as daily sacrifices, not the bodies of animals. Christians are to circumcise our hearts (Romans 2:25-31). All Christians are priests (1st Peter 2:5-9). All Christians, as priests, wear vestments of sinless white. Christians are to pluck the harp strings of their heart (Ephesians 5:1). Jesus is our high priest (Hebrews 2:17-3:1) and only potentate (1st Timothy 6:15). Each candle used in the temple is now a congregation of the church (Revelation 1:20-2:1,5). The incense of worship is the prayers of Christians (Revelation 8:34).

May we never substitute our glorious and New Testament with its spiritual law of grace for all the material and literal things that had to be practiced under the restricting Old Testament. The more we practice Old Testament forms of worship, the less we touch hearts and lives in our public worship.

While the Old Law of Moses brought God into a somewhat personal relationship with mankind, it was nothing compared with the New Law of Grace which brought us into the very presence of God's throne of grace. Who, in their right mind, would want to go back?

God literally poured out his heart in his Word (Proverbs 1:19, 23; John 1:1-3). How could anyone arrogantly believe they could improve on it? To worship God or man?

None of the Reformers sifted through all the hundreds of Catholic church laws. It was too difficult. So they kept a lot of it. Which ones do our congregations follow? By following them, whether or not we knew it before, we are still following the pope!

The only parts of the Old Law of Moses Christians are to keep are those things which were repeated in the New Testament. For instance, every one of the Ten Commandments was repeated in the New Testament except "Remember the Sabbath Day to keep it holy."

God, I didn't know. None of us did. Even our pastor didn't realize this. God, we're confused. We want to please you. How? How do we find out how, and then actually do it?

The Island and Blank Sheet of Paper

Let us try to pretend that we and our friends have been pagans on an isolated island somewhere, a Bible suddenly dropped out of the sky, and we were just converted to Christianity.

There are no church buildings around and no one we know ever heard of church buildings, so we have no concept of them. Our past pagan religion had few rituals for individuals, and did not require formal public gatherings, so we have no concept of a "worship service."

We were left with only a Bible. Is that enough? Now, what do we do? Obviously, we must start from square one.

In order to start from square one, we must pretend we haven't ever worshipped God before. Just keep as our motto: **Where the Bible speaks, we speak.** Can we do it? Yes! By getting out a blank sheet of paper, searching the New Testament, and noting only those things the Christians did in their first-century worship.

And remember the remainder of our motto: **Where the Bible is silent, we remain silent.** If it doesn't mention a particular form of worship, it cannot appear on our list.

We will end up with the Christian world that the first-century converts lived in. In the process, we will also find out why they attracted so many and grew so fast.

So, when the early Christians "came together on the first day of the week" (Acts 20:7), what did they do? Did they suddenly begin having all the formalism we have today? Or has formalism evolved to the detriment of a personal and personable type of worship?

If first-century Christians attended one of our worship services today, how comfortable would they be? Would much happen that they were familiar with? Would we be spending much more time on something they considered less important, and much less time on something they considered more important? Just what is important anyway?

Do you think any of them left their worship services feeling lonely? Do you think they avoided any visitors searching for answers? Answers to who and what they were? Answers to who and what God Is? Answers to how Jesus could touch their lives?

And, by the way, how comfortable would Jesus be?

God, everyone told me I had this talent to do things in front of the congregation. I want to use my talent for you. How can I do that and get intimate with the other members at the same time?

Meeting the Roots of Entitlement in the Heart

We have developed a presumptuous society that is covering up lonely hearts. We have developed an entitlement society that is covering up frightened hearts.

We have come full circle from the beginning of this chapter centering on fear of death via war and persecution. Kahoe and Dunn reported that people who attend religious services weekly are least afraid of dying.[33] In another study made of both denominational and self-declared spiritualized people, it was discovered that only those whose spiritual life centered around a congregation protected them against the fear of death.[34]

Just how fearful are we—even we healthy ones—on a day-to-day basis of death or bodily harm? The chairman and CEO of Gallup wrote in a blog in 2013. "Walking the streets in countries around the world carries a real risk....kidnapping [in] South America, and rape [in] India....sub-Saharan Africa." Rather than rely on police reports, Gallup asked a question of thousands of subjects worldwide that seemed to get to the heart of the matter: "Do you feel safe walking alone at night in the city or area where you live?"

One-fourth of Americans are afraid to walk alone at night. One-fifth of Canadians are afraid. Half of Russians are. Sixty-percent of Afghans are. Seventy-four percent of Venezuelans are.[35]

Indeed, fear of losing something important to life, coupled with an age of entitlement which masks itself in false pride in order to hide the fears is what we face, what the church faces.

It seems that we, in the church, need to address fear and

entitlement (pride) in our lessons. If it is fear that motivates us to do the drastic in our life, perhaps a little love-fear in our lessons wouldn't hurt. Usually fear comes first, and true, deep deep love follows.

But entitlement covering up fear of loss is nothing new. Back in the days when the Law of Moses was being kept, God condemned Jewish priests, even though they were doing exactly what God had told them to do in worship. Why? Because they were being self-serving and legalistic and not reaching out to others. They were looking out for number one. As long as they had job security in their religious hierarchy, that's all that mattered. Here is what he said:

"The multitude of your sacrifices—what are they to me?...Stop bringing meaningless offerings! Your incense is detestable to me. New Moons, Sabbaths and convocations—I cannot bear your evil assemblies....When you spread out your hands in prayer, I will hide my eyes from you....wash and make yourselves clean....learn to do right! Seek justice, encourage the oppressed. Defend the cause of the fatherless, plead the case of the widow" (Isaiah 1:11-17).

Then when the Christian Age started, did the early church grow because of the great choirs or magnificent bands? Did it grow because the church services were more exciting than the pagan temple services down the street? Did it grow because Sundays at church were more entertaining than Sundays at the amphitheater on the other side of town?

Christians in the first century were willing to die for the God they worshipped and the way they worshipped. Are we? Would we be willing to die for the way we worship? Or is the whole thing boring?

This is what was written about 150 AD in a *Letter of the Smyrnaeans*, and includes also an account of how far those early Christians were willing to go to defend their simple way of worshiping God:

"For it is the office of true and steadfast love, not only to desire that oneself be saved, but all the brethren also....seeing that when they were so torn by lashes that the mechanism of their flesh was visible even as far as the inward veins and arteries, they were endured patiently...

"...none of them uttered a cry or a groan....And they found the fire of their inhuman torturers cold....And in like manner also those that were condemned to the wild beasts endured fearful punishments, being made to lie upon sharp shells and buffeted with other forms of manifold tortures....

"....[a youth] used violence and dragged the wild beast towards him[self], desiring the more speedily to obtain a release from their unrighteous and lawless life."[36]

Dear reader, let us clear our minds now, as we begin our pursuit of first-century worship. Clear it of all the formalism and informalism, or all decorous buildings and uniforms, and all preconceived notions of what works and doesn't work.

We have become a presumptuous society, presuming God will take us to heaven no matter how much we avoid him in favor of pursuing things. Are we presuming too much? What is missing in our worship that makes most people in our society think they can do without it? What kind of presumptuous, entitled heart do we hide in the shadows because we are afraid we will sink alone without those attitudes?

Let us open our hearts to the possibilities in worship that may have escaped us. Grab hold of them, wrestle with them, and in the process perhaps even submit to them.

Loneliness and emptiness is at the root of entitlement. 1st John 2:16 summarizes it: Lust and pride. We deserve, don't get, then feel empty and lonely. We think happiness is right around the corner if we could just get what we're entitled to. But it isn't there, so we try something else. We're never truly satisfied. In the rest of the book, loneliness, emptiness, and entitlement will be interchangeable.

Think of all the loneliness in the world. Our own loneliness. The loneliness of others. The loneliness of God as he pursues us and cries out, "Look at me! Really look at me! I love you!"

Think of the Savior we all wish to find and embrace together.

Oh, God. We've got so caught up in our traditions. Forgive us. We didn't mean to. Help us see ourselves as we are, see the lost and lonely as they are, and see you as you are. Help us see clearly, even through the mist of our tears.

Second-Generation Church Accounts

Written about 95 AD, the Epistle of Clement, v. 59 relates this: "Save those among us who are in tribulation; have mercy on the lowly; lift up the fallen...convert the wanderers...raise up the weak; comfort the faint-hearted. Let all the Gentiles know...."

An Ancient Homily written about 120 AD by an unknown Christian says in verse 13: "Neither let us desire to please one another only, but also those men that are without, by our righteousness, that the Name be not blasphemed by reason of us....For the Gentiles, when they hear from our mouth the oracles of God, marvel at them for their beauty and greatness; then, when they discover that our works are not worthy of the words which we speak, forthwith they betake themselves to blasphemy, saying that it is an idle story and a delusion."

A letter written about 150 AD by an unknown Christian who called himself a **"disciple of Apostles,"** explains Christianity to a non-believer, **Epistle to Diognetus,** v. 1, 5, 9: "Since I see, most excellent Diognetus, that thou art exceedingly anxious to understand the religion of the Christians....they love all men...they are reviled and they bless; they are insulted, and they respect...being punished they rejoice...."....being convicted in the past time by our own deeds as unworthy of life, we might now be made deserving by the goodness of God....He hated us not, neither rejected us, nor bore us malice, but was long-suffering and patient....O the sweet exchange, O the inscrutable creation, O the unexpected benefits....we should believe in His goodness and should regard Him as nurse, father, teacher, counsellor, physician, mind, light, honour, glory, strength and life."

2. THE BAFFLING BIBLE
So I spoke to you;
yet you would not listen,
but rebelled against the command of the Lord, and
presumptuously went up into the mountain.
Deuteronomy 1:43 (NKJV)

Famous Theologians

About 450 AD, AUGUSTINE—PRE-CATHOLIC: "Antony, a just and holy man, who, not being able to read himself, is said to have committed the scriptures to memory through hearing them read by others, and by dint of wise meditation to have arrived at a thorough understanding of them." (On Christian Doctrine: Preface, Point 4)

About 1536 and 1543, JOHN CALVIN—REFORMED CHURCHES: "All may observe the legitimate order appointed by the church, for the hearing of the word...and public prayer....It is added 'Gather the people e together, men, women, and children...in their hearing.' to this end, therefore, did God desire the doctrine of His Law to be heard; viz., that He might obtain disciples for Himself....declares that He is not duly worshipped, except He shall first have been listened to." (Institutes of the Christian Religion, Book II, 8:34;and Commentary on the Last Four Books of Moses, Deuteronomy 31:9-10).

About 1721, MATTHEW HENRY—PRESBYTERIAN: "The reading of the scripture is very proper work to be done in religious assemblies; and Christ himself did not think it any disparagement to him to be employed in it....The Book is...to be brought before the congregation and read to them....Reading the scriptures in religious assemblies is an ordinance of God, whereby he is honoured and his church edified" (Commentary, Vol. V, Luke 4:16 AND Vol. II, Nehemiah 8).

About 1871 and 1875, CHARLES SPURGEON—BAPTIST: "It is God's word, not man's comment, but still it is true that the majority of conversions have been wrought by the agency of a text of scripture...Child of God, your portion is the whole word of God....Christ is yours, life is yours, death is yours, everlasting glory is yours. There is yours. It is very sweet to give you your royal meat. The Lord gives you a good appetite. Feed on it; feet on it." (Sermons in the Metropolitan Pulpit, London, 1871, pg. 589, and 1875, pg. 92).

Oh God, thank you for all you did over the centuries and millenniums to save mankind from our own sins. It took you all that time to straighten out the mess we made after Eden. It took you all that time for us to see just how far we had fallen, how serious our plight was, and that we could never lift ourselves out. Thank you for your Bible that explains all this.

He wanted to get his driver's license. The first thing the officer said was, "You have to take a road test."

"No sweat!" the young man replied. "I can drive circles around everyone else."

So the young man showed how well he could act like a good driver: He could make left turns that kept the car within the proper lines, he could parallel park, he knew which direction to turn the wheels when parking on a hill, he could bring his car out of a skid.

Further, this young man was so good that he knew all about how cars worked. He had a degree in automotive engineering and could build a powerful and efficient engine from the ground up.

This young driver also knew how to get more mileage out of the gasoline, more mileage out of the tires, and more mileage out of the brakes.

To top all this off, he knew how to paint a car and polish it and make it shine so well that you could see your face reflected in it.

So, when he got done with his road test, he reported in, got out his money, and began to pay the fee so he could get his driver's license.

"Sorry, I have to turn you away," the licensing agent said.

"You've got it all wrong!" the young man replied, rather edgy. "I can drive better than most people I know; I can build a car, get the best out of a car, and make a car look good."

"Sorry, I have to turn you away," the licensing agent repeated.

"Now wait a minute!" the young man replied, growing impatient. "You've got it all wrong! You have to give me a driver's license!"

"No, I don't have to give you a driver's license. You don't qualify."

"Why? Do I drive that bad?"

"No, you're a good driver. But you haven't passed the

written test. You don't know what's in the book."

"Of course I know what's in the book! Ask me any question," he replied desperately.

"When you make a right turn and your blinker isn't working, what should you do?"

"Uh, well...."

"What is the minimum speed limit on the expressway?"

"Well...."

"If you are in an accident, what should you do?"

"Uh...."

"If you run out of gas and have to leave your vehicle beside the road, how should you mark your car?"

"Um...."

God, I always went to church and sang the songs and gave to the poor and prayed. I never thought reading the Bible would make me any better. It's just a book.

Judged by the Bible

On the Day of Judgment, we will be judged by several books, one of them being the Bible. Psalm 139:13 talks about God listing all the members of our body in a book. Philippians 4:3 refers to names of the saved in the book of life. Malachi 3:16 mentions a book of remembrance "concerning those who feared the Lord and honored his name."

Will we pass the examination on that day? Do we have any idea what the standards are he wrote out for us?

Deuteronomy 29:19b-21 warned, "When such a person...thinks, 'I will be safe, even though I persist in going my own way.'...the Lord will blot out his name from under heaven...according to all the curses of the covenant written in this Book of the Law." Revelation 1:3 said we are blessed if we read, for judgment is near. And in 22:18f, we read, that if anyone adds to the book, God will add its plagues to him, and if anyone takes away from the book, God will take away his eternal life.

How are we supposed to know what the curses and blessings are if we don't read about them in the book?

Jesus said in John 10:35 "the scriptures cannot be broken." Paul warned in 1st Corinthians 4:6, "Do not go beyond what is written." Hebrews 4:12 says "the word of God...judges the thoughts and attitudes of the heart."

How are we supposed to know what scriptures not to break if we don't read them?

Just what is the word of God? Romans 2:2 says, "Now we know that God's judgment against those who do such things is based on truth." And John 17:17 explains, "Sanctify them by the truth; your word is truth."

You mean, when all those preachers preach different things, I can find out for myself by reading God's word, the truth? You bet!

Romans 10 works backward from salvation to how we are saved. In verses 1 and 2 Paul said he wanted the Jews to be saved, for they were zealous, "but their zeal is not based on knowledge."

Knowledge of what? That Jesus is the Son of God, and that we are to confess this truth to others (verse 9). But how can we prove Jesus is the Son of God in truth? Verse 17 says the knowledge that leads to faith in this truth and confession comes from the word of Christ.

Jesus said in John 12:48, "There is a judge for the one who rejects me and does not accept my words; that very word which I spoke will condemn him at the last day."

How are we supposed to know for sure what Jesus said if we never read it?

He also warned that the saved must do the will of God. How do we know the will of God? By reading it. Jesus said in Matthew 7:21-23, "Not everyone who says to me, 'Lord, Lord,' will enter the kingdom of heaven, but only he who does the will of my Father who is in heaven. Many will say to me on that day, 'Lord, Lord, did we not prophesy in your name, and in your name drive out demons and perform many miracles?' Then I will tell them plainly, 'I never knew you. Away from me, you evildoers!' "

Paul warned in Acts 17:30 "In the past God overlooked such ignorance, but now he commands all people everywhere to repent." How are we supposed to know what to repent of? What things are sin? We read God's word to find out.

One of the last things God said to us is in Revelation 20:12-15 through the apostle John. "And I saw the dead, great and small, standing before the throne, and books were opened. Another book was opened, which is the book of life. The dead were judged according to what they had done as recorded in the books....If anyone's name was not found written in the book of life, he was thrown into the lake of fire."

Oh, God, I always took for granted whatever anyone told me was your will. But now I'm seeing I will be judged directly out of the Bible. Am I ready for that? I've never read it completely through cover to cover. God, this is scary.

Is It Worth It?

Years ago a man named William McPherson lost his hands and eyes in a dynamite explosion. He even lost the feeling in parts of his face. He found it difficult to face a world of darkness. God's Word became extremely important to him.

He wanted to read the Bible, but he couldn't master Braille with artificial hands. He tried to read the raised letters with his lips, but the dynamite had seared them until there was no feeling left in them.

One day he discovered he could distinguish the letters with his tongue. As he sought to learn the Braille system, his tongue became sore, and so raw it bled. He would stay up all night just to learn one new letter of the alphabet. He prayed to God for grace and help to learn.

Over a period of 65 years spent in darkness, William READ THE BIBLE FROM COVER TO COVER FOUR TIMES WITH HIS TONGUE.

How many times have we read the Bible through from cover to cover?

George Barna reported in *What Americans Believe: An Annual Survey of Values and Religious Views in the United States,* only 15% of people who consider themselves Christians read the Bible one day a week, and only 12% read it daily. One-fifth of them never even pick up the Bible at home.

Only 47% of Americans, whether or not they attend church, strongly agree that the Bible is the written words of God and is totally accurate in all it teaches. Astonishingly, the figure is not much different for regular church attenders: 52%+ percent.

Without the Bible, the only standard for right and wrong is in our own wills. James Patterson and Peter Kim learned and reported in *The Day America Told the Truth,* 52% of Americans believe the Bible had some right to tell them what is right and wrong. Even then, only 37% said they accept its moral advice. Some people see the Bible and religion separately. The same percent believe the Bible had some right to tell them what to do, but only 34% live their lives by it.

The church has even less authority over our citizens than the Bible. Is it because people have read enough of the Bible for themselves to see some discrepancies? Only 44% of Americans say the church has any right to tell them what is right and wrong, but only one-fourth of Americans apply what the church says to their personal lives.

When I was a child and would hear discussions about God bringing in the spiritual sheaves at the harvest of souls, I thought the adults were talking about bringing in the sheeps. Children sometimes speak mistakenly of Pilate, the final judge at the trial of Jesus, flying his airplane. Some children have understood in their immature minds that Jesus died, was buried, and low in the gravy lay.

But are these any worse than the misunderstandings about the Bible adults have? Most adults, even those who go to church, do not know there is an Old and New Testament, don't know who came first, David or Moses, and think the Bible contains a few cute stories but no rules for our lives. Most adults don't even know for sure what things are sin. Test your own congregation to see if these things are not so.

Yet these same adults don't know that they don't know, and the thought of reading right out of the Bible seems either baffling or boring.

When cornered and not wanting to admit our dilemma, how many of us think, "Don't confuse me with the facts!"?

What is going to church all about? Where did the church get its information on how to worship? Did it just come out of someone's imagination? Who came up with the idea of meeting on Sunday? Why sing? Who is this God or god everyone prays to? Did someone just think up a name—Jehovah, Jesus, Adonai?

Without the Bible, we may decide anyone can worship God any way they want as long as the people like it. We could decide that apparently God doesn't care as long as we're sincere. And, of course, that's exactly what has happened in today's Christian world.

Even if the Bible is mentioned by name during a worship service, we might think it is some sort of confidential top-secret book made available only to a certain cloistered group of leaders. After all, no one ever actually reads out of it in front of the whole congregation.

How can we take the Bible for granted and let it just sit hardly ever read, even in church? A lot of us don't even take a Bible to church with us. Many congregations do not have pew Bibles, and if they do, they are not referred to. And even when they are, it is assumed everyone in the audience knows what a Zechariah is and that it's on page 592. Assumptions. Assumptions. So many assumptions and so much taking the Bible for granted.

God, the Bible is too long, too full of fine print, and too confusing. Surely you meant for only the clergy to read it. Didn't you, God? Is that what you meant to do- with it?

Taking It For Granted

There was a big, muscular logger (lumberjack) out west who

had to get up at 4:00 AM every day to go to work. This big guy was a Christian and wanted to read his Bible every day. But when? By the time he got home from the woods, it was 6:00 PM or later, then he'd eat and go to bed. It took a lot of courage, but he began taking his Bible up into the woods with him in his lunch bucket. At noon, he'd sit on a log, eat his four sandwiches and read out of his Bible.

You can easily guess how he was treated. One day this Christian guy found a page out of *Playboy* magazine in his lunch bucket. So, having figured out who had put it there, he got an old Bible, and the next day the other guy found a page out of the Bible in his lunch bucket.

But harassment grew. They either refused to talk to him any longer, or they taunted him, or they picked fights with him.

The loggers parked their cars at a parking lot on the edge of town and rode "crummies" (beaten up vans) up the back roads into the woods so as to not wreck their own cars. One day on their way down the mountain the harassment got so bad the Christian knew he would fight them if he didn't get out. He ordered the crummie stopped, got out, and walked several miles back to his car.

Months later another logger went up to the Christian in private and said, "You read your Bible. You know about God and things. My life is a mess. Would you help me know God too?" Months after that, another logger felt he had nowhere to turn. So he turned to the Christian. "I know I've harassed you about that Bible, but secretly I admired you. You've got guts. My life is falling apart. Can you help me?"

Oh, the power of God's Word!

In 1968 the *USS Pueblo* and its crew of 82 men were captured by the North Koreans and imprisoned for eleven months. Lt. Commander Stephen Harris, who was the chief intelligence officer aboard the ship, returned for his Bible "in the confused moments when capture seemed imminent." It was immediately taken from him at the point of a bayonet.

The *Pueblo* prisoners decided to make a Bible. "Snatches of hymns, elements of worship services, precious bits of scripture were written on left-over scraps of paper. This unorthodox, but living, vital document, became known as the 'Pueblo Bible'.

"In our unchurched, unlearned way we turned to God." Harris said when the Pueblo Bible was discovered, he received a new set of bruises, but he was "brought out of despondency" by the memorized scripture.[1]

In the mid-1970s when Bibles were still illegal in the Soviet Union, my niece helped smuggle Bibles into Moscow, the heart of the atheist world. This group of young people hid their Bibles under an artificial floor in their van.

They would play in a park and whenever they saw someone sit on a nearby park bench with a certain kind of shopping bag, one of them would go over there with an identical shopping bag with a Bible in it, and say the first half of a predetermined phrase. If the other person replied with the proper second half of that phrase, the young person would get up and carry the stranger's shopping bag away; the stranger would get up and leave with their newly acquired shopping bag and a precious Bible.

Not only were Bibles illegal in Russia, but meeting to worship was also. True, there were official churches they could attend. If they did, they often lost their jobs, were not waited on in the markets, and so on. But if they met secretly and were discovered, they were either shipped off to a concentration camp in Siberia or shot.

The young people stayed all summer. That fall they learned from the American Embassy in Moscow that some of the Christians were discovered meeting together and all were shot. Did they believe it was worth it? Obviously they did. Even at the risk of their very lives? Oh, yes.

In the Middle East and parts of the Far East, people have been arrested for just giving someone a Bible. (China is still officially Communist atheist, but is gradually easing anti-Bible regulations in some provinces.)

Voice of the Martyrs reported on April 14, 2011, "An Afghan convert to Christianity, Shoaib Assadullah, 23, was imprisoned in the city of Mazar-e-Sharif. He was arrested in late October 2010 for giving a Bible to a friend. While detained, Shoaib was physically abused and threatened with death by fellow prisoners. He refused to recant his faith in Christ in exchange for his freedom." [2]

On the other hand, orthodox Muslims perform a ritual cleansing with water before even touching a copy of the Qur'an. [3, 4] This is in response to Surah 56:77-80 in the Qur'an which states "That this is indeed a Qur'an Most Honourable, In a Book well-guarded, Which none shall touch but those who are clean. A Revelation from the Lord of the Worlds." [5] Therefore, In many Islamic countries, letting even a worn-out copy of the Qur'an touch anything dirty is punishable by imprisonment, and is punishable by death in Afghanistan, Somalia and Pakistan; e.g., Article 295-B of the Penal Code of Pakistan. [6]

In these modern times, people throughout the Middle East and much of the Far East have never even seen a Bible. Some are smuggled to them with false covers or as packing materials one page at a time. Those with computers are secretly downloading the Bible onto flash drives and burying them in their yard, behind bricks, or other hiding places so they can read the scriptures in secret behind locked doors.

Then there are all those who risked their lives to translate the Bible into the language of the common person so the common person could read it in their own language. Common people like you and me. How can we take it for granted?

God, I didn't realize so many people went through so much to get a Bible. But they were different. Most people aren't like that. We're just not.

Cost of the Commoner's Bible

Around 650 AD, Pope Leo I wrote, "It is not permitted...to think concerning the divine scriptures otherwise than the blessed Apostles and Fathers declared." [7]

In 1299, Pope Innocent III warned the people that, though the desire to study the scriptures was commendable, it was wrong to study them apart from the church's teaching authority and to presume themselves superior to the priests in Scriptural studies. [8]

In the 1378 John Wycliffe of Yorkshire, England, began translating the entire Bible into Middle English, at first releasing various portions as tracts. Thereupon, anyone found with such a tract had it tied about his neck and the person and the scriptures were burned at the same time.

Their translator Wycliffe was excommunicated from the Roman church and died six years later. But 41 years after that, his grave was broken into, his bones were burned, and his ashes thrown into the river. [9]

Around 1525 in Wales, William Tyndale was extremely distressed when told by a bishop, "We were better to be without God's laws than the pope's." To this Tyndale replied that if God would spare his life, a few years hence he would cause even a boy driving a plough to know more of the scriptures than this clergyman.

Tyndale declared that if the Bible was translated into common speech, even the poor could read and see the plain Word of God. He felt the main reason for the heresies in the church was that the scriptures of God were hidden from the people's eyes.

In 1525 William Tyndale printed his first copy of the New Testament in English. Cuthbert Tonstal, Bishop of London, with Sir Thomas More, plotted to destroy "that false erroneous translation." The bishop of Antwerp decided to purchase every copy of Tyndale's English New Testament "for I intend to burn and destroy them all at Paul's Cross."

The bishops and prelates convinced the king of England to declare the English New Testament illegal. In the town of Vilvorde, Tyndale was betrayed, arrested, and imprisoned.

Then in 1536 he was sentenced to be executed. Tied to a stake he cried, "Lord! Open the king of England's eyes!" Then he was strangled and burned by fire.

In reaction to having the Bible in common language, ten years later, the Roman Catholic Council of Trent formally stated, "the Council declares that no one, relying on his own ingenuity, in matters of faith and morals pertaining to the development of Christian doctrine, should distort Sacred scripture to suit himself, contrary to that sense which the holy Mother Church has held and continues to hold, whose place it is to judge concerning the true sense and interpretation of Holy scriptures."

At that same Council of Trent where the canon of the Bible was discussed, it was decreed that the traditions on faith and custom that "have been transmitted in some sense from generation to generation down to our times" were to be accepted "with as much reverence as Sacred scripture."

In 1564, according to the *Catholic Cyclopedia*, "indiscriminate" reading of the Bible with independent interpretation apart from the Mother church was forbidden by Pope Pius IV because "Bible reading...is not necessary for salvation." [10]

On December 13, 1898, Pope Leo XIII granted specific indulgences for reading the scriptures. [11] Indulgences were initiated in the early 11th century as a fleshly punishment due to sin, the guilt of which is already forgiven.

God, I appreciate all they did to get the Bible to me in English. I have a copy in my home and even look up the 23rd Psalm whenever someone dies. My priest marked it for me a long time ago.

Paying With Their Lives

Beginning in the early 1200s the Roman church tracked down people who, among other things, "read the Bible in the common language" along with those who read pagan writing or who were magicians. According to *Fox's Book of Martyrs*, such "heretics" who refused to repent were tortured and burned alive; those who repented were imprisoned for life. In both cases, their property was taken over by the church. Many accounts over the next centuries are left of the suffering, torture and death of countless Bible readers.

In 1415, Jerome of Prague was arrested for having translated much of the Wickliffe's Bible into his own language. For this he was arrested as an opposer of the pope, enemy of cardinals, persecutor of prelates and hater of the Christian religion. Sentenced to death and tied to a stake where they began lighting the fire behind him, he cried out, "Come here, and kindle it before my eyes; for if I had been afraid of it, I had not come to this place." As the flames consumed his body, he was last heard to cry out, "This soul in flames I offer Christ, to Thee." [12]

Did he think it didn't matter what was in the Bible?

In 1418 in Great Britain, Sir John Oldcastle was imprisoned and then taken to Lincoln's Inn Fields for execution for reading Wycliffe's translation and then applying it to worship.

Observing the crowd assembled to watch, he exhorted them to "follow the laws of God written in the scriptures, and to beware of such teachers as they see contrary to Christ in their conversation and living" (Fox, pg. 191). Then iron chains were placed around his middle, and his body was set afire. The few minutes he survived the flames he praised the name of God. [13]

Did he feel reading the Bible was dull and boring?

In 1507 at Norwich, England, Thomas Norris was burned alive for testifying the truth of the Gospel. [14]

Also in England in 1532, Richard Byfield, a former monk, was converted by reading Tyndale's version of the New Testament. In prison he was tied up by his arms until his joints were dislocated. He was beaten several times until most of the flesh on his back was gone. Then in "Lollard's Tower" (named after the followers of Wycliffe) in Lambeth palace, he was chained by the neck to the wall and beaten once a day. Finally he was burned at the stake in the Smithfield section of London. [15]

Did he think he had better things to do than read the Bible?

That same year, John Tewkesbury was arrested for reading Tyndale's translation of the New Testament and burned at the stake. [16]

Did he entrust Bible reading to ministers and elders?

In the Piedmont Valleys in Italy, the Waldenses had the New Testament and a few books of the Old Testament in their own language. Thousands suffered persecution for this "sin" in the early 1500s. Under the direction of the archbishop of Turin, one

Waldensian leader was ripped open, and his bowels were pulled out and placed in a basin in front of him until he died. Others were flayed alive, and others burned for having the scriptures and not following religious traditions as a result. [17]

Did he think he didn't have time to read the Bible?

In 1546, Peter Chapot brought Bibles to France in their own language and sold them publicly. Within a few days he was brought to trial, sentenced, and executed. Thereupon it was expressly forbidden for laity to read the sacred scriptures in France. [18]

Did he make fun of other people for reading the Bible so much?

In Bononia, Italy, John Mollius presented the Apostle Paul's writings to the church in Rome to the people in their own language. One of the things he objected to was the church of Rome holding services in an unknown tongue (Latin). He was arrested under the direction of Pope Julius III, hanged, and his body burned to ashes in 1553. [19]

Did he feel like God was beating him over the head with the Bible?

In the mid-1500s, great persecution arose in Germany. Henry Voes and John Esch were arrested for reading Luther's translation of the Bible. When representatives of the church of Rome asked what they believed in, Voes replied, 'In the Old and New Testaments.' When asked if they believed in the writings of the church fathers and decrees of the church councils, Voes replied, "If they agree with scriptures. ' Thereupon, they were burned at the stake. [20]

Did they care what their friends said about them reading the Bible?

In 1544 in Scotland, George Wishart shared the Epistle to the Romans with the public in a sermon at Dundee. When interrupted by an antagonist friend of the archbishop of St. Andrews, Wishart replied, "I have offered you the Word of salvation. With the hazard of my life I have remained among you."

Next an attempt was made on his life by a priest with a dagger but was thwarted. In Montrose the cardinal arranged for sixty men to lie in wait to murder him, but this too was thwarted. Finally Cardinal Beaton had him taken into custody where he refused to recant his beliefs which were based solely on the written gospel.

He was then led out to his execution. There, he fell to his knees praying, "Oh thou Savior of the world, have mercy upon me! Father of heaven, I commend my spirit into Thy holy hands. I beseech thee, Father of heaven, forgive them....I forgive them with all my heart." Then several bags of gunpowder were tied to different parts of his body, he was tied to a stake, and the kindling at his feet was set fire to, thus setting fire to the gun powder. [21]

Did he think he had better things to do than read the Bible?

In 1554, John Rogers, who backed William Tyndale and Miles Coverdale to translate the Bible into English which they called, *The Translation of Thomas Matthew*, was put under house arrest by the Bishop of London and later was sent to -Newgate prison. Then in February, under orders of Stephen Gardiner, bishop of Winchester, he was led out and torched to death. [22]

A few days later, Lawrence Saunders was led to his execution. There he said, "The blessed Gospel of Christ is what I hold; that do I believe, that have I taught, and that will I never revoke."; Then he walked slowly to a stake where a fire was about to be set. He grabbed hold of the stake and said, "Welcome, thou cross of Christ! Welcome everlasting life!" Then he was set fire to and burned to death. [23]

Did they care what their enemies said about them reading the Bible?

The following July, Dirick Carver of England was sentenced to be burned alive. Arriving at the stake, his Bible was thrown into a barrel. He reached down into the barrel, pulled the Bible out, and threw it into the crowd. Thereupon the sheriff of Lewes commanded in the name of the king and queen that anyone picking up the Bible would be executed. Then the Bible was thrown back into the barrel.

Being tied then to the stake, Carver prayed, quoting from the Bible, "O Lord my God, Thou hast written, he that will not forsake wife, children, house, and everything that he hath, and take up Thy cross and follow Thee, is not worthy of Thee! My soul doth rejoice in Thee!" The fire was lit and he was burned alive. [24]

That same year Thomas Cranmer of Northampton, England, was sentenced to execution. Some twenty years earlier he had begun saying that the Bishop of Rome had no authority to dispense with the Word of God. In 1537 he had encouraged a friend, Ossiander, to publish a Harmony of the Gospels. Cranmer also translated parts of the Bible into English. By the following year, the Bible in English was openly sold and people crowded into churches to hear it read.

When led out to the place of his execution, Cranmer was chained to a stake and the kindling around him set fire to. As the flames then began to engulf his whole body, he lifted his eyes up toward heaven and quoted Stephen in the book of Acts, "Lord Jesus, receive my spirit." [25]

Did they hide the Bible under blankets, magazines, or in closets?

In 1557, Joyce Lewes of Manchester, England, refused to go to mass and receive the communion from the bishop. "If these things were in the Word of God, I would with all my heart receive, believe, and esteem them." The bishop replied, "If thou wilt believe no more than what is warranted by scriptures, thou art in a state of damnation!" Although she was faint while being led to the stake, once chained to it, her countenance became cheerful. Set on fire, she raised her hands towards heaven until the flames destroyed them. [26]

In 1558, a Mrs. Prest of Cornwall knew the Bible so well she could tell in which part of it a particular scripture was found. Having been arrested, various clergymen sent for her to quote scriptures to them in answer to their questions, and then taunted her as a mad woman. Finally condemned to the flames, she announced, "This day have I found that which I have long sought." Her last words before being consumed were, "God, be merciful to me a sinner." [27]

Did they get the Bible out only to look up the 23rd Psalm?

In the Netherlands about that same time, Wendelinuta, a

widow, refused to recant her exclusive belief in the scriptures apart from church creeds. When a friend tried to dissuade her in prison, she responded by quoting scripture: "For with the heart we believe to righteousness, but with the tongue confession is made unto salvation." At her place of execution, a monk tried to get her to kiss a cross and she replied, "I worship no wooden god." She was strangled and her body burned at the stake. [28]

Did she think reading the Bible was too hard?

In 1560, Nicholas Burton, an Englishman in Spain, was arrested for telling people what was in the Bible in their own language. His tongue was forced out of his mouth and a stick fastened to it so he could not tell what was in the Bible again. Thereafter he was tied to a stake and burned alive. [29]

Shortly after, George Scherter of Salzburg, was imprisoned for instructing his congregation with knowledge of the gospel, and then beheaded. [30] Also in the Netherlands, in 1568, a Mr. Scoblant was set afire at a stake. As his flesh burned, he quoted the Lord's Prayer from the Bible and sang Psalm 40 from the Bible. Numerous others died in similar manner. [31]

Did they think Bible reading was only for weak sissies?

That same year, Coomans of Antwerp, the Netherlands, whose two imprisoned friends had already died for the sake of the Gospel, proudly confessed to his beliefs and proved the Scriptural part of his answers from the Gospel. The judge told him to recant or die, but he replied, "I am not only willing to die, but to suffer the most excruciating torments for it; after which my soul shall receive its confirmation from God Himself, in the midst of eternal glory." He was then executed. [32]

Did they think the Bible was a waste of time?

In the late 1500s in Islington, England, forty people were assembled to pray and read the scriptures. They were invaded by Catholic soldiers of Queen "Bloody" Mary. Several escaped. Two died in prison, and thirteen were burned at the stake. [33]

The duke of Savoy in the mid-1600s sent troops to the Piedmont Valleys of Italy to arrest anyone who read or owned a Bible. At first their houses were burned and possessions taken from them. Then they were kept from being schoolmasters or holding any position that brought a profit to them. Then their children were kidnapped and objecting parents murdered.

One leader, Sebastian Basan, was imprisoned 15 months and then burned at the stake. The rest were driven from their homes in mid-winter to die of the elements and starvation. Those who did not flee were murdered. [34]

Did they think the Bible was for goody-goodies?

In one town where people commonly read the Bible for themselves, 150 women and children were killed by beheading the women and dashing out the brains of the children. In the towns of Vilario and Bobbio anyone over age 15 was crucified upside down. The numerous other tortures are too hideous to print in this book, but are found in chapter six of *Fox's Book of Martyrs*. [35]

God, I don't understand all this. How could anyone want their own Bible enough to let themselves be tortured and killed for it. Why couldn't they just leave it up to the clergy? What was the big deal. I don't understand.

The Mind of God

If people willingly gave over their bodies to be mutilated and destroyed for the freedom of having a Bible in their own language so they could read it for themselves, how can we today take the Bible for granted?

Furthermore, how can we truthfully tell ourselves it's okay to trust other human beings—be they minister or whoever they are—to tell us what is in the Bible? What is it about us that trusts our souls to other people, regardless of how holy they act and how much they smile at us?

Don't we want to know for sure what is in it?

We are so lucky that God shared his mind with us. No other religion in the world other than Islam claims they have a book written by God through men.

In every other religion in the world, people have to guess what their imaginary god is thinking and expecting of them. They have to guess and imagine and wonder. In most of these other religions, their god never makes direct contact with them. They cannot know for sure what he is or what they are. They cannot know for sure who he is or who they are. They cannot know for sure how to reach him. Or if their god even cares.

In these other religions of the world, heaven is a vague state of being and their god is a vague state of being. Nothing is anywhere in particular, and no one is anyone in particular. How terrible to have to go through life like this. Always wondering. Always searching. Always failing to find out anything for sure.

How can we possibly take the Bible for granted? Have we ever read the entire Bible through in a year? It only takes about 20 minutes a day. Or have we ever looked up everything the Bible says on important spiritual subjects so we can have God's entire opinion rather than man's opinion? All we have to do is get a concordance (complete index to the Bible in unabridged dictionary size) from any bookstore or the internet++, and find out for ourselves.

How can we leave it up to other people to determine our eternal destiny? Jesus said "the children of this world are in their generation wiser than the children of light" (Luke 16:8, KJV). He was talking about people using more common sense in doing business in this world than in preparing to live in eternity. Do we read the fine print before signing documents? Have we ever read the fine print of the Bible?

What kind of example are we getting in our worship services? Are we learning just a few scattered things, or are we learning the entire Bible? A man who identified himself only as "Thomas" wrote this a long time ago.

"I was baptized...on a relation of my 'experience' as a Christian. Of my conversion there was no doubt entertained by our preacher....Our preacher generally explained a whole VERSE in one sermon; though I have known him sometimes explain only half a verse in one day's preaching. During nine years I had explained to me one hundred and eight texts—equal to two chapters in Matthew.

"About two years ago I became a warm anti-reformer...I

was a delegate to the Dover [Baptist] Association in 1831, and was consulting with some of my brethren on the best ways and means of putting down the reformers. Meanwhile I had a conversation with a very pious sister who I thought was quite orthodox; and in the course of her remarks she asked me for a reason of the hope which I entertained. I related my conversion. 'But,' said she, 'what do you hope for?' 'My salvation,' said I. 'Salvation from what?' she asked again. I hesitated; but finally said, 'From sin.' 'And,' said she, 'is the hope of salvation from sin, the hope which you now entertain?'

"I felt myself confounded....I was afraid to commit myself by any assertion; for I felt my ignorance of the scriptures...determined on changing the subject. 'Indeed,' said I, 'the Reformers have ridiculed this thing called Christian experience so much...it is now more than a year since I told my experience.' 'Well,' said she, 'I have never heard a reformer ridicule, or speak improperly upon Christian experience....Do you recollect what Peter has said on the subject of the present and future salvation?"

"I was struck dumb. I knew nothing about Peter's view in particular; and could not even tell to what part of the Testament she referred....to get out of this difficulty I said, 'Don't you, sister, lean a little more towards the Reformers than you did some time ago?' 'I always leaned to my Bible,' she rejoined....'I associate with all the brethren and sisters in the neighborhood and would advise you to read the Acts of the Apostles several times....'

"Our preacher preaches miraculous conversions and quotes Young and Milton twice for once Paul or Peter is honored with a place in his discourses. He is very fond of harmonious sentences and is smitten with the love of poetry. It throws such an air of fiction around his whole subject that his prose appears as visionary as his verse; and, therefore, the admirers of Sir Walter Scott are better pleased with him than any other preacher in our country. I have become a Reformer; and now I can pray with my wife and children, and I begin to delight in reading the oracles of God." [36]

God, I have my favorite verses just like everyone else. Those are the important verses. Why do I need to know any of the rest? I know all I need to know. Don't you think so, God?

Why? Just How Important Is It?

In the days the Bible was originally written, it was called "scriptures." During the days of Moses who gave the Ten Commandments and about 600 other laws to the Israelites/Jews, he quoted God in Deuteronomy 4:2, "'Do not add to what I command you and do not subtract from it, but keep the commands of the Lord your God that I give you.' "

Proverbs 30:6 says that adding to the Bible makes us liars. Yet there are many of us who can lie with a straight face, and even fool ourselves. How are we to know they are lying if we don't read it for ourselves?

Ezekiel was told by God to pass on his words. Ezekiel didn't want to do it because he would become unpopular. How did God answer?

"When I say to the wicked, 'O wicked man, you will surely die,' and you do not speak out to dissuade him from his ways, that wicked man will die for his sin, and I will hold you accountable for his blood. But if you do warn the wicked man to turn from his ways and he does not do so, he will die for his sin, but you will have saved yourself" (Ezekiel 33:8-9).

It is popular today to show God as one-sided. A God who smiles all the time is not really loving. If we never got angry at our children when they were doing self-destructive things, we would not really love our children. If we never got angry at people who treated the innocent wrongly, we would not really love rightness. We must protect ourselves and others from wrong.

This one-sided always-happy God concept in so many congregations is leaving many people empty.

What did God tell Ezekiel to say to the people?

"Son of man, say to the house of Israel, 'This is what you are saying: "Our offenses and sins weigh us down, and we are wasting away because of them. How then can we live?"' Say to them, 'As surely as I live, declares the Sovereign Lord, I take no pleasure in the death of the wicked, but rather than they turn from their ways and live. Turn! Turn from your evil ways! Why will you die, O house of Israel?'" (Ezekiel 33:10-11).

People may say that God is not just to punish people. But God has a reasonable answer to this too.

"Yet your countrymen say, 'The way of the Lord is not just.' But it is their way that is not just. If a righteous man turns from his righteousness and does evil, he will die for it. And if a wicked man turns away from his wickedness and does what is just and right, he will live by doing so" (Ezekiel 33:17-19).

God would not be a good God if he let people continue to do wrong and hurt other people any time they want. And there are very few sins that don't ultimately hurt someone else besides the sinner. Yet we lie and have worship services that talk only about the side of God that loves everyone in their sins (which he does), but never tell them how to turn from those sins. By withholding God's word on any subject, we are lying by omission.

Centuries later, the Apostle Paul told Christians in Rome that those who refused to recognize Christ as the Son of God were lost. In the following statement he referred to the Jewish unbelievers: "Brothers, my heart's desire and prayer to God for the Israelites is that they may be saved. For I can testify about them that they are zealous for God, but their zeal is not based on knowledge....Consequently, faith comes from hearing [reading], and hearing [reading] by the word of God" (Romans 10:1,2,17).

Paul wrote to the church in Galatia (part of today's Turkey), "I am astonished that you are so quickly deserting the one who called you by the grace of Christ and are turning to a DIFFERENT GOSPEL — which is really no gospel at all. Evidently some people are throwing you into confusion and are trying to pervert the gospel of Christ.

"But even if we or an angel from heaven should preach a gospel other than the one we [apostles] preached to you, let him be eternally condemned! As we have already said, so now I say again; if anybody is preaching to you a gospel other than what you accepted, let him be eternally condemned. Am I now trying to win the approval of men, or of God?" (Galatians 1:6-10). How are we supposed to know any of this if we do not read the Bible for ourselves?

We still face our Day of Judgment. On that day we cannot pass the buck to our minister, our bishop, or parents, our spouse, or anyone else. God is going to say, "Why didn't you read my last will and Testament for yourself?"

How in the world are we supposed to know whether a sermon is scriptural if we don't compare it with scripture? Paul wrote the young man Timothy, "All scripture is God-breathed, and is useful for teaching, rebuking, correcting and training in righteousness, so that the man of God may be thoroughly equipped for every good work" (2nd Timothy 3:16-17). What makes us thoroughly equipped? What people tell us is in the Bible? No, what we read for ourselves.

Have we convinced ourselves that God does not really have a will for us to do? Is God mindless?

In Matthew 7:21-23 Jesus warned that, just because we go to church all the time, we aren't necessarily saved. He said, "Not everyone who says to me, 'Lord! Lord!' will enter the kingdom of heaven, but only he who DOES THE WILL of my Father who is in heaven."

Jesus went on to say, "Many will say to me on that day, 'Lord, Lord, did we not prophesy in your name, and in your name drive out demons and perform many miracles?' Then I will tell them plainly, 'I never knew you. Away from me, you evildoers!' "

That's heavy! How are we ever going to know for sure we're pleasing God? We can know for sure by not trusting our knowledge of the will of God to other people. We can know for sure by reading the Bible for ourselves.

The Apostle Paul warned about religious rules "based on human commands and teachings. Such regulations indeed have an appearance of wisdom, with their self-imposed worship, their false humility...but they lack any value" (Colossians 2:20-23).

Believing Jesus is the Son of God is not all we must do to be saved. Jesus' own brother and later an apostle warned, "You believe that there is one God. Good! Even the demons believe that—and shudder" (James 2:19).

Timothy, who worked alongside several apostles, was told, "If anyone teaches false doctrines and does not agree to the sound instruction of our Lord Jesus Christ and to godly teaching, he is conceiting and understands nothing" (1st Timothy 6:3,4).

The church in Rome was warned to "watch out for those who cause divisions and put obstacles in your way that are contrary to the doctrine you have learned. Keep away from them. For such people are not serving our Lord Christ, but their own appetites. By smooth talk and flattery they deceive the minds of naive people" (Romans 16:17,18). How are we supposed to know whether we're being deceived if we do not read the Bible for ourselves?

Jesus warned, "Why do you break the command of God for the sake of your tradition? ....You have let go of the commands of God and are holding on to the traditions of men. You have a fine way of setting aside the commands of God in order to observe your own traditions....Thus you nullify the word of God by your tradition that you have handed down." (Matthew 15:2; Mark 7:8,9,13).

How are we supposed to know whether our traditional worship is according to God's command if we never read the Bible? If we're depending on our minister to do it, we must remember that our minister will not be judging us. The same God who judges us will also judge our ministers.

The apostle Paul warned, "See to it that no one takes you captive through hollow and deceptive philosophy, which depends on human tradition and the basic principles of this world rather than on Christ." We may think this isn't so important as long as everyone acts holy and is sincere. But in Acts 5:29, Peter and John said, "We must obey God rather than men." How are we supposed to know any of this if we don't read the Bible for ourselves?

Later the church in Rome was warned about Judgment Day, "for those who are self-seeking and who reject the truth and follow evil, there will be wrath and anger....Don't you know that when you offer yourselves to someone to obey him as slaves?" (Romans

2:5-8, 16).

Paul was greatly upset by a congregation who was blindly going along with whatever their leaders were telling them: "You foolish ones! Who has bewitched you that you should not obey? ....You were running a good race. Who cut in on you and kept you from obeying the truth? That kind of persuasion does not come from the one who calls you....The one who is throwing you into confusion will pay the penalty, whoever he may be" (Galatians 3:1; 5:7-10).

Why do we allow so much time for talking ABOUT the Testament and so little time reading directly out of it? It doesn't make sense!

Jesus said, "If you love me you will obey what I command" (John 14:15). How are we supposed to know what Jesus commanded directly and through his apostles? He said, "Your [God's] word is truth" (John 17:17). Romans 10:17 says, "Faith comes by hearing [reading], and hearing [reading] by the Word of God [not imagination]" (KJV).

David said in Psalm 19 that God's word appeals to our logic, for it includes laws, statutes, precepts, commands, ordinances and warnings. Then it appeals to our feelings, for it is perfect, trustworthy, right, radiant, pure, sure, and precious. The result is that is revives us, it makes us wise, it gives us joy, light, endurance, gives us simple eyes and heart, and provides a sure reward for our souls.

David further said in Psalm 119:32 that God's commandments set his heart free. Knowing God's commandments eliminates all the guesswork. Knowing God's commandments is the only way to bring us peace. Knowing God's commandments ultimately leads us to an intimate relationship with him, and an end to our loneliness.

But God, no one ever told me Jesus had any laws besides just believing in him. I believe in what others said about Jesus. Isn't that all I need? They've never read the Bible through either. You do understand, God, don't you?

Divide and Conquer

The Bible is full of commands that seem to contradict each other. In one place it tells us to offer animal sacrifices. In another place it tells us Jesus is our once-for-all-time sacrifice. In one place it tells us that only men of the Levite clan can be priests. In another place it says all Christians are priests. What's going on in these 66 books called the Bible?

If we divide up the Bible, we can understand and conquer our confusion. Imagine mankind as a person going through infancy, toddler, preteen, adolescent, apprentice, graduate and adult ages. Dividing mankind up by these ages helps us conquer our confusion with all 66 books of the Bible.

Infancy — Early Genesis (Book 1):

Mankind was innocent, not even knowing evil. That was our Garden of Eden Age. We were Adam and Eve. We lived only in a small corner of Iraq. This age was around 6000-7000 years ago.

Toddler — Mid & Late Genesis (Book 1):

Mankind started exploring and getting into a little trouble. So God gave us just a few rules, but not many. God just wanted us to treat each other fairly and for heads of families to sacrifice to him occasionally. This was our Patriarchal Age. We were Abraham, Isaac, Jacob, and the twelve descendants (tribes) of Jacob also called Israel. We covered Persia, Syria and Palestine. This age was around 5000 years ago.

Pre-Teen Age — Exodus-Samuel and Job-Song of Solomon (Books 2-10; 18-22):

Mankind started getting into major trouble. We subdivided ourselves into nations but were not very civilized. Actually we were quite barbaric with each other. So God gave us a lot of rules called the Law of Moses. It started with just Ten Commandments, but expanded into some 600 commandments.

It governed what we ate, who we married, how we did business, when-where-how we washed ourselves and our clothes, how far we could walk on Saturdays, who was allowed to be priests, and minute details on how to worship either weekly or annually. We tried to keep all those complicated laws, but it only made us feel like failures. This was our Mosaic Age. We were Moses, Aaron, Joshua, Gideon, Samson, Samuel, Kings Saul, David and Solomon. This age was around 4000 years ago.

Adolescent Age — Kings-Esther (Books 11-17):

Mankind became outright rebellious and out of control. We invented all kinds of imitation gods—gods of our imagination. Hardened, we broke every one of the Laws of Moses plus the laws of common decency, and we loved doing it. No one was going to tell us what to do—not even God. This was a continuation of our Mosaic Age. We were a multitude of kings who divided our country by civil war and then made us wallow in every invention of our imagination. This age was about 3000 years ago.

Simultaneous — Isaiah-Malachi (Books 23-39):

Mankind got so rebellious and headstrong that God sent many prophets to warn us to return to the Law of Moses he had given. Sometimes we did a short while, but always we returned to getting into trouble. He also sent prophets to other nations to at least be respectful toward each other and God. Sometimes we did a short while, but always they returned to getting into trouble too.

By the end of this period, most of the great world kingdoms of that era either became powerless or disappeared completely—Babylonia, Assyria, Egypt, Israel, Persia, Greece. This was a continuation of our Mosaic Age. We were Isaiah, Jeremiah, Ezekiel, Daniel and many other prophets sent to the kings of the world and turned away by them. But finally, after spending a lengthy time in captivity, some of us were released to return to Jerusalem and try all over again to do better.

Apprenticeship — Matthew-John (Books 40-43):

Mankind had settled down and gotten more civilized. We went back to following the Laws of Moses and even became radical about it. Still, we failed. No matter how hard we tried, we couldn't keep that law perfectly.

So God sent his Son, Jesus, to live in human form and show us how to live that Law of Moses perfectly. We tried, but we couldn't keep up with him. Finally the experiment with the Law of Moses was over. Someone had to pay the penalty for all those centuries of breaking the Law of Moses. The innocent Jesus stepped in and said, "Punish me." So he — the perfect Lamb of God — laid himself on the altar of mankind, shed his blood, and died in our place. Then he came back to life.

Jesus had shown us how to live, how to die, and how to come back to life. Then he said, "Just forget the Law of Moses. I'm giving you a new law of faith in me." This was the end of the Law of Moses. We were the Twelve Apostles, the 5000 miraculously fed from a few loaves and fishes, the lepers healed, Pilate, Mary and the thief on the cross. This was about 2000 years ago.

Graduate — Acts of the Apostles (Book 44):

Mankind was ready to go through the transition from childhood to full adulthood, from living physically to living spiritually, from living by works to living by faith in Jesus. Graduation day was for the 3000 on the day of Pentecost, the Ethiopian Eunuch, Saul (called Paul by the Gentiles) Lydia, Cornelius. This was the beginning of the Christian Age.

Graduation day for all of mankind is whenever each of us personally becomes a Christian.

Adulthood — **Romans-Revelation (Books 45-66):**

Mankind now left behind the "childish" Laws of Moses and were given fewer but more responsible laws by Jesus. Jesus' life and teachings were expounded by his apostles as well as James and Jude, his half-brothers.

It was easy to become Christians. The hard part was living the Christian life. Many letters were written to us explaining how. We were found in Rome of Italy; Corinth, Galatia and Ephesus of Turkey; Philippi, Colossae, and Thessalonica of Greece. We were Timothy, Titus, Philemon. We were the seven congregations of the province of Asia in Turkey. The Christian age—mankind's adulthood—is good.

That's it, God? That's the theme of the whole Bible? I never knew that? Now I know why I was so confused. I was applying things from mankind's toddler age to mankind's adolescence. And I was applying things from the Mosaic Age to the Christian Age. No wonder I was so mixed up. Why didn't anyone ever explain this to me? I'm anxious to learn more God. What a story!

Enough Time

Henry Halley in the now 70-year-old edition of his *Pocket Bible Handbook,* said that "widespread neglect of the Bible by the churches...is just simply appalling. Oh, we talk about the Bible, and defend the Bible, and praise the Bible, and exalt the Bible. Yes indeed! But many church members **Seldom Ever Even Look into a Bible**." [37]

Regarding the place of the Bible in our Sunday-morning worship, Halley said, "The scripture lesson, as commonly conducted, is given a very minor place, while the whole service is built around the sermon. [Today it is usually built around music.] What a mistake! The sermon [music] the big thing? The scripture lesson very insignificant? Usually, just a few verses read as a sort of lifeless form in the opening part of the service with the droning close, " 'May the Lord add his blessing to the reading of his Word.' " [38]

A hundred years ago, ministers of the churches of Christ used to say, "Here are the scriptures I am referring to in my lesson. Write them down. Go home and read them for yourself. Check on me. I may be wrong. But the Bible is never wrong. If you think I am wrong, come show me the scriptures and explain them to me so I may correct my error."

Preachers today don't say that sort of thing much anymore, perhaps because there aren't many scriptures in their sermons. They need to. And we need to hear it.

Preachers usually, in addition to knowing how to preach, also how to read aloud. Some even take courses called, "Oral Interpretation of the Bible," meaning how to read the Bible aloud meaningfully.

Most, if not all preachers today, take a single short passage from the Bible and expound on it. But in today's world, people don't know enough of the rest of the Bible. This pick-and-choose method only exposes people to a very limited part of the Bible.

Instead, the preacher could read an entire book of the Bible for the sermon, with brief explanatory comments as he goes. Look at how short 17 of the 27 books of the New Testament are, even in a large-print Bible:

Titus about 4 pages
Philemon about 2 pages
James about 6 pages
1st Peter about 7 pages
2nd Peter about 5 pages
1st John about 7 pages
2nd John about 2 pages
3rd John about 2 pages
Jude about 3 pages
Galatians about 8 pages

Ephesians about 8 pages
Philippians about 6 pages
Colossians about 6 pages
1st Thessalonians about 5 pages
2nd Thessalonians about 4 pages
1st Timothy about 7 pages
2nd Timothy about 5 pages

When this is done, don't just announce the book, chapter, and verses; also announce the page number in the pew Bibles. Give people time to get their Bibles out and read along with the oral reader. Hearing and seeing both enhance absorbency.

Another approach is for the preacher to look up every verse in the Bible on a certain topic, have all the verses typed up together, then read from the pulpit from God's own mouth everything he has to say on that topic. The congregation would be swept off their feet!

When doing this, the preacher may wish to show the verses on an overhead projector so people can read along.

The most effective and memorable sermon I ever heard was some 60 years ago. I still remember it so clearly. This man got up and quoted directly from the Bible about the creation, fall of Adam and Eve, major events in the Old Testament, the birth of Christ, major events of his life, the death of Christ, how the apostles told people to become Christians from the book of Acts, how to stay a Christian from some of the writings of Paul, and then Revelation describing heaven.

Finally he quoted Jesus' own words, "Come unto me, all you who labor and are heavy ladened and I will give you rest" (Matthew 11:28 KJV). Then, without a single word of his own, he raised his hands to indicate the audience should stand. We stood and sang an invitation song, encouraging people to come forward and become Christians. How amazing!

How many sermons do we hear today that are in large part quotations from the Bible? People hunger for the actual word of God. People hunger to learn how to read the word of God for themselves.

Another suggestion, if time permits, is to have a theme for

the day centered around the selected scriptures. Then teach one passage from the Bible on that topic to be repeated periodically by the audience throughout the service until it is memorized by them.

For those who have not taken a course in how to read aloud, here it is in a nutshell.

1. Read as though you're surprised. It won't sound that way to others, and will add excitement and vibrancy to the words.

2. Read sloooooowly. As children we read aloud fast to prove we can do it. But as adults, we need to read as though we're trying to explain something well enough the hearer(s) can soak in each word.

3.. Pause between sentences. This, too, helps the hearers absorb the sentence that was just read. Time is then given for meanings to be absorbed that were never thought of before.

4. Look intently at your audience when you pause. Make eye and heart contact.

God, all this time I thought the Bible could only be understood by the clergy. Now I know different. Knowledge is power. Has the clergy been keeping us in the dark so they could feel more important and smarter than us? We could still respect them if they'd share your actual words with us. We'd respect them more. Please, God, make my preacher want to share right out of the Bible more.

Undeniable Proof

Thirty-seven percent of America's church attendees believe that the god of the Buddhists, Muslims, Hindus, Shamanists, Shintos, and other world religions is the same god, even though the Bible describes a different God than the rest of the world religions have. [39] Thirty-five percent of church attenders say Satan is not a living being, even though the Bible says he is. [40]

Either we believe in all the Bible or none of it. The same God who said to love our neighbors also said the miracles were true. If part of the Bible is myth, it all is.

Is it possible to know for sure the Bible is true? There are three ways to prove it is true.

First, it is scientifically accurate. Things were written in the Bible centuries and millenniums before scientists knew these things. For example, the Bible said about 2500 BC that the earth hangs on nothing (Job 26:7) and there is fire inside the earth (Job 28:5); about 1000 BC that there are current "paths" in the ocean (Psalm 8:8); and about 600 BC the earth is round (Isaiah 40:22).

Second, it is historically and archaeologically correct. Lost cities and civilizations have been discovered by following descriptions given in the Bible. More ancient manuscripts have been found of Bible writings than any other document in the world. Inscriptions of pagan nations attest to the existence of many of the characters of the Bible.

Third, its prophecies always come true. Predictions of the destiny of well-known nations were written centuries before they occurred. The existence of the Persian Empire, Grecian Empire and Roman Empire were all predicted before their existence and in the correct order. One king, not even born yet, was predicted generations earlier by name and exactly what he would do.

The exact year Jesus would begin teaching was predicted. The city he would be born in, the fact that babies would be killed at his birth, the exact amount of money he would be betrayed for, how he would be executed at the hands of foreigners, how he would be buried in a rich man's tomb, and many many other events in Jesus' life—all predicted with super-human accuracy.

God, I'm so ashamed. I have not only not read the Bible through even once, but I've never encouraged our minister to read it aloud before our congregation. Maybe that's what it will take to get us reading.

God, Forgive Our Ignorance

The last thing Jesus ever said to his followers through all ages was this: "Go and make disciples of all nations, baptizing them in the name of the Father and of the Son and of the Holy Spirit, AND teaching them to OBEY EVERYTHING I have commanded" (Matthew 28:19-20).

There is no possible way we can teach others to obey everything Jesus commanded unless we ourselves know what he commanded. We cannot rely on other people to do this for us. We must all read the Bible for ourselves so we can teach people for ourselves.

How are we supposed to do that unless we know directly from him what he commanded? How do we do that? By reading the accounts of his life written by eyewitnesses, and by reading the other books of the New Testament written also by his eyewitnesses, his apostles.

Too many of us are relying on "he said" and "she said," or "Well, that's what my creed says," or "I think it's in the Bible somewhere." Jesus did not tell us to teach what he and she said. He did not tell us to teach what is in our creed. He did not tell us to teach what we think is in the Bible. He did not even tell us to teach just part of what he commanded. We are to teach EVERYTHING he commanded.

We cannot rely on other people to do our reading for us. We cannot rely on our parents, our spouses, our teachers, or minister. We must read it for ourselves. Otherwise, we will not be able to obey Jesus' final command to us. Remember, Jesus said, "If you love me, you will obey what I command" (John 14:15).

Jesus' commands are not grievous; he gives them to us to offer us his freedom, his peace, his salvation. His commands are not any more grievous than our commands are to tender little children. They are given out of love.

The purpose of our Sunday-morning worship is two-fold, as explained in Hebrews 10:24. We are to encourage each other to have love and good works. Who are we to love? It does not specify here. But the Bible as a whole says we are to love God, love each other, and love God's enemies — the unsaved.

In our public worship, we remind each other of God's love and try to impart that love to each other and our visitors. Visitors — or even regular attenders — who do not really understand God's love and have never really become Christians (in the saved sense —

not the generic sense), cannot know God's love unless they know what he has to say to them. God poured out his heart to us in his Bible (Proverbs 1:23).

Nearly everyone in the free world+ has easy access to the Bible. Why would we want to accept a second-hand message? Why would we be satisfied with just "he said" in classes and sermons? Comments about the Bible and how to apply it to our lives are good. But they are never and can never be substituted for God's very own words!

The whole thing of talking ABOUT what God said is like trying to have a friend with communication only from a mediator. The intimacy is not there. We want the intimate conversation ourselves. There can be no substitute to either Christians or the lost in our assemblies for hearing word for word what God has to tell us. This is what will capture the lonely heart.

"God actually said that?" the unconverted and lonely might comment silently. Well, there it was right in his word, read aloud for everyone to hear. "How amazing!" those people may think who never heard much out of the Bible before. And it's personal. Personal to the saved. Personal to the unsaved. Personal to the lonely. It says so right in John 10:3 — God knows us each by name.

Ultimately, we could tell people ABOUT the Bible and ask them to have faith in us so they can in turn have faith in God so they can in turn become Christians. That's wrong. We must take people directly to the Bible so they can have for-sure faith in God, not faith in us, so they can become Christians.

Why are we so round-about in reaching the lonely and lost? Are our egos so large we are willing to put our words above the actual words of God? The gospel is the power for the salvation of everyone (Romans 1:16). God's word — not ours — is that "word of truth, the gospel" (Ephesians 1:13).

Ultimately, would you want to hear what your best friend said always through a mediator with a few quotes thrown in now and then? You certainly would not remain best friends for long. Being best friends means direct communication. God talks to us through his Word. We talk to God through prayer. That is what will make best friends for God of the lonely and lost.

If we truly believe this, we will set aside significant time in our public worship for letting God — nay, insisting that God — talk directly to us.

In order to change our private lives and our private habits of Bible reading, church leadership must lead the way by reading the Bible when we are assembled together for worship. It must be read and re-read and re-read.

Paul told Timothy in his instructions on how a congregation should be organized, "Devote yourself to the public reading of scripture" (1 Timothy 4:13).

We must take time. We must make time. Otherwise, we are worshipping the god of our imaginations. Some day Jesus will say, "I never knew you" because we indeed never did really know him. We did not know the Bible or believe it was important enough to follow.

Oh, God, forgive me. Forgive our congregation. We have taken your Bible for granted. We've wasted so much time. This is your mind poured out to us. This is your heart laid open. From now on, our congregation is going make Bible reading the center of our worship.

Our Only Bible

In the book, *In the Presence of Mine Enemies*, Howard Rutledge, who had been a POW for seven years in Viet Nam, wrote: "Now the sights and sounds and smells of death were all around me. My hunger for spiritual food soon outdid my hunger for a steak. Now I wanted to know about that part of me that will never die. Now I wanted to talk about God and Christ and the church. But in Heartbreak Hotel solitary confinement, there was no pastor, no Sunday school teacher, no Bible, no community of believers to guide and sustain me....

"It took prison to show me how empty life is without God, and so I had to go back in my memory....If I couldn't have a Bible and hymnbook, I would try to rebuild them in my mind. I tried desperately to recall snatches of scripture, sermons, children's songs, and the hymns we sang in church. The first three dozen songs were relatively easy. Every day I'd try to recall another verse or a new song.

"....Most of my fellow prisoners were struggling like me to rediscover faith, to reconstruct workable value systems. Harry Jenkins lived in a cell nearby during much of my captivity. Often we would use those priceless seconds of communication [tapping on the wall] in a day to help one another recall scripture verses and stories.

"One day I heard him whistle. When the cellblock was clear, I waited for his communication, thinking it to be some important news. 'I got a new one,' he said. 'I don't know where it comes from or why I remember it, but it's a story about Ruth and Naomi.' He then went on to tell that ancient story of Ruth following Naomi into a hostile new land and finding God's presence and protection there. Harry's urgent news was two thousand years old.

"It may not seem important to prison life, but we lived off that story for days, rebuilding it, thinking about what it means, and applying God's ancient words to our predicament.

"Everyone knew the Lord's Prayer and the Twenty-Third Psalm, but the camp favorite verse that everyone recalled first and quoted most often is found in the Book of John:

" 'For God so loved the world that he gave his only Son, that whosoever believeth in him should not perish, but have everlasting life' (John 3:16). With Harry's help I even reconstructed the seventeenth and eighteenth verses....

"How I struggled to recall those scriptures and hymns! I had spent my first eighteen years in a Southern Baptist Sunday school, and I was amazed at how much I could recall; regrettably, I had not seen then the importance of memorizing verses from the Bible or learning gospel songs. Now, when I needed them, it was too late. I never dreamed that I would spend almost seven years (five of them in solitary confinement) in a prison in North Vietnam or that thinking about one memorized verse could have made a whole day bearable.

"One portion of a verse I did remember was, 'Thy word

have I hid in my heart.' How often I wished I had really worked to hide God's Word in my heart. I put my mind to work....Remember, we weren't playing games. The enemy knew that the best way to break a man's resistance was to crush his spirit in a lonely cell. In other wars, some of our POWs after solitary confinement lay down in a fetal position and died. All this talk of scripture and hymns may seem boring to some, but it was the way we conquered our enemy and overcame the power of death around us." [41]

Second-Generation *Church Accounts*

Justin Martyr wrote about 150 AD in Apology I, 67: "We always remember one another. Those who have provide for those in want....And on the day called Sunday there is a gathering together in the same place of all who live in a city or a rural district. The memoirs of the apostles or the writings of the prophets are read, as long as time permits. Then when the reader ceases, the president in a discourse admonishes and urges the imitation of these good things." [42]

Tertullian wrote about 170 AD in Apology xxxix:1-5: "We are a body with a common feeling of religion, a unity of discipline, and a covenant of hope. We meet together in an assembly and congregation....We meet together in order to read the sacred texts, if the nature of the times compels us to warn about or recognize anything present. In any case, with the holy words we feed our faith, we arouse our hope, we confirm our confidence. We strengthen the instruction of the precepts no less by inculcations; in the same place there are also exhortations, rebukes, and divine censures. For judgement is administered with great authority, as among those in the presence of God." [43]

Clement of Alexandria said about 200 in his Miscellanies V.xiv.113.3: "Always giving thanks in all things to God through righteous hearing and divine reading, true inquiry, holy oblation, blessed prayer, praising, hymning, blessing, singing; such a soul is never separated from God at any time." [44]

3. PLAY-BY-PLAY PRAYER

But the person who does anything presumptuously...
That one brings reproach on the Lord,
and he shall be cut off from among his people.
Numbers 15:30 (NKJV)

Famous Theologians

About 1536, JOHN CALVIN—REFORMED CHURCHES: "All may observe the legitimate order appointed by the church for the hearing of the word...and public prayer....Lest the public prayers of the church should be held in contempt, the Lord called the temple the 'house of prayer' (Isaiah 66:7). For by this expression he both showed that the duty of prayer is a principal part of his worship....As God in his word enjoins common prayer, so public temples are the places destined for the performance of them...the command of the Lord (Matthew 18:20)" (Institutes of the Christian Religion, Book II, 8:34; Book III, 20:29 and 20:30).

About 1721, MATTHEW HENRY—PRESBYTERIAN: "Our weeping for other people's sins may perhaps set those a weeping for themselves who otherwise would continue senseless and remorseless...this drew tears from every eye; men, women, and children wept very sore when he wept thus" (Commentary, Volume II, Ezra 9).

1861, 1862, 1868, CHARLES SPURGEON—BAPTIST: "I think I see the church as I fear she is now. There she is upon her knees with hands clasped; she mutters a few words; her head droops, for she is weary...she is a sleepy church in prayer....We stand up sometimes on the public platform and we charge the church of God with growing cold....Have we by our prayers added to her heat?...Are we ever without the sick and poor? Are we ever without the afflicted and wavering? Are we ever without those who are seeking the conversion of their relatives, the reclaiming of backsliders, or the salvation of the depraved....there should be frequent prayer meetings....They say that God does not bless the word. They say, 'Our conversions are not so numerous as they were.' " (Sermons in the Metropolitan Pulpit, London, 1861 pg. 52, 1862 pg. 260, 1868 pg. 129).

"Ten minutes! The guy took ten minutes! Broke his own record. Covered everybody in the county, like God needed his list. Then went on to preach to God. My knees were about to buckle. Quit calling on that guy to lead prayer. He's nuts!"

It is said that Benjamin Franklin, when a child, found the

long prayers of his father both before and after meals very tedious. One day, after he and his father had stored all the food necessary for the following winter, Benjamin suggested that his father pray over the whole supply, "once for all. It would be a vast saving of time."

Like it or not, a lot of people feel this way about public prayers. And perhaps they are right. Something must be very wrong for so many people to feel so uncomfortable with public prayer.

The book *What Americans Believe: An Annual Survey of Values and Religious Views in the United States"* revealed that 73% of the American population strongly believes there is a God who watches over them and answers their prayers. [1]

So what's going on?

The same survey discovered that half the population believes each person has the power to determine their own destiny. [2] We seem to be involved in some serious ambivalence.

Modern society has become a very controlling society, even in the realm of religion. We have how-to books on every possible area of life. We long for perfection, and somehow believe it is within our grasp. Books and websites abound on how to have the perfect body, how to have perfect health, how to raise genius children, how to become millionaires, how to have the dream vacation, how to build one's own house, how to have shining hair, how to find the perfect mate.

Religion is no exception. We see books and websites on how to pray, how to know the mind of God, how to testify to unbelievers, how to demand Satan leave someone, how to conquer sin, how to memorize the Bible, how to preach sermons no one forgets, how to take a neighborhood or even a city for Christ and on, and on, and on.

Have we made ourselves gods, and therefore only pay lip-service to God? Are we ashamed to admit we need outside help until there's nothing left we can do? Do we approach God on things we've tried and failed because now "we can do nothing but pray"?

If so, why? Perhaps it is our deep-down sometimes-unspoken disillusionment with prayer.

God, you know I pray sometimes. But I don't want you to think I'm a wimp. So I only pray when I'm in a jam I can't handle. Besides, if you don't answer it, I know I'll get frustrated and decide you don't really care about me. I don't want that to happen.

Problems With Prayer

Besides hypocrites, possibly the biggest reason people quit even believing in God is that God did not answer a critical prayer, a prayer that we knew was good. After all, did not Jesus say, "Ask and it will be given to you; seek and you will find" (Matthew 7:7) Indeed, he did. [3] But look what he's been talking about.

He's just spent the previous half hour or more saying we should be the salt and light of the world, we should not commit various sins, we should give to the needy, and we should "seek first his kingdom and his righteousness, and all these [necessary material] things will be given to you as well"(Matthew 6:33).

Then he says we should pray about these things. We should ask God to help us become the salt and light of the world, help us overcome our sins, help us give to the needy, help us seek first the kingdom of God. Why? He goes on to say how narrow the gate is into heaven.

Do we view prayer as a blank check that God gives us? Do we demand an answer to our prayers even if it creates major problems for other people?

Let us try to view answers to prayer from the other side of eternity, from the top side of heaven. God provided a way for us to do that; all we have to do is go to his Word, the Bible.

When we say our prayers are not answered, we do not stop to realize that God often has to do a lot of rearranging in people's lives to get that prayer answered. For instance, someone praying to be able to marry just the right mate might involve what? S/he may be living at the opposite end of the country. Someone would have to move. That probably means someone's boss has to see a need to either lay them off or transfer them. That's just the beginning, but it gets the idea across. How amazing God is to juggle all of us so he can answer our prayers at all!

Several years ago a study was made of people who did believe in prayer and did not believe in prayer. What each person wanted to achieve was recorded. A year later, people were identified who either had or had not attained their goals. The entire process was explained in the book *Prayer Can Change Your Life*.

"At the University of Redlands we conducted the first controlled experiment satisfying academic conditions in prayer as a specific therapy or healing agent." [4] They used the Rorschach Test, the Szondi Test, the Thematic Apperception Test, Sentence Completion Test, Word Association Test to set the "before" status of each person. Religion was never discussed. [5]

There were three control groups, each relying exclusively on (1) psychotherapy, (2) random prayer, (3) prayer therapy. At the end of the experiment, the psychotherapy group made 65% noticeable improvement in both tests and symptoms. The random prayer group made no improvement. The prayer therapy group had 72% improvement. [6] Descriptions of participants and how their lives did or did not change make this book come alive.

Well, yes, God, I believe you answer prayers. But it seems like you answer other people's prayers more, like maybe they have more faith than I do.

Unanswered Prayer Answered

Look at **Abraham**. God promised him a land for his many descendants who would someday make up an entire nation. What an elusive dream that was! Starting in Ur of today's Iraq, Abraham dragged Sarah and the rest of his household all over the place trying to take hold of his promise:

When they moved to Haran, it was 600 miles away, Abraham was 60, and they were there 15 years.
When they moved to Shechem, it was 450 miles away, Abraham was 75,

and they were there 2 years.

When they moved to Bethel, it was 20 miles away, Abraham was 77, and they were there 1 year.

When they moved to Negev, it was 100 miles away, Abraham was 78, and they were there 2 years.

When they moved to Egypt, it was 250 miles away, Abraham was 80, and they were there 2 years.

When they moved to Negev, it was 250 miles away, Abraham was 82, and they were there 1 year.

When they moved to Bethel, it was 75 miles away, Abraham was 83, and they were there 3 years.

When they moved to Hebron, it was 30 miles away, Abraham was 86, and they were there 3 years.

When they moved to Gerar, it was 50 miles away, Abraham was 89, and they were there 1 year.

When they moved to Negev, it was 25 miles away, Abraham was 90, and they were there 15 years.

When they moved to Beersheba, it was 25 miles, Abraham was 105, and they were there 15 years.

When they moved to Hebron, it was 25 miles away, Abraham was 120, and they lived there 17 years.

Not only that, but the first city Abraham moved to, Haran, was in the wrong direction and the wrong country. When he finally got to Shechem in the right country, there was a famine in his land of milk and honey (Genesis 12:4-7). He kept moving farther south, hoping things would be better, but they never were. Finally he had no choice but to abandon his promised land, which had been a bleak disappointment so far anyway, and go to Egypt.

He was kicked out of Egypt for lying (Genesis 12:10-20), so reluctantly headed back to his promised land. In Gerar he was kicked out also, again for lying (Genesis 20:1-14).

All those years Abraham prayed for the son God had promised him. Didn't his name—Abraham—mean father of nations? How people must have laughed at him. It wasn't until he had moved eleven times that Abraham finally got his first son, Isaac.

All those years he could have been bitter. He could have quit praying to God at all. He could have even quit believing in God. But he didn't. Why did God make Abraham wait so long to answer his prayer? God provided the answer so Abraham didn't have to guess.

"In the fourth generation your descendants will come back here, for the sin of the Amorites has not yet reached its full measure" (Genesis 15:16).

God was planning to use Abraham's descendants to punish the people who lived in Canaan at that time for their idolatry with terrible gods that demanded human sacrifices, religious prostitutes — both men and women — and were destructive. Later God would tell Abraham's descendants who did conquer the land that if they became like the Amorites, God would cast them out of the land too (Leviticus 18:28).

Sometimes God delays giving us our good answer because some other involved party is not yet ready.

Then there were **Isaac and Rebecca.** They'd married when Isaac was about 40 (Genesis 25:20), but remained childless for twenty years. Twenty long years of praying for a son. Isn't that too long? But their wait was worth it, for they had twin boys (25:24-26).

Trouble again. When the twins were about age 40 (Genesis 26:34), they had a terrible argument and Esau threatened to kill Jacob, his twin brother. Rebecca told Jacob to live with her brother a thousand miles away in a foreign country and "When your brother is no longer angry with you and forgets what you did to him, I'll send word for you to come back from there" (Genesis 27:45).

She never sent that word. Oh, how the parents of these twins must have prayed for their family to be reunited and for the twins to get along again. But it just didn't happen. Jacob stayed gone twenty long years (Genesis 31:38). Finally he went back to make up with Esau on his own. When he did, (Genesis 33:4), Esau took him to see their father Isaac (Genesis 35:27), but not their mother.

Rebecca had probably died believing that God had refused to answer her prayer for her sons. But he did answer her prayer. It just wasn't in her lifetime. The same is true with some of our own prayers. They're answered after we die.

Joseph was Abraham's great-grandson and Jacob's son. When Joseph was 17 years old (Genesis 37:2) he was sold by his brothers to a caravan headed for Egypt. There this teenager was sold again to be a forever slave in a foreign country with strange people, strange language, strange customs. What kind of sadistic trick was God playing on him?

He was bought by the captain of Pharaoh's guard. He kept a good attitude and his owner was so impressed that he gave him a lot of responsibility. But things went from tolerable to terrible. His owner's wife falsely accused him of trying to rape her, so he was imprisoned. There his feet were put in shackles and his neck was put in irons (Psalm 105:17-22).

Did he become bitter and turn against God? No. He made the best of an extremely bad situation. Eventually he was trusted so much that the jailor let Joseph, the prisoner, run things for him (Genesis 39:22). When Joseph was 28 years old (Genesis 40:1 — 41:1) it looked liked a personal servant of Pharaoh would be able to get him out of prison, but the servant forgot all about Joseph. How could God allow that to happen?

Finally, when Joseph was 30 years old (Genesis 41:46), Pharaoh personally released him from prison and made him prime minister of the entire land (Genesis 41:41). Ten years later when Joseph was about 40 years old (Genesis 41:53-54; 42:3, 8), his brothers came to Egypt and appeared before him, not recognizing him. Some time after that when Joseph was 42 (Genesis 45:6) they returned a second time, and that time he revealed himself to his brothers and actually forgave them (Genesis 45:1).

Instead of being bitter, and complaining God never answered his prayers, Joseph said he'd gone through being separated from his family and enduring slavery and imprisonment "because it was to save lives" (Genesis 45:6).

Sometimes God says no to us because he has much bigger plans for us that require us to stay in what we consider a bad situation.

Let us look at the **Israelites** who were enslaved in Egypt for some four centuries (Genesis 15:13-16). Do you think the Israelites prayed to God to release them? You bet they did (Exodus

3:7). But one after another of them died believing God did not answer their prayers.

God did answer their prayers. But not in the lifetime of most of them. God saw the big picture that they did not see. When Joseph's family first went to Egypt there were only 70 of them (Genesis 46:27). They were the grandson and great-grandchildren of Abraham. They were not nearly numerous enough to begin that nation God said would come from Abraham. Nor were they strong enough.

Four centuries later, when Moses led them out of Egypt, there were probably three million or more of them (Exodus 12:37). Now they were large enough. But they had the minds of slaves, all of them having been born into slavery to parents and grandparents of slavery. They had to have time to develop self-determining, mature minds.

So, God gave them the Ten Commandments and about 600 other commandments also called the Law of Moses. But they still needed time to get used to obeying God which they were in the habit of not doing. In fact, they were such cowards that, when God told them to take their promised land from the Amorites who by now had reached the height of their evil, they wouldn't do it (Numbers 13:31-33).

For forty more years, until a new generation was born and grown, the Israelites wandered as nomads, people with no country (Numbers 14:33-34). It wasn't until then that God answered their prayers and gave them their country, more as punishment to the bad inhabitants than a reward for how good they were (Deuteronomy 9:5). But at least they were strong enough now to develop their own nation.

Did they complain all those years? Yes, they did. In fact, over and over they said God just took them to the desert to kill them, and that God didn't care anything about them. They became bitter. But, even though they no longer believed God would answer their prayer, and long after they quit hoping, God did answer it.

About five hundred years after finally settling in their Promised Land, a great man was born of this nation. His name was

David and he became their king. And from David's descendants came Jesus, the Son of God, who came to us in the form of a human to save all of mankind from our sins (Matthew 1).

God, remember the old joke, "You'd better watch out what you pray for; you just might get it"? Well, that's me. I'm sometimes afraid you won't answer a prayer, and sometimes afraid you will.

Prayers We Wish Hadn't Been Answered

Sometimes God does not give us what we want because it would bring us heartache. We may not see it, and the bad effects may not even occur during our lifetime. But God knows. Sometimes he gives them their request anyway.

A couple was childless, for the wife had been sterile for a long time. They prayed and prayed for a son. Finally God answered their prayer and they named their baby Samson. He grew up to become a kind of supreme court judge for the Israelites before they had kings. That was an honor (Judges 13).

But **Samson** brought heartache after heartache to them. First he demanded that his parents arrange a marriage to a pagan (Judges 14:2). But when he was taken advantage of at his wedding reception, he divorced her (Judges 14:20). Then he started going to prostitutes (Judges 16:1).

Finally he fell in love with another pagan (Judges 16:4). She in turn betrayed him, and he was imprisoned by the enemy and his eyes gouged out (Judges 16:21). He finally died by suicide (Judges 16:30). They got their desired baby, and also great heartache.

Another such instance was when the Israelites decided they wanted to be like the other nations around them and have a **king** rule over them rather than a supreme court judge (1 Samuel 8:6-9).

They got their way. But it led to disaster. At first, the worst the king would do is take their children to be soldiers and servants, and tax them heavily (1 Samuel 8:11-20).

But it only took three generations for their kings to lead them into idol worship (1 Kings 11:9-10), and one more generation for the country to have a civil war and end up with two separate governments—one in the north and one in the south (1 Kings 11:43—12:1).

After that they went from bad to worse. Eventually the northern kingdom, made up of ten-twelfths of them, was taken captive by the king of Assyria and never released (2 Kings 17:1-23).

The southern king did not learn his lesson, however. Some time later the small remnant of the Israelites was taken captive by the king of Babylon. At that time Jerusalem and the great temple were burned to the ground (2 Kings 25:1-21).

They had prayed for a king, and God gave them what they thought they wanted. It led to their ruin.

King **Hezekiah** was one of the last kings of the southern kingdom. He became ill and was about to die, but turned his face to the wall and wept bitterly, praying to God to let him live. He was given fifteen more years (2 Kings 20:1-11).

But what happened during those fifteen years? He made peace with the king of Babylon and showed his emissaries all the treasures of his palace. As a result, even though Hezekiah died before it happened, the next king of Babylon returned and conquered Jerusalem, and Hezekiah's sons were castrated and exiled to Babylon to become servants until their deaths (2 Kings 20:12-18).

Hezekiah had prayed not to die, and God gave him what he asked for. But it spelled disaster for his own family and for his nation. When we pray, we must be careful to tell God that we are willing to accept his will and not our own.

Remember the other joke about prayer, God? You know, the one about being careful we don't pray for patience? That's me. Sometimes I'm not sure I'm willing to pay the price to end up getting what I say I want.

Bad to Good People

Another frustration people have in condemning God are the unanswered prayers that did not ever lead to anything good. Take for example all the innocent Israelite **babies** God allowed to be killed by the Egyptians (Exodus 1:22) and by King Herod fifteen centuries later in Bethlehem when Jesus was born (Matthew 2:16).

But we are nearsighted. Oh, yes, it brought unbearable grief to the families left behind. But what about the babies?

Jesus said, people who "become like little children" will enter the kingdom of heaven.... their angels in heaven always see the face of my Father in heaven" (Matthew 18:3 & 10). A little while later he said, "Let the little children come to me, and do not hinder them, for the kingdom of heaven belongs to such as these" (Matthew 18:14).

When those babies passed from this world, they immediately were taken by their angels to the arms of God. King David, whose own baby boy died, said in 2 Samuel 12:23, "Can I bring him back again? I will go to him, but he will not return to me." What a reunion that must have been when all those broken-hearted parents reached heaven and were able to hold their baby, this time forever.

Well, what about **Moses**? The Bible said that Moses was the meekest man in the world (Numbers 12:3) and the greatest prophet to ever live, "whom the Lord knew face to face" (Deuteronomy 34:10). In fact, when God considered destroying the entire Israelite nation, Moses prayed that God would send him to hell in their place (Exodus 32:33). What greatness!

Yet, after spending 40 years of his life leading the ungrateful and rebellious Israelites, God would not allow Moses to enter the Promised Land. Why? Because Moses struck a rock to get water from it instead of speaking to it, and then took the credit (Numbers 20:8-12). How could God just use Moses for so long like that and then discard him?

Yes, Moses died shortly after this event. But where did he go after this? He went to heaven. He was old and got to rest. How do we know for sure he went to heaven? Because fifteen centuries later, Moses appeared from heaven to Jesus and talked to Jesus shortly before Jesus' own death (Matthew 17:3). By the way, guess where he was when he appeared to Jesus? In the Promised Land (Matthew 16:21).

What about **Job**'s grown children? They were all killed in an apparent cyclone (Job 1:18-19). Their father was "blameless and upright" (Job 1:1), and even offered sacrifices on his children's behalf every morning (Job 1:5).

They lived some thousand years before Moses and his laws—probably about 2500 BC. During that early period of mankind, the father of each household took responsibility for leading his family to follow God. God had not yet established any kind of organized religion as such.

But Romans 1:19-20 and 2:14-15 explains that "since the creation of the world God's invisible qualities—his eternal power and divine nature—have been clearly seen, being understood from what has been made....Indeed, when Gentiles [non-Jews], who do not have the law [of Moses], do by nature things required by the law, they are a law for themselves, even though they do not have the law, since they show that the requirements of the law are written on their hearts, their consciences also bearing witness."

So, although it caused great grief to Job, his children were now in heaven and probably having the time of their life in that heavenly place where there are no tears, no death, no mourning, no crying, and no pain (Revelation 21:4).

Well, what about the wife of the great prophet **Ezekiel**? She died just so God could prove a point. Isn't God a crass user, a bully? Let us look at what happened.

"[God said] 'with one blow I am about to take away from you the delight of your eyes. Yet do not lament or weep or shed any tears. Groan quietly; do not mourn for the dead. Keep your turban fastened and your sandals on your feet; do not cover the lower part of your face or eat the customary food of mourners.' So I spoke to the people in the morning, and in the evening my wife died. The next morning I did as I had been commanded' " (Ezekiel 24:16-18).

But what else was going on at that time? Ezekiel had been

taken captive from the Promised Land by the Babylonians in today's Iraq, and was now in his 30th year of captivity. God had said the Jews who had been taken to Babylon would be there 70 years, long enough for a new generation to be born and grow up who did not worship idols.

It was Ezekiel's job to tell the people why they were being punished by this captivity. He quoted God as telling the Jews, "You adulterous wife! You prefer strangers [idols] to your own husband [the only true God]....Therefore, you prostitute, hear the word of the Lord! This is what the Sovereign Lord says: Because you poured out your wealth and exposed your nakedness in your promiscuity with your lovers, and because of all your detestable idols, and because you gave them your children's blood, therefore I am going to gather all your lovers [idolatrous nations], with whom you found pleasure, those you loved as well as those you hated. I will gather them against you from all around and will strip you in front of them, and they will see all your nakedness"(Ezekiel 16:32-37).

God needed for Ezekiel to understand God's own pain of being forsaken by his chosen ones, the Israelites, so they could worship idols. Further, God wanted Ezekiel to understand God's own pain of not showing remorse for their removal from their Promised Land (a kind of death). Oh, God cried for his people when they were taken captives, but he cried in private.

Now Ezekiel was able to feel what God was feeling for his "bride-wife," the Israelites. How many times Ezekiel must have secretly gone to his wife's gravesite to weep in private, and wish his wife could rise up out of that grave and return to him. God was going through the same feelings. He wanted to bring his "bride-wife" back from the living death they were existing in Babylon.

In Ezekiel 37 God gave his prophet a vision whereby he saw just that happen. Ezekiel saw a valley full of bones dried white by the sun. The bones came back together, then tendons and flesh were added, and finally skin covered them. Then God breathed into them his breath and they came back to life. Maybe one was his wife. What a reunion! Temporary, but a reunion.

Can you imagine Ezekiel rushing to the others in exile

excitedly and saying, "God's not going to leave us here in this living death! Some day he's going to take us back to our Promised Land. We will live again!"

Also God did not leave Ezekiel hopeless concerning his wife either. Ezekiel was a priest, which meant he belonged to the tribe of Levi (Ezekiel 1:3). Revelation 7:7 tells us that all the saved from the tribe of Levi are in heaven. That means Ezekiel's wife was now in heaven. Did Ezekiel miss her? Terribly. Did he mourn for her? Yes, in private. Did he gain a new understanding of God and his deep love for his people who had betrayed him? Indeed he did. Did Ezekiel ever get to see his wife again? Oh, yes. For all the saved from the tribe of Levi are in heaven. What a reunion theirs must have been.

What about **Stephen** who was such a dedicated Christian in the New Testament that he was executed by stoning rather than renounce the fact that Jesus was the Son of God? How could a good God allow such to happen to him?

Once more we look on the other side of eternity. Our lives on earth are but a drop in the sea compared with eternity in our final destination. When the early church selected its first deacons, although they were all outstanding men of faith, Stephen was singled out as "a man full of faith and of the Holy Spirit" (Acts 6:5). 1 Corinthians 12:7-10 lists various gifts of the Holy Spirit, and faith is listed just prior to healing as a special gift.

We have all known people who find faith so easy and, no matter what they go through, their faith never seems to waver. They inspire us. Stephen was the very first Christian martyr. When, at his court hearing, the verdict of guilt was being decided for declaring Jesus was actually God, Stephen cried out, "Look! I see heaven open and the Son of Man standing at the right hand of God!"

He died a few minutes later by their hand. Hebrews 11:35-38 says of such martyrs that they were "tortured and refused to be released, so that they might gain a better resurrection. Some faced jeers and flogging, while still others were chained and put in prison. They were stoned, they were sawed in two; they were put to death by the sword....THE WORLD WAS NOT WORTHY OF

THEM."

Polycarp, a student of the Apostle John was burned at the stake probably 70 years later. In the events leading up to this he was taken into a stadium. "When the magistrate pressed him hard and said, 'Swear the oath and I will release you; revile the Christ,' Polycarp said, 'Fourscore and six years have I been His servant, and He has done me no wrong. How then can I blaspheme my King who saved me?'

"....Whereupon the proconsul said, 'I have wild beasts here and I will throw you to them, except you repent.' But he said, 'Call for them....' Then he said to him again, 'I will cause you to be consumed by fire, if you despise the wild beasts, unless you repent.' But Polycarp said, 'You threaten that fire which burns for a season and after a little while is quenched: for you are ignorant of the fire of the future judgment and eternal punishment, which is reserved for the ungodly. But why delay? Come, and do what you will!'

"....Forthwith then the instruments that were prepared for the pile were placed about him; and as they were going likewise to nail him to the stake, he said, 'Leave me as I am; for he that has granted me to endure the fire will grant me also to remain at the pile unmoved....

"....looking up to heaven [Polycarp] said, 'O Lord God Almighty, the Father of your beloved and blessed Son Jesus Christ, through whom we have received the knowledge of you, the God of angels and powers and of all creation and of the whole race of the righteous, who live in your presence; I bless you for you have granted me this day and hour, that I might receive a portion among the number of martyrs in the cup of Christ unto resurrection of eternal life, both of soul and of body, in the incorruptibility of the Holy Spirit.

"....I praise you, I bless you, I glorify you through the eternal and heavenly high priest, Jesus Christ, your beloved Son, through whom with him and the Holy Spirit be glory both now and for the ages to come. Amen' " [7]

Indeed, Romans 8:31-39 encourages us thusly: "If God is for us, who can be against us....Who shall separate us from the love of Christ? Shall trouble or hardship or persecution or famine or nakedness or danger or sword? As it is written: 'For your sake we face death all day long; we are considered as sheep to be slaughtered.' No, in all these things we are MORE THAN CONQUERORS through him who loved us.

"For I am convinced that neither death nor life, neither angels nor demons, neither the present nor the future, nor any powers, neither height nor depth, nor anything else in all creation, will be able to separate us from the love of God that is in Christ Jesus our Lord!"

While we're at it, we may as well think about, "If God is so good, why does he allow bad? For instance, how could he possibly stand by and let them torture and kill his own Son?" It was because of their love for us.

Everyone in the whole world sins (Romans 3:23). The Old Testament is not much fun to read. It covers some four thousand years of people trying every way possible to attain perfection and heaven for themselves. They tried it through their wits, through their physical strength, through their intelligence, through their emotions. They tried through having the Law of Moses and through creating their own laws to be perfect. They tried creating gods that would save them. They tried denying all gods and Jehovah God and even calling themselves god. Instead of attaining salvation, they got themselves into wars, built strong nations and then lost them, and built great indestructible temples that were then destroyed.

Nothing worked for man's ever-present and ever-threatening disease of sin. And the "wages of sin is death" (Romans 6:23). Man needed a vaccine. A vaccine can only come from someone who experiences a disease but does not die. With the antibodies now in their blood, they can provide a vaccine so others who are weaker will live through the disease.

So God sent a part of himself, his Son, to live on earth in the form of a man and be faced with the same disease of sin. Jesus was, therefore, tempted every way that we are, but he never sinned (Hebrews). But he was crucified as though he were a sinner. God then, in a way we do not understand, took all the sins of mankind—yours and mine—and injected them into Jesus (2nd Corinthians 5:21). Then Jesus bled for us and died. He paid the price. Satan could no longer accuse (Revelation 12:10) the world of sin because Jesus paid the price of death for us (1st Corinthians 6:20).

Then Jesus came back to life! The disease of sin could not keep this God-Man dead. Now Jesus was ready with the serum that came from his blood. All mankind had to do was believe all this really happened, and then imitate Jesus' death, burial and resurrection (Romans 5:20-21; 6:3-8).

Don't you see that if Jesus had not died, he could not have proven his power over death? He could not have proven to us that when Christians die, we too will be brought back to life?

But, you may say, "If God is so good and powerful, why does he allow bad to exist at all?" It is like up and down. For up to exist, there has to be the possibility of a down. Otherwise up wouldn't be up. It wouldn't be anywhere. And like light and darkness. For light to exist, there has to be the possibility of a darkness. Otherwise light wouldn't be light. It wouldn't be anything significant. And so for good to exist there has to be the possibility of bad. Otherwise good wouldn't be good. It wouldn't be anything.

There is a church song called "Victory in Jesus." How can we have victory in Jesus unless we have something to be victorious over? Satan can cause people to get sick, but God can heal them. Satan can cause people to die, but God can bring them back to life. Satan can cause people to sin and go to hell, but God can forgive them so that they end up in heaven instead.

God's glory is most obvious and powerful and wonderful when Satan tries and fails.

You're right, God. I got angry at you when my little brother died in that car-bike accident, and when my grandmother suffered so long with cancer, and when I lost that good job, and.... I've had trouble dealing with those times when I thought you had let me down.

Prayer and the Spirit World

Another amazing thing about prayer is that it influences what is going on in the spirit world—the world of angels and demons. Ephesians 6:12 explains, "our struggle is not against flesh and blood, but against the rulers, against the authorities, against the powers of this dark world and against the spiritual forces of evil in the heavenly realms."

We are to wear the armor of God which is truth, righteous living, readiness to face anything, peace, faith, salvation, the word of God. And with all that, we are to pray "on all occasions with all kinds of prayers and requests" (Ephesians 6:18).

To understand how our prayers influence the spirit world, let us go back to the book of Daniel. In chapter 10, Daniel fasted and prayed for three weeks—21 days (10:3). Three days later on the 24th day Gabriel appeared (see 8:16, 9:21).

He said that God had heard Daniel's prayer from the very first day (10:12). But Gabriel was busy fighting the prince (angel) of the Persian kingdom for 21 days (three weeks) and couldn't come. So Michael, one of God's chief princes (angel), helped him. Now, with Michael holding off the prince (angel) of Persia, Gabriel could come explain what Daniel wanted to know about a previous vision.

First, we learn that God uses his angels to answer our prayers, and although God can be everywhere at once, God's angels cannot. So, sometimes we have to wait because larger, more critical things are occurring. However, no one is unimportant, and God does send an angel to help.

Also, there seems to be some inference that Daniel's prayers were giving strength to God's angels so that Michael was able to come and help Gabriel. Daniel prayed 21 days, and that is how long it took for Gabriel to break free and come to Daniel. How amazing if this is true.

There is another way that Christians help angels. This is why the world was created. It is explained in Ephesians 3:9-11:

QUANDARY: "To make plain to everyone the administration of THIS MYSTERY, which for ages past was kept hidden in God, who created all things.

EXPLAINER: ....His intent was that now, through the church, the manifold wisdom of God should be made known

QUESTIONER: to the rulers and authorities in the heavenly realms

MEANS: ....according to his eternal purpose which he accomplished in Christ Jesus our Lord."

"Rulers and authorities in the heavenly realms" — good and bad angels of God and Satan — do not understand something; it is a mystery to them. An examination of the word "mystery" in the Bible reveals that the mystery is complete forgiveness. The church is here to prove God does forgive, and it was made possible by Jesus and his death.

So, we see there is a definite interaction between the spirit world and our world. The link is prayer and salvation.

God, that's heavy. I wish I understood all about angels, and the fight between good and bad, but it's too hard. Maybe you communicate with me on a higher level, like the language of angels. Maybe that's what I've been missing.

The Language of Prayer

There are some people who say the tongues of men and of angels referred to in 1st Corinthians 13:1 is unintelligible gibberish. To find out for sure, all we have to do is find out in what language angels speak.

Genesis 16:7-12 and 21:14-18 says an angel spoke to Hagar. Genesis 16:3 said she was Egyptian. Therefore, the angel spoke Egyptian.

Genesis 19:10-21 says two angels spoke to Lot's family. Genesis 11:31 says Lot was Chaldean. Therefore, the angel spoke Chaldean.

Judges 13:2-17 says an angel spoke to Samson's parents. Judges 13:1-2 says they were Israelites. Therefore, the angel spoke Israeli (Hebrew).

2nd Kings 1:3-4 says an angel spoke to Elijah. It also says he was a Tishbite which was part of Israel. Therefore, the angel spoke Israeli (Hebrew).

Daniel 8:16-25 and 9:21-27 says an angel spoke to Daniel. Daniel 1:1-4 says Daniel was from Jerusalem of Israel, but now in Babylon everyone spoke in Aramaic. Therefore, the angel spoke in either Israeli (Hebrew) or Aramaic.

Luke 1:8-20 says an angel spoke to Zechariah, John the Baptist's father. Luke 1:5 says Zechariah was a priest of the Israelites/Jews. However, many now spoke in Greek; this account was written in Greek. Therefore, the angel spoke Israeli (Hebrew) or Greek.

Luke 1:28-38 says an angel spoke to Mary. Luke 3:24f, Mary's genealogy, says she was an Israelite. Therefore, the angel spoke Israeli (Hebrew) or Greek.

Luke 2:8-12 says angels spoke to shepherds. Luke 2:4 says these shepherds were from Bethlehem in Israel. Therefore, the angels spoke Israeli (Hebrew) or Greek.

Matthew 28:1-9 says an angel spoke to Mary Magdalene and others. Mary was from the city of Magdala in Israel. Therefore, the angel spoke Israeli (Hebrew) or Greek.

Acts 10:1-8 says an angel spoke to Cornelius. Acts 10:1 says he was Roman. Therefore, the angel spoke Italian/Latin.

Acts 12:5-10 says an angel spoke to Peter. John 1:44 says Peter was from a city in Galilee, Palestine/Israel. Therefore, the angel spoke Israeli (Hebrew) or Greek.

Revelation 5:2, etc., etc. says an angel spoke to John. Matthew 4:18-21 says John was from a city in Galilee, Palestine/ Israel. Therefore, the angel spoke Israeli (Hebrew) or Greek.

All of this is to demonstrate that at no time did the person angels spoke to say they did not understand. They conversed at ease in each person's native language. Therefore, the language of angels is the language of whoever they are speaking to. They are multi-lingual. They never spoke in gibberish.

You mean, God, that you hear me no matter how much I stutter and struggle? You understand even when I don't understand my problem or what the answer could possibly be? I just can't ascend to where you are. Could you lean a little lower for me?

Where the Rubber Meets the Road

Praying in private is not complex. But it is more so in public where the leader tries to represent what the others want to be praying. But how is this possible?

Several years ago I went through a period when I wrote notes to the prayers that were being offered in church. (God, forgive me for peeking.) This is what a typical prayer covered: The sick of OUR number, OUR weak members, OUR leaders, OUR worship, OUR blessings. Another typical prayer was about worship, love, Jesus, serving, everyday life, next week, travelers, sermon, sins, members' lives, parents, children, wonders of the world.

On the other hand, the prayer of a former missionary I took notes to covered the delights of Christianity, open-hearted people, congregation, backsliders, unchurched, the general public, our feeble human efforts, missionaries, World Bible School, prayer, glory of God.

Someone from another country prayed for congregational love, being a light in the community, families, the sick, worship, the word, our sins, God's Spirit.

All these are good in their own way. But very seldom did they get specific. How are we going to know if our prayers are answered if we don't get specific?

How specific are our prayers? Do we pray for "all those it is our duty to pray for the world over"? Our public prayers are a mirror of our private prayers. If our prayers are general, then our private Christian life has not become very specific and likely will not. If we are drifting through our Christian life, our public prayers will too. And as our prayers drift, so do the hearers we are supposed to be leading; they will drift from thought to thought on things that have nothing to do with the prayer.

On the other end of the scale, if we have a busy Christian life in private, we need not include everything in our public prayers. If everyone did that, we'd be praying for hours on end.

The hours-on-end prayers are for private discussions with God, and they are good.

But what about public prayers? What should God's people pray for when they are together?

In the 1960s I attended a congregation in California, that learned to get specific. I think it started on New Years Eve when the congregation decided to pray the new year in. It seems we began praying about ten o'clock. "Ten o'clock? You prayed for two hours?" you might be thinking. "What a bunch of fanatics. Did you roll on the floor too?" Actually we prayed longer than that.

Someone stood up front with a blackboard. People stood who had prayer requests. When recognized, they explained the situation and who they wished to be prayed for. The person in charge wrote the name and the situation in a couple of words. When the blackboard was full, he called on someone to lead a prayer for those people. Then those were erased and we continued around the auditorium with people standing and explaining their prayer requests.

There were all kinds of prayers regarding sickness, finances, relationships, travel, jobs, souls, thanksgiving and praise.

If we were worldly, we would have said something magical happened that night. But as Christians, it was something spiritual and holy and wonderful. We got into each others hearts. No more masks. Gradually people began standing and sharing their own personal burdens, things the rest of us never guessed. They began confessing a particular type of sin they needed help with. They cried softly and we cried with them.

But prayers were not just requests. Some were thanking God for answers to prayer. Some were thanking God for sending his Son to us in our desperation and sin. Some were thanking God for the numerous things we take for granted. How do we think of what we take for granted? Think of people living in a country that is in famine, or war-torn, or run by atheists. Think of people who are blind, deaf, mute, lame.

Some prayers were praising God. Isn't praising kind of like thanking? Actually praising centers around someone's traits. What are God's traits? He is love. He is life. He is justice. He is mercy. He is patience. He is might. He is power. He is light. God is so large the universe cannot contain him. God is so small he can hide within our heart. When Satan causes illness, God heals. When Satan causes sin, God forgives. When Satan causes death, God brings back to life.

It was hard to break up that night. For the first time many of us had allowed others into our lives and hearts, exposing the raw and so-easily-wounded part of us. Our masks came down.

That's what happens with prayer. The most successful marriage counselor I ever knew was a minister who has now gone to live with his Lord in heaven. Other ministers within a hundred-mile radius or more would call him after they had tried everything they knew to keep a marriage together. A day or two before the court date, the divorcing couple would consent to see this minister with the "magic touch".

But once again, it wasn't magic. It was God's power that can only be tapped in prayer. The minister did not ask them about their marriages and why they were so bad. Instead he told them one thing. He told them to pray together. Then he left them alone in his apartment all night so they could have the night to pray together with no distractions. He had about a ninety-percent success rate. Actually, of course, it was God who had such a phenomenal success rate.

So what happened to the congregation that prayed in the new year? The following week one of the elders got up before the congregation and said he'd counted something like seven answers to prayer since that night. He got up the following week and said, "I've counted 29 answers to our prayers since that night." The next week he counted 43 (or whatever the actual number was).

Members started writing their prayer requests down and turning them in. Someone in the office wrote the prayer requests on a large sheet for distribution. Members began praying for these lists in private. Wednesday night got so it began earning the name we used to call it decades ago—"prayer meeting night."

And each week that elder would get up and say, "This past week we had 12 more answers to prayer," or whatever the number was for the week. We began to understand prayer. We began to see that prayer had to be specific in order for us to see when it had been answered. Once we knew that, we could thank and praise God more.

This was a large congregation of many hundreds, and they took whatever time was necessary to have a long session of prayer. However, this may not be conducive to your congregation. In that case, divide up into smaller groups in classrooms or even in various corners of the auditorium. Dividing up by men and women is a little more conducive to closeness since men will say things among other men they wouldn't with women around, and visa versa. Allow those with prayer requests time to explain their request. They are pouring out their heart. They have learned to trust.

Yes, prayer is done with trust. Not only trust in God, but also trust in each other. Things discussed in prayer time should never be discussed outside of that group. If the person with the prayer request wants others to know, they will tell them themselves. If anyone wishes to tell anyone else, the person making the request must give their permission; otherwise it is tabu.

Not Enough Time

Some may be saying their congregation does not have time for so much praying. It would add another half hour to their worship period. Friends, we all know Christians are to pray for each other daily. The early church did. How did they know about each other's needs? They saw each other every day (Acts 2:46)!

Although we have innumerable time-saving gadgets that we should have much more time than the Christians of the first century, we keep adding more and more activities to our lives. As a result, we have ended up with less time for each other.

For most Christians, we are lucky to see each other once a week. So if we are to pray for each other, and to know just what to pray for, we're going to have to take the time to do it in our public worship. Either that, or not at all.

Congregations who have begun entertainment type

worship rely on small groups to provide the intimacy for the lonely. But, once again, with the time-poor situation of society, how many miss those groups? And how many need it more than those who attend?

Why is it we have to have two songs, a prayer, three more songs, a scripture reading, another two or three songs, another prayer, another couple of songs?

Young people in Cuba were interviewed about any religion they might have in their lives in 1998 when the pope went there for a visit. Surprisingly, many of those young people who grew up without God began flocking to church. Why?

One young man, age 30, said, "I needed a change in my life." Another said, "My life was so turbulent with too much drinking, too many parties." [8] Too many parties? You mean partying at church as part of the worship isn't what they're looking for?

It is a proven fact that on any random Sunday, half the members will not be at church. [9] Why? Probably because they do not feel attending is doing them any good. How do you feel after you have attended a worship service? Do you feel any more loved than you did? Do you have any more love for the others than you did?

People are feeling empty even in church. Or perhaps especially in church. Of all places, they come hoping the church can help fill their emptiness. Solomon said God has "set eternity in the hearts of men" (Ecclesiastes 3:11).

People's personal concerns are too vital to substitute with a perpetual party atmosphere in church worship.

Entire bookstores are being dedicated to "spiritualism." These are "new-age" bookstores wherein books on all the religions of mankind are available. Anything to feel spiritual. People are so empty. They meditate by themselves trying to find the god within them, or to find an elusive perfection. It gnaws at everyone including you and me. It is an emptiness only God can fill.

In one of the last speeches Moses made before his death, he said, "What other nation is so great as to have their gods near them the way the Lord our God is near us whenever we pray to him?" (Deuteronomy 4:7).

Friend, when we meet for our times of worship, let us take time to touch God. Really touch him. And in the process, touch each other with eternity.

Second-Generation Church Accounts

Justin Martyr, about 150 AD, said in Apology I, 67: "The memoirs of the apostles or the writings of the prophets are read, as long as time permits. Then when the reader ceases, the president in a discourse admonished and urges the imitation of these good things. Next we all rise together and send up prayers." [10]

Tertullian, about 170 AD, said in Apology xxxix:1-5: "We are a body with a common feeling of religion, a unity of discipline, and a covenant of hope. We meet together in an assembly and congregation so that praying to God we may win him over by the strength of our prayers. This kind of force is pleasing to God. We pray also for emperors, for their servants and those in authority, for the order of the world, for peaceful circumstances, for the delay of the end." [11]

Clement of Alexandria, about 190 AD, said in Miscellanies VI.xiv.113.3: "Always giving thanks in all things to God through righteous hearing and divine reading, true inquiry, holy oblation, blessed prayer, praising, hymning, blessing, singing, such a soul is never separated from God at any time." [12]

4. THOSE BORING ANNOUNCEMENTS

That his heart may not be lifted above his brethren,
That he may not turn aside from the commandment
To the right hand or to the left,
And that he may prolong his days in his kingdom,
He and his children....
Deuteronomy 17:20 (NKJV)

Famous Theologians

About 450, Augustine—PRE-CATHOLIC: "...that not the voice alone may praise, but the works too....So, too, do thou whensoever thou singest 'Halleluia,' deal forth thy bread to the hungry, clothe the naked, take in the stranger: then doth not only thy voice sound, but thy hand soundeth in harmony with it, for thy deeds agree with thy words. (Expositions on the Psalms: Psalm CXLIX)

About 1370, THOMAS AQUINAS—CATHOLIC: "To assist a man against any distress that is due to an extrinsic cause comes to the same as the ransom of captives." (Summa Theologica, Secunda Secundae Partis)

About 1536, JOHN CALVIN—REFORMED CHURCHES: "The closer the relation the more frequent our offices of kindness should be...more duties in common between those who are more nearly connected by the ties of relationship, or friendship, or neighborhood. And this is done without any offence to God, by whose providence we are in a manner impelled to do it" (Institutes of the Christian Religion, Book II, 8:44).

About 1682, JOHN BUNYAN—BAPTIST: "If thy faith be not accompanied by a holy life, thou shalt be judged...a sounding brass and a tinking cymbal. For, they say, shew us your faith by your works, for we cannot see your heart....This is the man also that provokes others to good works. The ear that heareth such a man shall bless him....What do men meddle with religion for? Why do they call themselves by the name of the Lord Jesus?...God, therefore expecteth fruit....Let them work, or get them out; the vineyard must have laborers in it....A church, then...not place where the workers...may hide." (The Works of John Bunyan, "Christian Behavior" and "The Doom and Downfall of the Fruitless Professor").

About 1721, MATTHEW HENRY—PRESBYTERIAN: "Those that are not able to help...with their purses should help them with their pains...lend them a hand....Lazarus in his distress had nothing of his own...no relation to go to, nor did the [church] take care of him. It is an instance of the degeneracy of the Jewish church at this time that such a godly man as Lazarus was should be suffered to perish....He was hard-hearted to God's poor, and therefore he...has judgment without mercy and falls under a punishment" (Commentary, Vol. V, Luke 11:19f and Luke 10).

1859, 1872, 1875, CHARLES SPURGEON — BAPTIST: "The worst part of the Christian church...lost their hearts. Step into your churches and chapels, everything is orderly and precious; but where is the life?...You cannot pray well for those you know nothing about....They fuss about that wonderful point in the fourth verse of the fifteenth chapter of this and that, but no soup kitchen brings down upon them the blessings of the poor....We think our nose detects the faintest possible smell of hypocrisy in all this....To sunder ourselves in sympathy from our fellow-men is certainly inhuman, and therefore it can hardly be divine" (The New Park Street Pulpit Sermons pg. 277, Sermons in the Metropolitan Pulpit pg. 258, The Sword and the Trowel pg. 328).

Oh Jesus, you did so much for me. You didn't have to leave heaven, but you did it for me. You didn't have to take the persecution for being so good, but you did it for me. You didn't have to die such an excruciating death, but you did it for me. You didn't have to descend to hell and then break out again, but you it did, for me. How can I ever repay you?

Our wedding was part of the closing announcements one Sunday night. We had both been widowed and decided that, in this busy world, we did not want to inconvenience our friends who struggle even to make it to young people's first weddings.

During the closing announcements, we disappeared into a couple of side rooms along with our best man and matron of honor (an elder and his wife). Meanwhile, when the man was through with the ordinary announcements, he just told everyone, "Dick and Kathryn are now going to get married, so you may be seated if you'd like to stay and share in their joy."

Nearly everyone sat back down. What an exciting announcement! And they were part of it. The podium was moved, an old fashioned wedding song was sung, then we walked out and got married in front of probably 300 friends.

See there! Announcements don't really have to be so bad after all.

Come on now, you may be thinking. That was different. Announcements? How boring can you get? For the rest of us, there is no way you can ever make the regular announcements interesting. Tolerable maybe. But never interesting.

They're a waste of time, anyway. Nobody pays any attention to them. It just gives a job to one of the men so they can do something in public. That's all.

We have all experienced the frustration with the announcements. Often, all this person does is stand in front of us and read the bulletin. Ever feel like he should just say, "Let us all together stand and all together read the announcements"?

Get ready for a surprise. A surprise like you've never experienced before regarding Christian worship. A delightful surprise! A surprise full of serendipity, fascination, victory.

All that? Get real.

But that's been the problem all along. Getting real. The announcements mean nothing to us. Nothing because we've never participated in them.

Dr. Greg L. Bahsen has many blogs on the internet (+he is now deceased), some of which are about the church. In speaking of several things he believed have died in the church, he spoke of the death of fellowship: " 'But you need fellowship,' I'm often told. But I don't get fellowship listening to Christian rock/praise music, or looking at the back of someone's head during a sermon. The word translated 'fellowship' in the Bible is 'koinonia' which doesn't allow for one party to be a passive audience as is found in most churches. The best time for 'fellowship' is usually during the coffee and doughnuts between services. Sometimes 'Sunday School' can be a time of lively dialogue, heartfelt sharing, and informative 'questions-and-answers.' I was once a full-fledged member of a church, and I stopped attending 'church' and started attending only Sunday School and doughnuts. They excommunicated me…Proverbs 29:18 says, 'Where there is no vision, the people perish' Even if I were to put my body in a pew every Sunday, I would still feel very alone. I would be passively observing what went on up front."

God, I think things would be much more holy in worship if we didn't break the spell, so to speak, by talking about each other. Putting in the bulletin who is sick is enough. Don't you agree?

Where's the Meat?

Why do we gather together with other Christians in the first place? Technically, we could do everything alone that is a part of our worship services. We could sing alone, read the Bible alone, pray alone, listen to a tape of someone preaching alone, even keep the Lord's supper alone. People who say they can worship God just as well walking through the woods would be right if these are the only reasons for our gatherings.

But there is one thing we cannot do alone. It is explained in Hebrews 10. It is the reason we are told to gather together.

WHO?   CHRISTIANS — VERSE 22: "Let us draw near to God with a sincere heart in full
assurance of faith, having our hearts sprinkled to cleanse us from a guilty conscience and having our bodies washed with pure water."
WHAT?   REMAIN FAITHFUL — VERSE 23: "Let us hold unswervingly to the hope we profess, for
he who promised is faithful."
HOW?   ENCOURAGE — VERSE 24: "And let us consider how we may spur one another on
toward love and good deeds."
WHEN?   GATHER — VERSE 25: "Let us not give up meeting together, as some are in the habit of
 doing, but let us encourage one another, and all the more as you see the Day
approaching."
WHY?   SALVATION — VERSE 26: "If we deliberately keep on sinning after we have received
the knowledge of the truth, no sacrifice for sins is left."

Have you ever wondered why so many congregations are relatively inactive out in the world around them? The plain answer is that we're teaching by example that Christianity is an inactive, passive state of being.

We teach, by our example, that Christianity is (1) going to a building, (2) listening, (3) talking, (4) going home. For all the neighbors around our building know, they see us entering a building and coming out again. We are not any different, and they are not any different. No wonder people of the world think Christianity is boring. If that is all we do, then it is.

We must show each other how to express love and be filled with good works (God said that!), and then encourage each other to actually do them (God said that too). Otherwise we sin willfully (and God said that); there no longer remains a sacrifice for our sins but rather a terrifying judgment. Remember, the devils know all about God and believe and tremble (James 2:19), and it does not benefit them anything.

We must put behind us always being a learner. Just being at the church building "every time the doors are open" is being a "hearer of the word and not a doer...like unto a man who beholds his natural face in a glass; for he beholds himself, and goes his way, and straightway forgets what manner of man he was" (James 1:23, 24 KJV).

Sacrifice was part of worship under the Law of Moses for the Jews. It is still part of worship under Jesus' law for Christians. There we "offer to God a sacrifice of praise—the fruit of lips that confess his name." But this is not all, for we are also urged to "not forget to do good and share with others, for with such sacrifices God is pleased"; (Hebrews 13:15, 16).

The worship service is only the beginning of our service. Romans 12:1 tells us to "offer your bodies as living sacrifices, holy and pleasing to God—this is your spiritual act of worship." The King James Version states that it is "your reasonable service." It is only reasonable to expect a Christian to be full of acts of kindness and to encourage others to be also. This is the fulfillment of worship to God.

Matthew 7:16 and 20 both quote Jesus as saying, "By their fruit you will recognize them." John 15:16 says Jesus' followers were appointed to "go and bear fruit—fruit that will last."

Romans 7:4 and 5 explains the difference in what we use our bodies for as Christians compared with non-Christians: "So, my brothers, you also died to the law through the body of Christ, that you might belong to another, to him who was raised from the dead, IN ORDER THAT WE MIGHT BEAR FRUIT TO GOD. For when we were controlled by the sinful nature, the sinful passions aroused by the law were at work in our bodies, so that we bore fruit for death."

Is our congregation bearing fruit? Do we claim to be Christ-like? Jesus said in John 15:5, "I am the vine; you are the branches. If a man remains in me and I in him, he will bear much fruit; apart from me you can do nothing." Is our congregation apart from Jesus? Has it been accomplishing nothing in the name of Jesus?

Jesus went on to warn in verse 6: "If anyone does not remain in me, he is like a branch that is thrown away and withers; such branches are picked up, thrown into the fire and burned." Jesus said we must bring forth fruit. He commanded it.

Let us not be one of those to whom he said, "Not everyone who says to me, 'Lord! Lord!' will enter the kingdom of heaven, but only he who does the will of my Father who is in heaven. Many will say to me on that day, 'Lord! Lord! Did we not prophesy in your name, and in your name drive out demons and perform many miracles?' Then I will tell them plainly, 'I never knew you. Away from me, you evildoers' "(Matthew 7:21-23).

Right or wrong, we are in an instant society. We have instant potatoes, instant cataract removal, instant weather forecasts, instant startup of our cars, instant music at the flick of a switch, instant microwave cooking, instant worldwide internet.

Right or wrong, people want what they are searching for in church instantly also. People are church hopping, looking for an instant feeling of being accepted by the congregation and of being accepted by God. They may give a congregation one week or one month, but they won't stick around much longer if they're really serious about their search.

The only problem with this is that they become tired of always being the visitor and never belonging, and so most eventually settle for a congregation that will turn them into a clone, or they quit searching altogether and stay home on Sundays.

God, I'm glad we have a preacher who talks to us about our good works.
Most of us don't have time to do them, but we can slip in one or two every once
in awhile. We know our preacher means well.

From the Horse's Mouth

In his book, *What Americans Believe: An Annual Survey of Values and Religious Views in the United States,* George Barna reported that less than half of Americans strongly believe the Christian faith is relevant to the way they live. More disturbing is the fact that this figure applied equally to people who are regular church attenders. [1]

Since some people separate the Christian faith with the church, the same question was asked about the church: Do you strongly agree that the churches in your area are relevant to the way you live today?

Startlingly — or maybe it shouldn't surprise us — only 28% of the entire population agree that the churches are relevant to their lives. Of regular church attenders, 34% think churches are relevant to the way they live. Of those who never, ever attend church, only 10% think churches are relevant to the way they live. [2]

On the average, regular church attendees miss attending church about half the time; that is, only half the membership of any congregation is likely to be there on any Sunday morning.

In Barna's survey, of people who said they had not attended church in the past month, 63% had not attended for a year or more. [3]

So, why do people attend church? Less than half of regular church attendees attend to worship God. The next most important reason given for attending church was to become a better person. [4]

Of those who regularly attend church, only half believe the preaching impacts the way they live. Also, only half of regular attenders believe the congregation is friendly. [5]

In his book, *A Generation of Seekers: The Spiritual Journeys,*

Wade Clark Roof reported throughout his book the religious questions that people are typically seeking to be answered by the church:

1. Where is God when I need him?
2. What is moral and immoral?
3. Aren't my parents' values good enough?
4. Can't I be a Christian in my home?
5. Why aren't churches concerned with social justice and community problems?
6. Why are churches so boring and lifeless?
7. Do churches have to be so prejudiced against women?
8. Can I find a more fulfilling life with the church?
9. Can I exercise my individualism in church?
10. What is truth?
11. Can the church help me understand myself better?
12. Can the church help me fulfill my potential?
13. How can I trust the church?
14. Why doesn't the church get involved in the community more?
15. Why is the church so impotent?
16. Why shouldn't I be suspicious of the church?
17. Why so much ritualism which is so death-like to the spirit?
18. Is there a church anywhere who can make a difference in people's lives?
19. Can I have immediacy in my religion?
20. Can I encounter God and people on the feeling basis?
21. Are there any churches that exist in the real world?

Mr. Roof summarizes, "Just showing up and going through the motions is what many boomers abhor about churchgoing." [6]

Highly active seekers are trying to find a church where they are personally involved and feel fulfilled with their involvement. One-third of seekers said, "I feel the need to find more excitement and sensation in my life." [7] They want a church to be a warm, supportive place over against a world that is very dangerous and corrupt." [8]

People who dropped out of the church in their youth, tend to return for the following reasons:

1. To have a family experience
2. To provide moral standards for children
3. To work out marital and family problems
4. To ease some of the suffering in the world
5. To fill feelings of emptiness
6. To fill the need to belong [9]

One minister said this: "I think people are lonely. I think people's lives feel empty and dead for a lot of people, no matter how much money they have. I mean we haven't developed a middle-class theology to address our emptiness....then we stick them on a committee....There's a gap in there." [10]

Another minister said, "What really matters is how you treat people in the here and now, because that's really the only thing, despite what religion teaches you, that you can ever really know about. You don't know why you're here, and you don't know what happens when you die, and so you sort of have to make the best of what you have now." [11]

Church dropouts and those who hold back from affiliating with any congregation put great stress on getting their personal needs met as the reason why they'd go back to church. They want the emphasis to be on feelings, awareness of needs, freedom, and spirituality. [12]

People are saying they dropped out of church and even quit looking elsewhere because of boring and uninspiring worship services, stiff people in the pews, lifeless programs, cold and unfriendly atmosphere. [13]

When people refer to a congregation they can relate to and feel a part of, it is nearly always in relation to what goes on in the church "basement" — small groups sharing and doing things.

People feel congregations have lost "spirituality" which they generally define as genuine connectedness between religion and everyday life. "The struggle is to get beyond the facade, the external shell of religion, to its 'embodiment,' or the link between spirituality and responsible action....Boomers are willing to make commitments that express their deepest convictions; what they have difficulty doing is giving of themselves to programs and causes that do not connect with their own lives." [14]

Forty-eight percent of liberal protestants and 76% of conservative protestants say that churches have lost spirituality. The disillusionment is indeed widespread.

"Boomers will commit themselves to religious activities and organizations, including traditional congregations, where they feel there is some authentic connection with their lives and experiences." [15]

You know, God, I think the same way. But there isn't a church anywhere that is like this. It's impossible in these days when people are always rushing. An hour on Sunday can't include everything.

A Few Moments in Time

Oh, we know what you're leading up to, you may be thinking, not sure you want to keep reading. Forgetting our own craving for "feeling" our religion and making a difference in the world with it, we turn right around and say, "Well, don't expect me to put any time into this. I'm already overloaded. Up at 5:30 every morning, to bed at midnight. I can't handle any more obligations."

So, what we're basically doing is saying, "I want whatever takes time to do, but I don't have the time to do it. I want instant spirituality. I want it automatically by osmosis." That, in turn, adds to our feelings of guilt over a religion we cannot spend time with.

This is a busy rush-rush world full of time-savers that our ancestors never had; but still they ended up with more leisure than we have. Indeed, Christians in previous generations had a sense of "feeling" their religion more than we do. In a few moments a modern solution to this problem will be suggested; but first let us look at how previous generations found time to "feel" their religion. In those generations most women stayed home during the day, whether or not they had children (unless, of course, they were the sole breadwinner).

So, what did the women do during all that time? Those who

went to church got involved in "church work." They went to ladies Bible classes once a week, often combined with luncheons and a group project for the needy. Before, during, or after those classes, they discussed the needs of their own congregation and anyone in the community they knew about. Those, by the way, were their "announcements." But there was more than just talk.

On their own or in twos, these women went out into their community and busily met those needs. That was then. This is now. Things are different now. Indeed they are. Time is at a premium, and we're so caught up in all there is to do, we sometimes get lost in the forest and just wander, not even realizing it.

Well, that's the kind of world we've created. So, rather than jump into drastic changes, let's work with what we have—a few moments in time. Those moments will be on Sunday....

Okay, we've gotten up when our neighbors were still in bed or at least still in their pajamas. We got into the car, stopped at a fast-food place for a donut and coffee to go, and slipped into the church parking lot just before worship begins. So far, so good.

Now, what are we going to spend this time in worship services doing? Let's look at it from the point of view of visitors. They walk in and watch and listen. For an hour they watch and listen. They don't feel any different about the life they're going back to. They haven't been convinced in that one hour that anyone really cares about each other, let alone about the strange visitor.

That instant sense of belonging they crave from the congregation is not there. That instant sense of connecting with God and that God really cares about what's going on in their daily life is not there. They arrive and they leave in their perpetual lonely vacuum.

According to Hebrews 10 above, we must spend a majority of our time when we meet together encouraging each other to have love and good works.

"Like when?" you may be asking, rather impatient by now. "The singing and sermon take up most of the time we're together."

Perhaps we need to reduce the singing. After all, when Jesus established the Lord's Supper, the most important and divine part of Christian worship, the Bible says they say one hymn (Matthew 26:30).

There are things we can do on the spot while we're still with each other. Wouldn't that break up the formality? Oh, yes, it would. But is that bad? Who said we have to be formal?

A trend that keeps growing in the religious world — whether Christian, Buddhist, or whatever — is more emotionalism. People want to feel their religion. They want immediacy in it. So they raise their hands, turn around and around, sway, clap their hands, shout, put on dramas — anything to feel.

Even after this, however, many people finally give up, because it did not really and truly fill that emptiness in their heart, the part of them that wants to feel and experience religion.

Why not substitute all the time spent in emotionalism and formalism for some real experiencing? Experiencing the love of God by giving it and receiving it? If we don't have time the rest of the week for love and good works, why not do it while we're together? Are you serious?

Harmonious Notes of Encouragement

Let the person in charge of announcements get up and say, "Here are some people that could use some expressions of love."

On the back of each pew have a supply of the following: (1) Plain white bond paper, (2) envelopes, (3) a directory of members and hospital addresses, preprinted messages on colored bond paper done by a member who writes poetry or prose.

Then the announcer says, "These are the people from our congregation who are in the hospital. Sister Smith just had surgery. Who would like to send her a note? Any volunteers? Okay. And Brother Jones is still in the nursing home. Who would like to write him a note? Any volunteers? Okay, now, the Greens just had a baby girl. They named her Candy. Any volunteers to send them a note during the rest of the announcements?"

A few people who want to can raise their hands, and then begin immediately writing their note, or finding a pre-printed get-well note, thinking of you note, sympathy note, or congratulations note.

But it need not stop with the obvious. The announcer can then open up the newspaper. "Last week there was an accident on South Main which resulted in Hal Haley and Bryan Bullard going to General Hospital. Who wants to send them a note? Any volunteers?

"On the next page is a story about the Discount Pharmacy being robbed. The clerk's name was Yvonne Yelton. The robber's name was Bubba Black. Who would like to write Yvonne a note expressing our thankfulness that she was not hurt? Any volunteers? We have her address in the office, so you do not have to address an envelope. Any volunteers to send Bubba Black a note telling him that God loves everyone regardless of what they have done? He is out on bail bond and we have his address in the office also.

"On page 5 is the story of the parking garage murder last June. The man was sentenced to 20 years in prison. We do not know where he is going yet, but we have his family's address. Who would like to write to them a note of encouragement?

"On the obituary page, these are from our neighborhood: George Green age 62, Holly Hamilton age 3, and Fannie Fatima age 91. Who would like to send a note to the family of George Green? Any volunteers? How about Holly Hamilton's family? Any volunteers for Fannie Fatima's family?

"The birth announcement pages contains these from our neighborhood: A girl to Mr. & Mrs. Daniel Davis and a boy to Mr. and Mrs. Bevis Blue. Who will send them notes of congratulations?

"The engagement pages contain the announcement of Gloria Gonzales to Edward Effingham from our neighborhood. Who will send them notes? Also married were Harriet and Harry Hendrix. Who will send them a note?

"Now then. We obtained the following names from the electric company that Mr. & Mrs. Victor Varnish have just moved into our neighborhood. Who will volunteer to send them an invitation to church?

"In our congregation next week we will have two birthdays.

Cards to these people are being passed down the aisles now. Be sure and sign it and pass it on quickly. If the card is addressed to you, pretend you haven't seen it yet.

"In the nursing home down the street, there are three birthdays. And in the orphan home we send money to there is one birthday. Those cards are now being circulated also. Sign them quickly and pass them on. Oh yes, a Loretta Young off at the university is having a birthday next month and her card is being circulated, along with Harold Shaw who is stationed with the Army in Fort Freight on Mount Ararat. Be sure to sign their cards."

Then allow some time to write. Five minutes of silence should do it. If some who are not talented with writing notes would like to begin singing softly during this time, that might be good.

Don't discourage the children. If they want to use some of the paper on the back of the pews to draw on, let them. Then turn in their picture to be sent to one of the people who has been announced. What a wonderful opportunity to teach encouragement to your child.

Benevolence

But this is not the end of the announcements. There are other things that need to be done that may require use of the fellowship hall or some classrooms briefly after church services.

HUNGRY: "Next week, we are requesting that everyone bring cans of green beans to place in the barrels in the lobby. Now, there was a young father who stopped by the building this week who is between jobs and has a family. He lives over on Second Street. We have his address. Do I have any volunteers to go into the pantry after services, bag up what they need, and deliver it and a Bible to them on your way home?"

COLD: "On page two of the newspaper is a family who was burned out a couple nights ago. We have a list of clothing they need. Do I have any volunteers to go into our clothes closet and select a few basic items for them? Anyone? Raise your hand. Okay, we have the address of the motel they are staying it. Can you deliver them along with a Bible on your way home from church? Anyone with furniture they don't need? Call us this week with what you have and someone will call them to ask if they need it."

BEREAVED: "We have contacted the families in our neighborhood listed on the obituary page. One of them does not have any arrangements to feed the funeral attendees afterward. We are volunteering our building. Who can come at 11:00 next Thursday with some food? How many volunteers do we have?"

DISABLED: "Sister Conrad is home from the hospital, but is unable to cook for her family. Do we have any volunteers who will take dishes of food over there this week? How about Monday? Tuesday? Wednesday? Thursday?"

ORPHANED: "The orphan home we support is in need of toys. We have had some good donations. But we need to fix them now. Any volunteers to stay an hour after services and go to the basement to paint and repair? Come on, men. We've already lined up dinner for you. Any volunteers? Or if you're good at wood carving, sewing, or some other craft, please join the group and spend an hour making new things. Who would like to help in this way?"

WIDOWED: "Several of our single ladies need the oil and other things checked in their cars. If they will take their cars immediately after services to the west end of the parking lot, some men will be there to help out. Okay, men. Do we have any volunteers to help these ladies?"

FATHERLESS: "We have two young men who want to be included in a father-son banquet at school on February 1. Do we have two volunteers to go with them? Raise your hand. There's one. We need two. One more volunteer, guys? And we have a young man who got a 100-pound bow for Christmas. Do we have an archery buff who will take him out sometimes?"

CELEBRATORS: "As you know, Scott and Janice are getting married next month. They would like to have some love songs sung by some of you. Whoever likes to sing on key, meet them in classroom 4B after services. They will hand out the sheet music to what they want. They have pizza available to eat. Then you can go through the songs a couple times. Who can volunteer your time to practice every Sunday after church for a month?"

ABSENTEES: "In the telephone room are sandwiches and coffee. While the telephoners are eating, we need people to put our attendance cards from this morning in alphabetic order and determine who was absent. Then they can eat while the telephoners call to see if there's a problem we can help with, the filers can eat. Okay, any volunteers to put the cards in order? We need two. And volunteers to make phone calls. It'll only take an hour. Who can help out there?"

TEACHERS: "In the teachers' workroom will be three elementary level teachers needing help cutting out visual aids for next Sunday's class. Also, one adult class needs help collating and stapling some handouts for next Sunday. Do we have any volunteers to help out these teachers? It'll only take a few minutes. Anyone?" [16]

Soul Saving

Are the announcements over yet? No, not yet. Remember, according to Hebrews 10:25, the reason we are to meet together is to encourage love and good works toward each other and toward others.

But we can do all the good works in the world and not be any different from good moral people who never go to church. The reason we do good works is to open up the hearts of people to let them know God loves them. Christians need constant reminding of this. Non-Christians need to learn this for the very first time. Until they are approached about their salvation, our work is not yet done.

Romans 10:1-3 says we can have a zeal for God but not according to knowledge, and therefore be lost. So where do we get knowledge of God? Romans 10:17 says knowledge which leads to faith comes from the Word of God. We need to get God's word out to people. Otherwise our work is not done.

A poll taken several years ago revealed that 9% of people chose a particular congregation because of the architectural beauty of the building; 3% made their choice because the minister came to visit them; 18% chose on the basis of their prior denominational ties; 22% were influenced to attend because they knew and respected certain members; 34% because they were invited by a neighbor or friend.

Every Sunday morning, the strongest emphasis must center around the unsaved, the seekers. Other assemblies, such as Sunday night, Wednesday night, or Saturday night, can emphasize the needs of the regular members.

Every Sunday morning, someone needs to stand up and say, "Have you brought a visitor with you today?" Do not make the visitors stand and embarrass themselves. But just ask the members if they have. Then welcome the visitors.

But we can even go farther than this. The congregation can be divided up in groups of four or more (one for each week of the month). Each Sunday that group holds a potluck dinner in the fellowship hall for newcomers. Visitors and new members of the congregation are personally invited to the dinner. Also people in the community are called and invited—possibly along with the telephoners calling absentees. The rest can be done from someone's home or by the church secretary.

Before you say you don't have time, everyone has to eat, including the members. If you eat at home, you have to consider cooking time as well as eating time. If you eat out, you have to consider ordering time and waiting time as well as eating time.

At your newcomers dinner while they are eating, you can explain the types of work the congregation is involved in. Perhaps a few of the members who like to sing can entertain them while they eat.

After their meal, you may wish to show the first five minutes of a Bible survey film or a film proving the Bible is true, or so on, and have sign-up sheets available for people who would like to see them in their home. You may also wish to give a Bible to every family who would like to have one.

You could even have a skit about someone deciding to

become a Christian, or about someone in the Bible.

Some larger congregations have information centers for visitors in their lobby. This is a more personable form of accomplishing what the information center tries to do. You can have at each place last week's bulletin, a list of good works the congregation is involved in, and even a budget. In the chapter on giving, surveys are explained showing that money and the suspicious use of money is the main reason people leave churches or never go in the first place. Individual members who are business owners could have discount coupons at each seat.

The idea for new people is to give, give, give, not take, take, take. They are a little suspicious. Let them know they do not have to be.

Another way to reach out to souls is to offer Bible correspondence courses. This may be a world-wide evangelistic outreach, or a local outreach. At any rate, people's courses need to be graded and their questions answered. In another classroom a few members could gather to eat sandwiches they've brought, then grade lessons together.

Another outreach may be in yet another classroom. This would be the prayer room. Some people have a special gift of prayer. It is meaningful to them and they have no trouble with it.

On the other hand, there are some people who just do not have a long attention span. They didn't in school growing up, and they still do not. It just isn't one of their gifts. Rather than hold the congregation hostage with long, drawn-out prayers, the people who are comfortable with prayer can meet together after services. They may not be there long enough to need a meal.

They are needed to pray about everyone who was included in the announcements. Also they may have confidential access to the names of people who are studying the Bible and are showing an interest in becoming Christians.

On the attendance cards may be private prayer requests. Those can be referred to and prayed for at this time. Prayers of thanksgiving are also vital. And prayers of praise.

People wishing to contribute extra money to a special cause, or who have low incomes, may wish to gather after services once a week to fast together and use the money they would have spent on dinner for a worthy cause. They could do any number of things during their hour or so together.

Why?

But, you may object that the announcements during the services would take too much time. There wouldn't be any time left for the preacher.

Perhaps the preacher would like to incorporate the announcements into his sermon. Or perhaps the preacher would like to spend his time presiding over the Lord's Supper, or prayer requests, or reading the scriptures (all discussed in other chapters).

Or perhaps the preacher really wants to spend more of his time teaching the Bible on an individual basis during the week to these new people who have begun worshipping with your congregation. Even though they finally feel religion makes a difference in their lives, they may still not be sure how to become Christians, or they have a multitude of philosophical, moral, and theological questions they need answered.

Or perhaps he really wants to spend more time following up on the contacts made in the community through the newspaper outreach of the congregation.

In preaching a sermon, he must make general applications. Talking to people individually, he can zero in on certain spiritual questions people have and, after finding God's opinion of them in the Bible, help people find applications to their own lives.

Well, isn't that what the clergy for? To preach a sermon every Sunday?

In the church as set up in the Bible, there is no clergy and laity. In Revelation 2:6, Jesus from heaven praised one congregation because "you have this in your favor: You hate the practices of the Nicolaitans, which I also hate."

Then in Revelation 2:15-16 Jesus warned another congregation, "Likewise you also have those who hold to the teaching of the Nicolaitans. Repent therefore! Otherwise, I will soon come to you and will fight against them with the sword of my mouth."

The word Nicolaitan comes from the combined words Nicholas and laity. Nicholas means victory, and laity means people. Therefore, what we have here is power over the ordinary people.

Actually, we are all priests. Peter said, "You also, like living stones, are being built into a spiritual house to be a holy priesthood, offering spiritual sacrifices acceptable to God through Jesus Christ....You are a chosen people, a royal priesthood, a holy nation, a people belonging to God, that you may declare the praises of him who called you out of darkness into his wonderful light" (1st Peter 2:5, 9).

As spiritual kings and priests (Revelation 1:6), we have crowns. Over and over in Revelation chapters 2 and 3, Jesus sent his messages to the congregations and said, "I know your deeds." Then in chapter 3, verse 11, our Savior admonished, "I am coming soon. Hold on to what you have, so that no one will take your crown."

We are reassured about our Christian works in 1st Corinthians 15:57 and 58: "But thanks be to God! He gives us the victory through our Lord Jesus Christ. Therefore, my dear brothers, stand firm. Let nothing move you. Always give yourselves fully to the work of the Lord, because you know that your labor in the Lord is not in vain"

And Galatians 6:9 and 10 encourages us by saying, "Let us not become weary in doing good, for at the proper time we will reap a harvest if we do not give up. Therefore, as we have opportunity, let us do good to all people, especially to those who belong to the family of believers."

In the last day when our eternal destination is pronounced, we can depend on the righteous judgment of God who "will give to each person according to what he has done. To those who by persistence in doing good seek glory, honor and immortality, he will give eternal life" (Romans 2:6-7).

"God is not unjust; he will not forget your work and the love you have shown him as you have helped his people and continue to help them. We want each of you to show this same diligence to the very end, in order to make your hope sure. We do not want you to become lazy, but to imitate those who through faith and patience inherit what has been promised" (Hebrews 6:10-12).

When, after a long hard week, and a weekend where you have rushed around to get your grocery shopping done, the lawn mowed, and the myriad of other things necessary, but you get up on Sunday morning and worship and serve, you may sometimes wonder if you can stick it out another ten years. Think of Revelation 14:13: "'Blessed are the dead who die in the Lord from now on.' 'Yes,' says the Spirit, 'they will rest from their labor, for their deeds will follow them.' "

Does this, then, mean that we earn our salvation? Definitely not. We can never be good enough to be saved, "for all have sinned and fall short of the glory of God, and are justified freely by his grace through the redemption that came by Christ Jesus" (Romans 2:23-24).

Why, then, do good works? It is to imitate Jesus whom we have grown to love. He said in Mark 10:43-45, "Whoever wants to become great among you must be your servant, and whoever wants to be first must be slave of all. For even the Son of Man did not come to be served, but to serve."

God, that's scary. I'm going to be judged partly on my good works? I don't have time. I care about all those hurting people, but I really don't have time. Could you change your mind about this one thing, God?

I'd Rather See a Sermon....

Edgar A. Guest wrote a poem beginning, "I'd Rather See a Sermon than hear one any day."

I'd rather see a sermon than hear one any day.
I'd rather one should walk with me than merely tell the way.

The eye's a better pupil and more willing than the ear.
Fine counsel is confusing, but example's always clear.

The best of all the creatures are the men who live their creeds;
For to see good put in actions is what everybody needs.
I soon can learn to do it if you'll let me see it done.
I can watch your hands in action, your tongue too fast may run.

And the lecture you deliver may be very wise and true,
But I'd rather get my lessons by observing what you do.
For I might misunderstand you and the high advice you give,
But there's no misunderstanding how you act and how you live. 16]

How hard would we work for the church if we were paid $500 for each soul, $25 for each person visited, $20 for each visitor brought to worship, $250 for each home Bible study you conducted?

God came to us in the form of a man. When Jesus walked the earth, God too walked the earth. Jesus left. God's Spirit remained. God still walks the earth. Through those who have God's Spirit.

What would our lives be like today if God hadn't taken the time to come to us? What would our everyday lives be like if God took as much time for us as we do for him?

E. Stanley Jones, missionary to India, wrote in his *The Christ of the Indian Road:* [17]

"Jesus was never in a hurry. He never ran, never fussed, never worried. But he was always busy, so busy that sometimes he didn't even take time to eat. But he always had time for that next person with that next need.

"At the end of Jesus' day, he was fresh and adequate. Why? He was not worn out with inner conflicts. He was inwardly adjusted to the will of God.

"Modern advocates of 'spirituality' put too much emphasis on introspection, too much emphasis on absorption with oneself. Eventually we must dismiss ourselves from the focus of attention, and get on with the work of God. That, ultimately, will bring us the leisured heart.

"Jesus did not argue that life was a growth, and character an attainment. He 'grew in wisdom and stature, and in favor with God and man.'

"He did not speculate on why temptation should be in this world. He met it straight on. And after forty days' struggle with it in the wilderness, he conquered and 'returned in the power of the Spirit' to his home.

"He did not discourse on the dignity of labor. He worked at a carpenter's bench and his hands were hard with the toil of making yokes and plows, and this forever makes the toil of the hands honorable.

"He did not try to prove the existence of God. He brought him. He lived in God, and men looking upon his face could not find it within themselves to doubt God.

"He did not argue, as Socrates, the immortality of the soul. He raised the dead.

"He did not teach in a didactic way about the worth of children. He put his hands upon them and blessed them. And setting one in their midst he said, 'Of such is the kingdom of God.

"He did not paint in glowing colors the beauties of friendship and the need for human sympathy. He wept at the grave of his friend.

"He did not teach in the schoolroom manner the necessity of humility. He girded himself with a towel and kneeled down and washed his disciples' feet.'

"He did not discuss the question of the worth of personality as we do today. He loved and served persons.

"He did not discourse on human equality. He went to the poor and outcast and ate with them.

"He did not prove how pain and sorrow in the universe could be compatible with the love of God. He took on himself at the cross everything that spoke against the love of god. And through that pain, tragedy and sin, he showed the very love of God.

"He did not discourse on how the weakest human material can be transformed and made to contribute to the welfare of the world. He called to him a group of weak men, transformed them, and sent them out to begin the mightiest movement for uplift and redemption the world has ever seen.

"He wrote no books. Only once are we told that he wrote anything, and that was in the sand. But he wrote on the hearts and consciences of people about him, and it has become the world's most precious writing.

"He did not paint a utopia, far off and unrealizable. He announced that the kingdom of heaven is within us, and is 'at hand' and can be realized here and now.

"He did not discourse on the beauty of love. He loved.

"He told us that the human soul was worth more than the whole material universe. And when he had crossed the storm-tossed lake to find a storm-tossed soul, ridden with devils, he did not hesitate to sacrifice the two thousand swine to save this one lost man.

"He did not merely ask men to turn the other cheek when smitten on the one, to go the second mile when compelled to go one, to give the cloak also when sued for the coat, to love our enemies and to bless them. He himself did these very things. The servants struck him on one cheek, he turned the other, and the soldiers struck him on that one. They compelled him to go with them one mile from Gethsemane to the judgment hall. He went with them two, to Calvary. they took away his coat at the trial and he gave them his seamless robe at the cross. Then, in the agony of the cruel torture of the cross he prayed for his enemies, 'Father, forgive them, for they know not what they do.'

"He did not merely tell us that death need have no terror for us. He rose from the dead, and told the world we could too.

"Many teachers have tried to explain everything, yet changed little or nothing. Jesus explained little and changed everything.

"Many teachers have tried to diagnose the disease of humanity. Jesus cured it.

"Many philosophers speculate on how evil entered the world. Jesus presented himself as the way by which it shall leave.

"He did not go into long discussions about the Way to God and the possibility of finding him. He quietly said to me, 'I am the Way.'

"The philosophical, the mystical, the spirituality-centered person is weak. The mere practical person is weak. But Jesus, glowing with God and yet stooping to serve, is Strength Incarnate."

I have read somewhere of a wild duck on migration that came down into a zoo where tame ducks were feeding. This one particular duck liked the food so well that he stayed a day, a week, a month, then the whole season.

One day he heard a familiar honking high overhead and he recognized the call of his erstwhile companions winging their way home. His eyes sparkled, his heart beat faster, and he rose to join them. But he had fed too well and could get no higher than the tops of the zoo trees.

So he said to himself, "Oh well, what difference does it make? I like it here." So he spent the rest of his life in the zoo. The day came when his old companions passed over and he never even heard their call.

Reader, did you once mount up with the wings of eagles, but are now content to live in the zoo? Does your heart sometimes beat a little faster and your eyes be filled with tears?

But have you fed too well on the feasts of the Word in the church building? Do you like it too well there until you have finally reached the sad state that you no longer respond to the call from on high to go and share and tell those around you?

An unknown author once wrote this:

When the great plants of our cities have turned out their last finished work;
When our merchants have sold their last yard of silk;
And dismissed the last tired clerk;
When our banks have raked in their last dollar,
And paid the last dividends;
When the Judge of the earth says, "Close for the night,"
And asks for a balance – WHAT THEN?

When the singers have sung their last anthem,
And the preacher has made his last prayer;
When the people have heard their last sermon,
And the sound has died out of the air;
When the Bible lies closed on the pulpit,
And the pews are all empty of men;
And each one stands facing his record,
And the Great Books is opened – WHAT THEN?

When the bugle's call sinks into silence,
And the long, marching columns stand still;
When the captain repeats his last orders,
And they've captured the last fort and hill;
When the flag has been hauled from the masthead,
And the sounded afield check in,
And a world that rejected its Savior
Is asked for a reason – WHAT THEN?

When the actors have played their last drama,
And the mimic has made his last fun;
When the film has flashed its last picture,
And the billboard displayed its last run;
When the crowds seeking pleasure have vanished
And gone out in darkness again;
When the trumpet of ages has sounded,
And we stand up before Him – WHAT THEN?

Have we set proper priorities in our life? Read Ecclesiastes. Solomon tried everything possible to feel fulfilled in life, but felt complete emptiness in everything he did except where it concerned his God.

Some day our life will be over. It may be fifty years from now. Or five years. Or one. Or less. How do we want to be remembered? For what will people remember us? For building the largest building? For going the fastest? For being the best?

*They were going to be all that mortal could be **tomorrow**.*
*No one would be better than they **tomorrow**.*
*Each morning they'd stack up the letters to write **tomorrow**.*
It was too bad indeed they were too busy to visit,

*But they promised to do it **tomorrow.***

*The greatest of workers they would have been **tomorrow.***
*The world would have known them had they ever seen **tomorrow.***
But the fact is they died and faded from view,
And all that was left when living was through
*Was a mountain of good they intended to do **tomorrow.***

What kinds of plans do we have? Do our announcements at church center around getting it over with so we can go on to the important parts of the worship? Do we discuss in our classes and sermons how much good we should be doing? But it is always rhetoric? Then we go home unchanged? And our friends untouched?

First I was dying to reach my teens,
Then I was dying to graduate from college,
Then I was dying to get married,
Then I was dying to have children,
Then I was dying to get on with my career,
Then I was dying to retire,
Then I was dying.
And I suddenly realized
I had forgotten to live.

Second-Generation Church Accounts

Some of the quotations below refer to monetary gifts, but can also be applied to working toward helping in other ways.

Clement of Rome about 96 AD wrote in 55:2, "We know many among us who have given [sold] themselves into bondage in order that they might ransom others. Many delivered themselves into slavery and taking their price provided food for others." [18]

Aristides, a Christian from Athens wrote the earliest surviving explanation of Christianity and addressed it **to the emperor Hadrian about AD 125.** In his Apology 15 he said: "They love one another. They do not overlook the widow, and they save the orphan. He who has, ministers ungrudgingly to him who does not have. When they see strangers, they take him under their own roof....

"And if they hear that some are condemned or imprisoned on account of the name of their Lord, they contribute for those condemned and send to them what they need....And if there is any that is a slave or a poor man, they fast two or three days, and what they were going to set before themselves they send to them, considering themselves to give good cheer even as they were called to good cheer. [19]

In the Epistle to Diagnetus by an unknown writer, 10:4,5: "But whoever takes upon himself the burden of his neighbor – he who wills to benefit another who is worse off in respect of those things where he is better off, who taking the things which he has received from God distributed them to those who are in need – this one becomes a god to the ones who receive. He is an imitator of God." [20]

Lucian of Samosata, a pagan author of satires, was born about 120 AD, and wrote in The Death of Peregrinus 12-13: "At dawn there were to be seen waiting at the prison aged widows and orphan children, and their [church] officials even slept inside with him....Varied meals were brought in, and their sacred words were spoken....They exhibit extraordinary haste whenever one of them becomes such a public victim, for in no time they lavish their all....For these poor devils have altogether convinced themselves that they will be immortal and will live for all time; for which reason they despise death.... Therefore they despise all things equally and consider them a common possession." [21]

Hermas of Rome, wrote in the early 2nd century, Similitudes V.ii.7, 8: "On that day in which you fast, you shall taste nothing except bread and water. Of the foods which you were going to eat, reckon how much the food of that day when you fast was going to cost, and give the amount to a widow or orphan or one in need.

"Therefore instead of fields, purchase afflicted souls, as each is able. And visit widows and orphans and do not neglect them....For the Master made you rich for this purpose that you might perform these ministries for him." [22]

Justin, who lived about 150 AD, said in his Apology I, 67: "We always remember one another. Those who have, provide for all those in want....for the orphans and widows, those who are in want on account of sickness or some other cause, those who are on bonds and strangers who are sojourning." [23]

Barnabus, who lived about 190 AD, said in his writings 4:10: "You are not to retire by yourself and live alone as if you were already righteous, but you are to come together in one place and seek the common good." [24]

Sextus lived about 190 AD wrote in Sentences 47; 217: "Kindness to men on behalf of God is the only suitable sacrifice to God. God does not hear the prayer of the one who does not hear men in need." [25]

5. LAST SUPPER OR LOST SUPPER?

Not forsaking the assembling of ourselves together, as is the manner of some,
but exhorting one another,
and so much the more as you see the Day approaching.
For if we sin willfully after we have received the knowledge of the truth, there
no longer remains a sacrifice for sins....
How much worse punishment do you suppose will he be thought worthy who
has trampled the Son of God underfoot,
counted the blood of this covenant by which he was
sacrificed a common thing....
Hebrews 10:25-29 (NKJV)

Famous Theologians

About 1536 — JOHN CALVIN — REFORMED CHURCHES — "And truly this custom, which enjoins communicating once a year, is a most evident contrivance of the Devil, by whose instrumentality soever it may have been determined....Every week, at least, the table of the Lord should have been spread for Christian assemblies, and the promises declared by which in partaking of it we might be spiritually fed" (Institutions Book 4, chap. 17, sect. 46; and Book 6, chap. 18, sect. 56)

About 1775 — JOHN WESLEY — METHODIST — "If we are not obliged to communicate constantly, by what argument can it be proved that we are obliged to communicate frequently? Yeah, more than once a year? Or once in seven years? Or once before we die?" (106th Sermon, Vol. III, on Luke 22:19, "The Duty of Constant Communion").

About 1800 — JOHN MASON — PRESBYTERIAN — "It is evidence [Acts 20:7] not only that Christians assembled on the Lord's day for public worship, but that they did not part without commemorating his death....sacramental communion was a principal, if not the principal object of their meeting" (Letters on Frequent Communion, Edinburgh Edition of 1799, pg. 34-42) [1]

Oh Jesus, you were so determined to stand by Truth no matter how angry people got. You confronted religious leaders who persecuted you over it, and you refused to back down. Even to the death. What a man! What a God! The God!

I heard it was done out west several decades ago. I do not know if it is true. But what I heard is that a young preacher felt as though his congregation was taking far too much for granted the Lord's Supper and the horror of Jesus' sacrifice for us.

So he brought a lamb to services, tied it up, and put it on the covered communion table. Then, before anyone could grasp was about to happen, he raised a knife over his head and plunged it into the lamb so that it died.

The congregation gaped and gasped in disbelief at the atrocity done to the innocent lamb, some also wondering what the Humane Society might do to them.

The young preacher, then announced, "This is what Jesus, our Lamb of God, did for us."

Perhaps it was "overkill." But, have we gone to the other extreme? Most leaders in the denominational Christian religion world believe that having the Lord's Supper every week makes it so commonplace, that partakers begin taking it for granted.

Are they right?

Tom Sine, in his book, *The Mustard Seed Conspiracy*, says, "I believe the Lord's Supper is the very center of worship....Those of us who are from sermon-centered backgrounds could profit from moving the pulpit over a bit and restoring communion and prayer to the center of our common life. We have so much to learn from the liturgical churches regarding the awesomeness of worshiping the Almighty....need to learn to worship the Lord in the beauty of silence." [2]

Jesus said in all the gospels that the Lord's Supper was to be kept to "do this in remembrance of me" (Luke 22:19, etc. and also 1st Corinthians 11:23-26). He said the bread represented his body given for the world of sinners. The wine represented the New Testament put into effect by the loss of his blood and hence his life. So, we have two things to reflect on as we partake of the Lord's Supper.

God, I look forward to Easter every year. What Jesus did for us all on that day so long ago, is so special. It demands everything special I can dedicate on that day. Thank you, Jesus.

Jesus' Body Torture for Us

When we partake of the Lord's Supper, we recall his terrible crucifixion where his body was broken open by the nails and his blood poured out. How could we ever take that for granted? How could remembering this make it commonplace? Let us allow our minds to go back to that horrible and amazing day........

.....The hammer fell and the first cruel blow sent the pain shooting up Jesus' arms, racing through his body, and exploding in his head.

"*Oh, Father. Help me,*" he perhaps cried out deep in his soul.

Jesus instinctively reached with his free hand for the punctured one, but another soldier grabbed it and pulled it back out of the way. Another brutal blow fell on his quivering flesh. Trembling fingers strained to fold down in an impossible attempt to grasp the spike and remove it.

Finally, with two contemptible spikes piercing his flesh and torturing his ever-weakening body, Jesus was forced to stand. He probably nearly fainted. Two soldiers supported the beam, keeping Jesus from falling backward. They backed him up to the tall upright beam darkened with the blood of countless other victims of justice.

With each step his flesh was torn and the punctures in his mutilated wrists stretched larger. They moved slowly so that his wrists did not go back through the spikes and free themselves. Still the torture. His muscles cramped and fiery pain shoot helter-skelter through every inch of his body.

Once there, two more soldiers on ladders lifted up Jesus' crossbeam a few tormenting inches to wedge it into the cut-out section of the upright beam. The two beams were secured together.

Jesus' entire weight was now supported by two thin tearing spikes and the bones at the bottom of his hands. He writhed in agony. In his wildest imagination, he had not anticipated such torment. Such horrible, hideous pain.

The soldier then knelt on the ground before Jesus. He took the victim's left foot and placed it over the right foot. Jesus, preoccupied with the pain in his upper body, perhaps was not yet aware of what they were about to do to him next.

A larger and much longer spike was handed to the soldier. Once more with the hammer. With three skillful blows, the spike was sent mercilessly shooting through the top and arch of one foot, then the top and heel of the other foot, and finally into the upright beam.

The pain shot like fiery arrows through every nerve in Jesus' body. He shuddered in agony. The cold spikes held on, refusing any help, defying any relief.

Jesus perhaps was temporarily oblivious of any voices around him, for the trauma seized all thoughts.

Another soldier climbed on one of the ladders at the side up to the top of the beam. His hammer had one last job. The sign declaring the felon's crime was nailed to the top of the cross over the Savior's head. Each blow of the hammer shook the entire structure and sent shock waves through Jesus' body.

Suddenly, without warning, Jesus' lungs begged for air, for now he could not get his next breath. He gasped and struggled for oxygen.

Blood gushed out in mocking pulsating rhythm from the half severed arteries in his wrists and feet, almost as if from the nails themselves. Most of it spilled to the ground, but some of it streamed treacherously across his arms as if in search of something.

"Father!" He groaned, and lifted his head toward the heavens. But a sharp pain again shot through his body. He jerked, and for a moment stiffened, then slowly gave over to a spasmodic twisting, twisting, twisting.

"Father!" he pleaded, "give them..." his voice choked and broken, "a full...pardon...."

Jesus' head fell forward. His eyes filled with tears of agony.

"They don't realize," he choked, "what...they've... done...."

Oh, Jesus. Your death. It was so terrible. I don't deserve all you did for me.

Jesus' Soul Torture for Us

His terrible death is not all we must think about during the Lord's Supper. We must think about the reason he had to go through it. That reason was us. That reason was our own sins. The sins of action and attitude we commit every day, often don't admit, then take for granted that, if God is really good, He will feel honored to take us into his heaven.

During the Lord's Supper, we must remember the Old Testament (old covenant) of Moses where forgiveness of sins was impossible. We were supposed to keep the Old Law perfectly for salvation and we couldn't do it (Romans 3:23). It only takes one sin to make us sinners (James 2:10).

True, the Old Testament (old covenant) allowed for sacrifices, but they couldn't take away our sins (Hebrews 10:4-11). Creating a New Testament (new covenant) and putting it into effect required that the testator die (Hebrews 8:13; 9:16f).

Look at what Jesus rescued us from! Try reading through some of the 600 laws in the Law of Moses (that's the indomitable Exodus, Leviticus, Numbers, and Deuteronomy that few of us have ever plodded through!) to see what Jesus saved us from. He rescued us from the impossible requirement of keeping all those laws perfectly.

He also rescued us from the numerous sins listed in the New Testament—sins of action, attitude, and inaction; in other words, bad things we did, bad attitudes we had, and good things we left undone.

But ultimately, what Jesus really saved us from was hell. Biblical accounts of hell describe it as flames and screaming (Luke 16:22-31; Revelation 20:10-15), crying and gnashing teeth as if freezing (Matthew 8:12), bottomless and always falling (Revelation 9:1-6), darkness (Revelation 16). Which of us will be there? Cowards, immoral, and liars, to name a few (Revelation 21:8). Is it fun to read about? How about spending eternity there?

Body death is not all that Jesus had to go through to save us from hell. Many thousands had been crucified before Jesus and would be afterward. And yet Hebrews 5:7 says, "During the days of Jesus' life on earth, he offered up prayers and petitions WITH LOUD CRIES AND TEARS to the one who could save him from death." Jesus was conqueror of the ages. Jesus had already conquered storms and leprosy and even death itself. What was it that he had not yet faced that he was so terrified of?

Jesus knew he would be temporarily forsaken by God. How and why?

Look, now at Acts 2:27 — "Because you will not abandon me to the grave, nor will you let your Holy One see decay."

Many think that this verse refers merely to Jesus' body. But in the original Greek, "grave" is *hadas,* sometimes also translated "hades." According to *Thayer's Greek-English Lexicon of the New Testament, hadas* literally means unseen. In Greek classical literature of that period, it referred to the lower regions where Pluto reigned, or the netherworld, the realm of the dead, not someone's cemetery plot six feet under.

The *Septuagint* was the Greek translation of the Hebrew *Old Testament* completed two centuries before Christ and accepted as authentic by all Jews. The *Septuagint* used the word *hadas* in Job 10:21 and Job 11:8 as the place of no return, the land of gloom and deep shadow.

The word was used by Jesus in Matthew 11:23f and Luke 10:15 saying that the citizens of Capernaum will go down to *hades* on the Day of Judgment for not believing Jesus was the Son of God. He was not referring to six feet under, the grave.

The word was used by Jesus in Luke 16:23 to explain where the rich man was in torment. Jesus also used it in Matthew 16:18 to declare that its gates will not prevail against the kingdom of heaven.

Both physical and spiritual death were personified in 1st Corinthians 15:55 where it is said, "'Where, O death [physical in the grave], is your victory? Where, O death [spiritual in hell], is your sting?'" The second death is *hadas.*

In Revelation 6:8, the difference in physical and spiritual death is made where the rider of the pale horse was Death [physical], with Hades [spiritual] following close behind him. Further, in Revelation 20:13 it explains that both those in the sea [dead bodies] and in hades [souls] were judged, then thrown into the lake of fire.

Therefore, Acts 2:27 is talking, not only about Jesus' fleshly body, but also his soul. More specifically, it seems Jesus descended to hell. Some people believe this happened during his three days in the grave. Evidence seems strong that it happened the last three hours on the cross during the darkness when Jesus said nothing. A few minutes before his death, Jesus cried out in a loud voice, "My God! My God! Why have you forsaken me?" (Mark 15:34).

Of course, he knew the answer to his own question. Perhaps he wanted us down through the ages to try to think seriously about the answer. Why did God forsake him?

Technically, death means separation. Physical death is separation from the body. Spiritual death is separation from God. Romans 3:23 says the wages of sin is death. 2nd Corinthians 5:21a says, "God made him who had no sin to be sin for us."

For a few minutes, or perhaps during those last three hours on the cross, some people believe Jesus descended to hell in our place!

This may be what Jesus meant when he said he would build his church and the gates of hell would not prevail against [Jesus the head of] it in Matthew 16:18.

Can you just hear him? Shouting out to Satan as he plunges to the farthest depths away from his Father? Let us for a few minutes imagine what it might have been like....

"Punish me! Not them! Punish me! I've got all their sins! I am now them! Punish me! Punish me! Not them! Punish me...."

Why? To complete the process. Sin deserves punishment and separation from God. But he descended for even more than this. It was also to get the keys.

Revelation 9:1 and 11 says that, when Satan fell, he had the keys to the Abyss—hell. By the time Jesus appeared to John, Jesus said he now had the keys (Revelation 1:18).

No one had ever escaped from hell before. It was an impossibility. It would, of course, be impossible for all of us. That is, until Jesus. If Jesus did, indeed, plunge briefly to hell, that may have been what Jesus dreaded so, not only in the Garden of Gethsemane where an angel had to be sent to encourage him, but his entire life (Hebrews 5:7). Thousands of other people had been crucified, but no one had ever or could ever escape from hell.

Let us imagine for a moment what it might have been like if this indeed was the case (italics are only inferred words/thoughts of Jesus)......

.....*Punish me! Not them! Punish me!* [3]

With the power of ultimate love, Jesus plunged with an iron will. Resolutely, he burst through the gates of hell where he did not belong so mankind could burst through the gates of heaven where we do not belong!

The sacrificial flames leaped and lunged lustily around him. Good is eaten alive by Bad. *Stop the pain! Stop the pain!*

The raging fire. Forever incinerating. Forever blazing. Forever the inferno.

Ghosts and forever shadows. Night. Murky night. Terrible darkness. Forever darkness in the forever night. So lonely. So terribly lonely. Screams, but no one can be seen.

Then the cold and chattering teeth. So cold! Teeth gnawing and grinding. Forever exhausted from the shaking and trembling, the spasms and chilling. [4]

In a sense, Jesus' soul was falling. Falling through the bottomless hole. No place to stand. No sidewalk, no road, no floor, no earth. Just the falling.

The stench. It engulfed his senses. The rank, foul smell. Forever the retching and heaving.

Then Jesus' energies must have turned from pain to anger. Love demands anger. Anger at sin and self-destruction. Anger at the god of hatred who convinces people the God of Love is against them.

No! I will not allow it! perhaps Jesus declared.

Satan must have been shocked at Jesus' burst of courage.

You will never destroy them! I will take the keys of hell away from you! Jesus was determined to take control.

I will break out of here and save them forever! I will no longer allow you to accuse them, Satan! I forgave them from the cross. [5] That means, their sins no longer exist.

"But," Satan perhaps reminded Jesus, "Their sins are what sent you here to hell. They're the cause of all this, you know. It's their just punishment."

I forgive them too.

The moment Jesus forgave the world of its sins, all the burning and falling and cold and stench and darkness was gone. Jesus was once more strong. [6] And once more Jesus was the Water of Life, the Foundation of the Saved, the Wall of Salvation, the Light of the world. [7] How Satan hates the light.

Perhaps, just as Jesus debated Satan in the wilderness after his baptism, he debated him now again. Perhaps their final debate before Jesus crushed Satan's head went something like this:

I have come to do the will of my Father in heaven. [8] Satan, hand me the keys!

"You know, that so-called Father of yours probably doesn't even exist," perhaps Satan said.

My Father and I are united forever! [9]

"Stop kidding yourself! He was only a figment of your imagination. All that power you had to perform miracles? That was me, not him. If you are the Son of God...."

Those words again. Those doubting words: IF.... Just like at the beginning. If you're God's Son, turn these rocks to bread.... If you're God's Son, jump off a tower.... If you're God's Son, come down from the cross.... [10]

"IF you are the Son of God, go ahead and grab the keys, but you'll never get them to work. You can't break out of hell. No one has ever done that."

N O O O O O O ! ! ! ! ! ! Jesus was angry.

"Your father, if he exists, has deserted you. If you are the Son of God, he would rescue you. You have been forever forsaken by God."

N O O O O O O ! ! ! ! ! Jesus has had enough of Satan's lies, his anger at Satan now out of control.

Father, where are you? Father, I have a gift for you. It's all the forgiven ones. I completed my sacrifice! And the keys! I have the keys!

[11]

Jesus raced courageously through the corridors of hell. He must escape. For their sakes. He must escape. Zooming. Looming higher and higher. Soaring! And defiantly, Jesus burst out through the gates of hell!

....Now, his soul back on the cross, he said, "It is finished."

Oh, Jesus, I cannot even begin to imagine your strength. I am so weak compared with you. You went into the prison of my soul and rescued me. I couldn't do it alone.

Paradise Purchased

Paradise (Abraham's bosom) is in the Bible in two different places. Before Jesus, paradise was so close to hell that the saved could talk to the condemned. The saved could see the condemned.

It was as though paradise was not completely freed from Satan's control until Jesus came to finish his work. Hebrews 9:15 says that Jesus "died as a ransom [held ransom by Satan?] to set them free from the sins committed under the first covenant." That means no person was truly saved until Jesus completed his ransoming work (read about this in Hebrews).

Revelation 7:17 says God will forever wipe away the tears of all the saved. Yet, being that close to hell, and even being able to see it and talk to people in it, would not be completely heavenly.

Apparently, if indeed Jesus descended to hell, then broke out, he took paradise with him (see Ephesians 4:8-10) to heaven. Then he returned to his body. For in Revelation 22:2, paradise, where the tree of life is, was now in heaven.

At the end of the three hours on the cross, he shouted frantically, "My God! My God! Why have you forsaken me?" (He knew the answer.) He then quietly announced, "It is finished" (John 19:30) and died.

He'd accomplished everything required on his part. Now he would rest for three days before his Father brought him back to life and return to his friends to prove he will do the same for all who believe on him.

Think about this, and stand amazed. Amazed that Jesus, who abhorred sin, became exactly what he hated — sin. For himself? No, he was already safe. It was for you and me.

Jesus and his Father spared nothing to keep us out of hell. How can we even think of remembering his death just occasionally because it might become commonplace and we might take it for granted? Take Jesus for granted? After all he did for us?

Oh God, I knew Jesus suffered on the cross. I never understood what it meant for him to suffer for my sins. He became me and took my punishment for me. How could he?

Golden Silence

But there is more. More that we must think about during the Lord's Supper. Yes, we must think of the body torture Jesus endured in our place. Yes, we must think of the soul torture Jesus endured in our place. We must also think of the reason he had to endure it all. It is explained in 1st Corinthians 11:27-32. Let's look at it progressively.

First, we are told not to eat and drink the bread and cup in an unworthy manner. This does not say we are supposed to be worthy of the bread and wine. We are not now, and never will be. What it does say is that our manner must be worthy. We're to concentrate on, not rush through, the death of Jesus. But there's even more.

We are to examine ourselves before taking of the bread and cup. That means we could hold the emblem in our hand for a few minutes considering what we're about to do. Or the person in charge of the Lord's Supper may announce a few minutes of silence to consider our sins before the ushers distribute the emblems. It takes time to think back over the week and consider what we did each day and how we may have sinned.

In verse 30, the writer explains that many are spiritually

weak and sickly, and still others are completely asleep spiritually because they haven't been doing this. Then verse thirty-one says: "If we judged ourselves, we would not come under judgment."

Yes, the Lord's Supper serves partly as a time to examine ourselves and judge what we did the past week. This is our weekly pop quiz which we give ourselves. As a result, the final exam given by God on the Day of Judgment isn't full of surprises, and we've been able to correct a lot of things that might have been left "on the books" so to speak.

This takes time. This means going over last Monday, Tuesday, Wednesday and so on all week. And if we don't know how, perhaps we need to take this time to look up a few lists of sins. It is not the obvious sins like murder that get us. It's what we call the little sins; either the sins of attitude, sins resulting from poor attitude, or sins of not doing good things we should have done.

Is it masochistic to think of our sins like this? Many people would think so. Many people would arrogantly declare there is no such thing as sin. Many who admit we do sin, arrogantly declare we can't think of what they are. God helps us. Let's look at some of the lists of sins in the New Testament:

>Romans 1:29-31 lists greed, depravity, envy, murder, strife, deceit, malice, gossip, slander, insolence, arrogance, boastfulness, disobedience, senselessness, faithlessness, heartlessness, ruthlessness.

>1st Corinthians 6:9-10 lists sexual immorality, idolatry, adultery, prostitution, homosexuality, thievery, greed, drunkenness, slander, swindling.

>Galatians 5:19-21 lists sexual immorality, impurity, debauchery, idolatry, witchcraft, hatred, discord, jealousy, fits of rage, selfish ambition, dissensions, factions, envy, drunkenness, orgies.

>Ephesians 4:31; 5:4f lists bitterness, rage, anger, brawling, slander, malice, obscenity, foolish talk, coarse joking, immorality, impurity, greed.

>Philippians 2:3, 14 lists selfish ambition, vain conceit, complaining, arguing.

>Colossians 3:8-9 lists anger, rage, malice, slander, filthy language, lying.

>1st Timothy 1:9-10; 5:13; 6:3-5 lists lawbreaking, rebellion, ungodliness, unholiness, irreligion, murder, adultery, perversion, slave trading, lying, perjury, idleness, gossip, false teaching, conceit, controversial, quarrelsomeness, envy, strife, malicious talk, evil suspicions, constant friction, robbing truth.

>2nd Timothy 3:2-8 lists loving self, loving money, boastfulness, pride,

abusiveness, disobedience to parents, ungratefulness, unholiness, without love, unforgiving, slanderous, without self-control, brutal, not lovers of good, treacherousness, rashness, conceit, lovers of pleasure, denying power of godliness, controlling the weak-willed, never acknowledging truth, opposing the truth, depraved of mind.

>Titus 3:3, 9-11 lists foolishness, disobedience, deceit, enslaved by passions, malice, envy, hatred, foolish controversies, arguments, quarrels, divisiveness.

>James 3:14-16; 4:1-3; 5:3-6 lists bitter envy, selfish ambition, boasting, denying the truth, disorder, fights, quarrels, murder, covetousness, quarrelsomeness, fighting, wrong motives, hoarding wealth, failing to pay wages, living in self-indulgence, condemning the innocent.

>1st Peter 2:1; 4:3 lists malice, deceit, hypocrisy, envy, slander, debauchery, lust, drunkenness, orgies, carousing, idolatry.

>2nd Peter 2:14-19 lists adulterous eyes, seducing, greedy, boastful, lustful, enticing, slaves of depravity.

>Jude 7-8, 16 lists sexual immorality, perversion, rejecting authority, slandering celestial beings, grumbling, faultfinding, boastful, flatterers.

>Revelation 21:8 lists cowardliness, disbelief, vileness, murder, sexual immorality, false healing, idolatry, lying.

We are also to develop plans on how we are going to try to overcome our sins.

We always were and still are so unworthy. When we take of the Lord's Supper, our souls cannot help but fall at the feet of Jesus weeping, and whispering,

"Thank you! Thank you...."

Two Firsts

But there are people who will tell us keeping the Lord's Supper monthly, quarterly or yearly is enough. In fact, they will also say it doesn't really matter on which day we take it, suggesting that Friday, the day Jesus died, might be a good day to take it. It could be a lot of people honestly believe there is no directive on this, but there is.

There is only one directive in the New Testament telling us when and how often to keep the Lord's Supper. But it only takes once for God to say something for it to be true. It is found in Acts

20:7. It mentions two firsts, two priorities. The first first is the day of meeting. The second first is the primary reason for meeting.

"On the FIRST day of the week we came together TO break bread."(NIV) The original Greek reads, *En de ta mia-ton sabbaton, sunag-menon hamon klasai arton....*

Let's take a brief look at a few of those Greek words, for they uncover a marvelous new world.

"Ta" is a little word but with great meaning. It is another word for *ho*. These interchangeable words are used in connection with the official affairs of state, such as THE constitution, THE governor, THE budget deficit. In the Judeo-Christian state of affairs it is used regarding THE Ten Commandments, THE Savior of the world, THE Sabbath. In Acts 20:7 it refers to THE first day of the week as the official day of Christians. Other places in the Bible Sunday is called THE Lord's Day (see Revelation 1:10).

"Mia" is the feminine form of neutral *heis* and is translated one. *Heis* is 283 times in the New Testament as one. *Mia* is translated as first. Even more dynamic is to discover that it refers to EACH and EVERY one WITHOUT EXCEPTION, as in Acts 2:6 where every man heard the apostles speak in their own language.

Does this mean we get to keep Easter every Sunday? You bet it does! With all the agony propelling into ecstasy! All the impossible zooming into reality! All the hopelessness exploding into victory!

Nothing can stop us now! We will declare it and declare it and declare it! Not one Sunday in the year, not one Sunday in the quarter, not one Sunday in the month, but every Sunday of every week! This is the main purpose of our meeting on Sunday! All other forms of worship we can do any day of the week.

Are we sure of this? Let's look at some more Greek words. **"Ton"** means a certain day, a particular day, not just any day. It never appears alone. In Acts 20:7, it appears as "mia ton."

When **"ton"** is combined with **"pro"** to create the word "pro ton", it gives the significance of copying another first, an original first, a prototype. **"Mia ton"** and **"pro ton"** have basically the same meanings. Therefore, Sundays are set aside to recreate the prototype of the meaningful thing that happened on the first

Sunday of significance to the Christian.

So, what happened of significance to Christians on Sunday? That question is an understatement. What DIDN'T happen? is more like it.

On Sunday, Jesus, after being dead three days, came back to life (Mark 16:9, etc.)! On Sunday he kept the Lord's Supper with two of his disciples (Luke 24:28)! On another Sunday he appeared to his loyal apostles (Luke 24:33); and yet another Sunday (John 20:26-29)! On Sunday he gave power to his Apostles to carry on his work after he leaves (John 20:21-23)! And on Sunday, the church of Christ was born (Acts 1:20, 21)!

What more do we want in order to make Sunday a special day? Oh, God created all days equally. But Sunday became special because of what Jesus did that day, and remains special to Christians everywhere throughout all ages.

Well, you may have spotted the word *"Sabbaton"* in that sentence, and being the intelligent person you are, quickly figured out it refers to the Sabbath day. Shouldn't, therefore, the Lord's Supper be kept on Saturday? Since the previous words in Acts 20:7 already referred to the first day, this word is used as a contrast to the Sabbath, and to help people understand when the first day was. In other words the first day after the Sabbath was to be remembered. This is clear in Matthew 28:1 which refers to late on the Sabbath before dawn being just before the first day of the week. Early Christians sometimes called Sunday the "eighth" day of the week. Since the word Sabbath is plural, it refers to every first day after every Sabbath.

Some may be thinking that this just means the early Christians met on every Sunday to have a meal. After all, verse 11 says they ate a meal. Is it talking about two different things?

"Sunag" refers to a religious congregation or assembly and we get the word synagogue from it. *"Menon"* refers to people who are present together as a group. They met together for religious purposes, specifically to "break bread" of the Lord's Supper. Later, after midnight, they broke bread for a different purpose. This time they "ate" a meal, a term also used in Acts 10:10 where they were very hungry.

Are there other references to having the Lord's Supper daily? No, those daily experiences were meals. Acts 2:46 says the Christians in Jerusalem daily broke bread together, EATING their MEAT with gladness. The word translated eat here comes from the Greek word, *metalam* from whence we get our word metabolism.

Okay, you may be thinking, it looks like the Christians broke bread as part of the Lord's Supper at the beginning of their meeting, then Paul preached to midnight, then after midnight they ate a meal. But don't you think this was a practice for just the early church? After all, many of them had seen Jesus for themselves. Meeting every Sunday for the Lord's Supper would mean more to them. Let's look at the last of that sentence.

"Harmon" is extremely important. Basically, it means to perpetually espouse or adopt in harmony with something. It is NEVER TEMPORARY. Vine's *Expository of New Testament Words* says *harmon* refers to something that is PERPETUAL and ongoing, such as each and every such day perpetually.

So, what part is perpetual? The day appointed to keep the Lord's Supper is perpetual. Does it say year? No, it says day. Does it say any day of any week of the year? No, it says the first day of every week in the year. And not just in the first century, but in the 21st century also.

Think about the Old Testament Mosaic command, "Remember THE Sabbath Day to keep it holy" (Exodus 20:8). Did they keep the Sabbath day once a year? No, they kept it every week. Did they keep any day of the week? No, they kept the seventh day. THE Sabbath day meant EVERY Sabbath Day.

No Jew ever said, "Well, it doesn't specify, so we'll keep the Sabbath once a month, or quarterly or yearly." So, why would a Christian keep THE first day of the week for breaking bread monthly, quarterly, or yearly?

Okay, you're convinced. But the kind of bread does not make any difference, some say. For sure, they certainly don't want to copy the Catholics who use unleavened bread. So they'll use leavened bread to prove we're not following the pope. Would it really be following the pope to use unleavened bread?

"Klasai Arton" refers to bread, often the shewbread used by the priests in a Jewish religious ceremony. What kind of bread was it? Did it matter?

When Jesus instituted the Lord's Supper, he was actually keeping the Passover Feast, also called the day of Unleavened Bread (Luke 22:7, Deuteronomy 16:5-8). Observers were to clean their house and make sure there was nothing with yeast in it anywhere.

In 1st Corinthians 5:7, it says Jesus became our Passover lamb that was eaten at that feast. Therefore, we do not have meat at the Lord's Supper. However, he took that same unleavened bread which originally referred to the Jews being in a hurry to eat and leave slavery in Egypt (Exodus 12:8ff) and said it now represented his body.

Jesus gave new meaning to the yeast also. He referred to the "yeast of the Pharisees" (Matthew 16:6 & 12) being their distorted teachings of God. Still later, the Bible referred to the "yeast of malice and wickedness" (1 Corinthians 5:8).

Therefore, the kind of bread we use for the Lord's Supper does have significance. If Jesus specifically used unleavened bread, and he referred to yeast as evil, who are we to change the symbols and use any kind of bread we want? If we begin using leavened bread, we may as well add sugar and chocolate and make it chocolate cake while we're at it.

So, what are the two firsts in this Acts 20:7 scripture? We are to meet on every first day of every week in the year. AND, the primary purpose we are to meet that makes the first day unique is that we are to keep the Lord's Supper.

Every other day of the week we find Christians singing, praying, reading scriptures, and preaching. But they never kept the Lord's Supper just any time they wanted. They were to meet on the FIRST day of the week TO (FOR THE PRIMARY PURPOSE) break bread.

Every Sunday, God? I get to keep the Lord's Supper every Sunday? Deep down I always wanted to. But no one agreed with me. They thought we had to get fancy that day. All you want is for us to compare our sins with your power to forgive. That's all.

Not In the Body

What happens to us if we do not partake of the Lord's Supper every Sunday? What happens if we do not go through the process of considering what Jesus did for us, and our sins that caused it?

Jesus spent some time on this in John 6:53. It is dynamic. It is warning enough to get us to never take the Lord's Supper for granted again.

"I tell you the truth, unless you eat the flesh of the Son of Man and drink his blood, you have no life in you!"

In fact, 1st Corinthians 11:33 says that, if anyone missed the Lord's Supper, we are to wait for that person. Most congregations "wait" by returning to worship again in the evening to provide that opportunity for those who had to work or were otherwise tied up during the morning.

Well, can we take the Lord's Supper alone? We could say that the church is the body of Christ, and based on the above verse, we would have to take it with the body. But that is stretching the meaning a little. Let's just return to the examples God included in his Bible. And while we're at it, does a church leader have to hand it to us or put it in our mouth?

In the gospels, the Lord's Supper was instituted by Jesus with eleven of his twelve apostles (Judas having left by then).

Acts 20:6 and 7 says Sopater, Aristarchus, Secundus, Gaius, Timothy, Tychicus, and Trophimus were joined by Paul and "the others" at Troas. There, they "came together" on Sunday in order to have the Lord's Supper.

The church in Corinth was having trouble distinguishing between a regular meal and the Lord's Supper. Paul led into this discussion by saying, "In the following directives I have no praise for you, for your MEETINGS do more harm than good. In the first place, I hear that when you come together....When you come together, it is not the Lord's Supper you eat....Therefore, whoever eats the bread or drinks the cup of the Lord in an unworthy manner will be guilty of sinning" (1st Corinthians 11:17, 18, 20, 27).

Here is a suggestion for those who lead the congregation in the Lord's Supper. Why not read scriptures about Jesus' death, burial, resurrection and the importance of his blood. Below are listed fifty-two passages from the Bible that might be read before, during, or after the Lord's Supper.

1. Matthew 17:22-23; 20:28
2. Matthew 26:1-4
3. Matthew 26:26-29
4. Matthew 26:36-50
5. Matthew 26:57-67
6. Matthew 27:1-2, 11-25
7. Matthew 27:27-31
8. Matthew 27:33-50
9. Matthew 28:1-10
10. Mark 14:22-26
11. Mark 14:32-46
12. Mark 14:53-65
13. Mark 15:1-20
14. Mark 15:22-39
15. Mark 15:42-16:7
16. Mark 16:9-14
17. Luke 22:14-20
18. Luke 22:39-53
19. Luke 22:63-71
20. Luke 23:13-24
21. Luke 23:33-48
22. Luke 24:1-12
23. Luke 24:13-53
24. John 1:9-11, 29
25. John 18:12-14; 19-24
26. John 18:28-39
27. John 19:1-15
28. John 19:16-30
29. John 20:1-18
30. John 20:19-31
31. Acts 1:1-11
32. Acts 2:14-36
33. Acts 4:8-12
34. Acts 10:34-43
35. Acts 13:23-36
36. Romans 6:3-11
37. Romans 8:1-11
38. Romans 8:28-39
39. I Corinthians 10:16-17

40. I Corinthians 11:23-26
41. I Corinthians 15:1-8
42. I Corinthians 15:12-22
43. Ephesians 2:4-7
44. Philippians 2:5-11
45. Colossians 1:12-22
46. Colossians 2:8-15
47. Hebrews 9:13-17; 10:4-18
48. I Peter 1:18-21
49. Revelation 5:6-9
50. Revelation 1:5-7
51. Psalm 22:6-10, 14-18
52. Isaiah 53:3-12

The following refers to all the times the church gets together. That would include Sunday, of course, which is the minimum. "Let us not give up meeting together, as some are in the habit of doing, but let us encourage one another—and ALL THE MORE as you see the Day approaching. If we deliberately keep on sinning after we have received the knowledge of the truth, no sacrifice for sins is left, but only a fearful expectation of judgment and of raging fire that will consume the enemies of God" (Hebrews 10:25-27).

Why so forceful? It is explained in an introductory statement: "Let us consider how we may spur one another on toward love and good deeds" (Hebrews 10:24). It is explained further by the brother of Jesus: "What good is it, my brothers, if a man claims to have faith but has no deeds? Can such faith save him? Suppose a brother or sister is without clothes and daily food. If one of you says to him, 'Go, I wish you well; keep warm and well fed,' but does nothing about his physical needs, what good is it?" (James 2:14-16).

In other words, while we're examining ourselves before the Lord's Supper, we need to consider whether we've done any good deeds the previous week. To make us worthy to be saved? No, to prove our faith in, gratitude for, and love toward God. James goes on to say, "You believe that there is one God. Good! Even the demons believe that—and shudder. You foolish man...faith without deeds is useless" (James 2:19-20).

Oh God, there is so much to think about during the Lord's Supper. But we've never allowed for much silence. We need the silence to commune with you. There's so much to commune about.

But the Depth of Easter....

Some readers may have concluded that everything noted is true, but they cannot let go of that one very special Sunday of the year when there are special programs proclaiming Jesus' death, burial, and resurrection.

Let us never think that officially remembering Jesus' death, burial, and resurrection once a year is sufficient. Let us never think we can thank Jesus for what he did for us in the way he prescribed for us just once a year, no matter how grand.

However, if it is against the conscience of some to stop celebrating with a special service once a year, then don't. Romans 14:6 and 19 says, "He who regards one day as special, does so to the Lord. He who eats meat, eats to the Lord, for he gives thanks to God; and he who abstains, does so to the Lord and gives thanks to God.....Let us therefore make every effort to do what leads to peace and to mutual edification." Just remember to keep it as one of all 52 Sundays in the year you remember Jesus' sacrifice.

If a special celebration of Jesus' death, burial, and resurrection can attract people who normally never darken a church building door, do it. But, again, not to the elimination of the all the other Sundays of the year.

The same is true of Christmas. All Bible scholars agree that there is never any command or example in the Bible for us to set aside a special day or days to remember Jesus' birth until he comes. This is the one time of the year that even atheists are forced to say the word Christ, for they cannot say Christmas without doing so. Infamous atheist, speaker and writer, Madolyn Murray O'Hare, celebrated Christmas!

Do atheists and agnostics celebrate Christmas for selfish reasons? Certainly. Most of us do too, if we are willing to admit it.

But, Paul saw good even in the selfish proclamation of Jesus. He said,

"The former preach Christ out of selfish ambition, not sincerely, supposing that they can stir up trouble for me while I am in chains. But what does it matter? The important thing is that in every way, whether from false motives or true, Christ is preached. And because of this I rejoice" (Philippians 1:17-18).

But, do not neglect the other 51 Sundays of the year to remember Jesus death until he comes. Once these special days take precedence to the point of eliminating the ones stipulated in God's Word, they become misleading.

Besides, who would want to eliminate the special time once a week when we consider the depth of Jesus' sacrifice, and the reason—our sins?

Yes, God, I appreciate Easter. But I'll never see it again like I used to. I could never come back to life alone. Jesus did it first to prove you'll do the same for me! Oh resurrection day! How I long for it. Every day.

The Grandest Statement of Faith

But, there will be visitors mingled in with the congregation each Sunday who are not used to the Lord's Supper occurring suddenly without fanfare. They are used to more pomp and ceremony in connection with it. Many are confused because they are used to it being kept only on Easter Sunday in March or April.

Not having personally investigated the scriptures regarding the Lord's Supper, visitors may think that your congregation is being sacrilegious. Be sensitive to their feelings and be prepared.

Make a statement about it in the bulletin or order of worship handed to everyone when they enter the building. Explain what will be happening during the service and why. Further, the person in charge of the Lord's Supper must explain what is about to happen, referring to applicable scriptures.

The person in charge also needs to talk about what Jesus'

death means to him and try to represent everyone in the audience. (It may be that, since this will take up part of the sermon time, the minister may be put in charge of this each week.)

The message of the Lord's Supper is the basic gospel message. In a nutshell, the gospel is this, as found in 1st Corinthians 15:1-4:

"I want to remind you of the gospel I preached to you, which you received and on which you have taken your stand. By this gospel you are saved, if you hold firmly to the word I preached to you. Otherwise, you have believed in vain.

"For what I received I passed on to you as of first importance: That Christ died for our sins according to the scriptures, that he was buried, that he was raised on the third day according to the scriptures."

The Lord's Supper is the most dynamic sermon that could ever be demonstrated. The Lord's Supper spells out the gospel. The Lord's Supper makes a connection between Jesus' death on the cross and our sins. This is a connection most people in the world do not understand. What an opportunity to explain it!

As a result of being told this, after the first gospel sermon, "When the people heard this, they were cut to the heart and said to Peter and the other apostles, 'Brothers, what shall we do?' " (Acts 2:37).

Do we want people to ask us what to do to be saved? Then have the Lord's Supper every week and proclaim every week that Jesus took our punishment for our sins and died in our place on the cross. This should prick the heart of anyone except the most hardened.

"He actually did that for me?" they will think. "For me? I had no idea. What can I do to accept his gift of salvation?"

Second-Generation Church Accounts

Around 90 AD, an unknown Christian in Syria wrote in his **Didache** 14:1: "Having earlier confessed your sins so that your sacrifice may be pure, come together EACH Lord's day of the Lord, break bread, and give thanks." [12]

And in Didache 9; 10; 14 he wrote this: "Concerning the [Lord's Supper], give thanks in this way: First concerning the cup, 'We give thanks to you, our Father, for the holy vine of David, your Servant, which you made known to us through Jesus your Servant. To you be the glory forever.

"Concerning the broken bread, 'We give thanks to you, our Father, for the life and knowledge which you made known to us through Jesus your Servant. To you be the glory forever. As this broken bread was scattered upon the mountains and being gathered together became one loaf, so may your church be gathered together from the ends of the earth into your kingdom. Because the glory and the power are yours through Jesus Christ forever.'

"No one is to eat or drink of your [Lord's Supper] except those who have been baptized in the name of the Lord.

"Having earlier confessed your sins so that your sacrifice may be pure, come together EACH Lord's day of the Lord, break bread, and give thanks. No one who has a quarrel with his fellow is to meet with you until they are reconciled, in order that your sacrifice may not be defiled. For this is what was spoken by the Lord. [13]

Ignatius, a friend of the Apostle John, said in his Magnesians 9: "If therefore those who lived according to the old practices came to the new hope, no longer observing the Sabbath but living according to the Lord's day, in which also our life arose through him and his death (which some deny)...." [14]

Justin Martyr wrote this around 100 AD in his Apology I,65: "After we thus wash him who has been persuaded and agreed entirely with our teachings....we pray that we who have learned the truth may be counted worthy and may be found good citizens through our works and keepers of his commandments so that we may receive the eternal salvation.

"When we cease from our prayers, we salute one another with a kiss. Next there is brought to the president of the brethren bread and a cup of water mixed with wine. Taking these he sends up praise and glory to the Father of all through the name of his Son and of the Holy Spirit and makes thanksgiving at length for the gifts we were counted worthy to receive from him.

"When he completes the prayers and thanksgiving, all the people present sing out their assent by saying 'Amen'....When the president has given thanks and all the people have made their acclamation, those called by us deacons give to each of those present to partake of the bread and wine mixed with water for which thanksgiving has been given, and they carry some away to those who are absent." [15]

ADDENDUM I — Who Serves It?

Historically, in the early church the elders often led the Lord's Supper because it was the Christians' main reason for meeting on Sundays. Then the deacons distributed it to the congregation. Actually, who is to lead and distribute the Lord's Supper is not in the Bible; therefore it is left to the discretion of the congregation. It certainly is not listed among the duties of elders or deacons found in 1st Timothy and Titus.

However, by the last of the first century, many made it a regulation that the elders had to administer the Lord's Supper, and the higher the leader's position, the better.

Christians are to keep the Lord's Supper every Sunday. But the denominational world's religious hierarchy's insistence that only they be allowed to "administer it," keeps Christians from obeying God's higher command to keep it every Sunday if they don't have someone "ordained" by the church hierarchy in their assembly.

Indeed, Paul warned the Ephesian elders that it would be from among their own eldership that the first heresy would originate. "Even from your own number men will arise and distort the truth in order to draw away disciples after them" (Acts 20:30). Luke 22:17-19 says that Jesus gave the bread to his disciples and told them to divide it among themselves. He never handed it to each of them individually.

ADDENDUM II – Is He Really There?

Some well-meaning people believe (because they've been taught this by "religious" people) that the bread and wine actually become the body and blood of Jesus.

In the mid-1500s in England, a Mrs. Prest of Cornwall continually talked with others about the inconsistencies of believing Jesus was actually present in the bread and wine of the Lord's Supper. When taken before the bishop, she said,

"I will demand of you whether you can deny your creed, which says that Christ doth perpetually sit at the right hand of His Father, both body and soul, until He come again; or whether He be there in heaven our Advocate, and to make prayer for us unto God

His Father? If He be so, He is not here on earth in a piece of bread....If He did not offer His body once for all, why make you a new offering?...If He is to be worshipped in spirit and in truth, why do you worship a piece of bread?"

The bishop falsely accused her of starting her own church and had her imprisoned. Many visits followed by people trying to get her to recant, but she would not. Finally she was sentenced to be burned at the stake, to which she replied, "This day have I found that which I have long sought." As they lit the fire, she prayed, "God be merciful to me a sinner." Then, patiently enduring, she was consumed by the flames and her body reduced to ashes. [16]

So, how can we know whether the bread and wine are the actual body and blood of Jesus? All we have to do is look closely at the above scriptures which recount Jesus instituting the Lord's Supper. When he said, "This is my body" and "This is my blood" he was still in his actual body, and still circulating his actual blood. Since Jesus had only one body, his body could not have been in two places at once.

In the early 1600s, in Lisbon, Portugal, an Englishman of Bristol, settled to set up business for his merchant employer. William Gardiner continued to worship as he had in Britain where historically the apostle Simon had started the church late in the first century.

One day he went to a wedding which included celebration of the mass (Lord's Supper). He was shocked at the superstition he saw. He returned the following Sunday where once again he witnessed people worshipping the bread.

Gardiner could not hold back his outrage at such misuse of the Lord's Supper. He sprang forward, snatched the bread from the cleric and trampled it underfoot. Someone in the congregation stabbed him with a dagger. When they demanded to know why he had done such a thing, he replied he had done so "out of an honest indignation, to see the ridiculous superstitious and gross idolatries practiced here."

Thereupon he was sent to prison and tortured excruciatingly. Finally he was ordered executed. A large fire was created. He was pulled up over the fire by pulleys, then let down near the fire where he was roasted by slow degrees. He bore it patiently, and to the last thanked God for the privilege of defending his truths on earth. [17]

As we investigate the Bible further on this subject, we learn that Jesus' Apostles, soon after the beginning of the church, clearly said Christians were not to drink blood: "James [Jesus' brother] spoke up....'we should write to them, telling them to abstain from food polluted by idols, from sexual immorality, from the meat of strangled animals and from blood' " (Acts 15:13, 20).

Further, the following letter was written: "The apostles and elders, your brothers, to the Gentile believers....You are to abstain from food sacrificed to idols, from blood, from the meat of strangled animals and from sexual immorality" (Acts 15:23, 29).

Also in the early 1600s in Italy, Daniel Rambaut of Vilario was imprisoned because he did not believe in the real presence of Jesus in the bread and wine (the "host") along with several other beliefs that were not in the Bible. Although interrogated numerous times by various priests, he continued to say that his understanding of the Bible and his conscience would not allow him to subscribe to such a belief.

Continually he told them that to believe the real presence in the host is a shocking union of both blasphemy and idolatry. Further, the words of consecration said by the priests called "transubstantiation," which supposedly turned the bread and wine into the actual body and blood of Jesus "is too gross an absurdity for even a child to believe who was come to the least glimmering of reason...nothing but the most blind superstition...." [18]

Even in the early church writings, the Lord's Supper was continually defended to pagans who complained that Christians were guilty of cannibalism (as well as incest) because they regularly ate someone's flesh and blood (and were married to those they called their brothers and sisters). The Christians explained to their accusers that these were both spiritual in nature, and not fleshly.

Theophilus wrote about 180 AD: *To Autolycus* III.xv: "Consider then if those who have been taught such things are able to live indifferently and to be joined in unlawful intercourse or most ungodly of all to eat human flesh....With them temperance is present, self-control is exercised, monogamy is preserved." [19]

6. UNEXPLOITED GIVERS
For all that is in the world
~ the lust of the flesh, the lust of the eyes, and the pride of life ~
is not of the Father but is of the world.
I John 2:16 (NKJV)

Famous Theologians

About 450, AUGUSTINE — PRE-CATHOLIC: Give without a qualm: it's the Lord who receives, the Lord who is asking. You wouldn't have anything to give him unless you had first received it from him....acts of charity. (Sermon 390)

About 1836, JOHN CALVIN — REFORMED CHURCHES: "Wherefore the Papal priests draw a silly inference when they claim the tithes for themselves, as if due to them in right of the priesthood; else must they needs prove that those whom they call the laity are their tenants...it would be sacrilege to appropriate the tithes to their own use....'The priesthood being changed, the right also is at the same time transferred' (Hebrews 7:12)...whatever the Law had conferred on the Levitical priests now belongs to Christ alone." (Commentaries on the Last Four Books of Moses, Numbers 18:20)

1682, JOHN BUNYAN — BAPTIST: "Upon the first day of the week let every one of you lay by him in store as God hath prospered him....The work now to be done was...to bestow their charity upon the poor; yea, to provide for time to come." (The Works of John Bunyan, "The Seventh-Day Sabbath" Vol. II, pg. 377)

1721, MATTHEW HENRY — PRESBYTERIAN: "Markets in the temple...rob God of his honor....The priests lived, and lived plentifully upon the altar; but, not content with that, they found other ways and means to squeeze money out of the people." (Commentary, Vol. 5, Matthew 21:12)

1868, CHARLES H. SPURGEON — BAPTIST: "Much has been said about giving the tenth of one's income to the Lord....But it is as great a mistake to suppose that the Jew only gave a tenth. He gave very, very, very much more than that...but after that came all the free-will offerings...so that, perhaps, he gave a third....I do not, however, like to lay down any rules....for the Lord's New Testament...teacheth us rather the soul of liberality....Give...proportionately, as the Lord has prospered you....You are not under the Law but under grace; you are not, therefore, to give or to do anything to God as of compulsion, as though you heard the old Mosaic whip cracking in your ears."

Oh, Jesus, how hard it must have been for your apostles to say goodbye to you. But you assured them you'd always be partners with them. Your promise is true today also. You are as close to us as our heart. We feel you smiling somehow. Where are you, Jesus? You're inside of us. That's why we cannot see you. Thank you for your friendship.

A disaster happened one Sunday morning in church when my twin brother and I were maybe a year old. It was during the collection. And, by the way, our World War II era church building only had a basement at the time due to building-supply shortages, and so had a cement floor.

You understand that men do not have laps. Women have laps — at least whenever they wear skirts. Women back then always wore skirts. Well, I was sitting on my mother's lap, and my twin brother was sitting on my father's non-lap.

The collection plate slowly made its way down the rows back and forth, back and forth between the ushers in each aisle. When it got to our row in the back, either my father got his hands mixed up, or forgot he had my brother on his non-lap.

Letting go of my brother, he reached up and took the collection plate from the usher. Then it happened.

My brother commenced to slip through my father's legs and fall upside down onto the cement floor. Immediately the collection plate commenced to slip through my father's hands and fall upside down onto the cement floor.

The collection plate clanged all over the floor, and my brother screamed all over the floor. Immediately both my father and the usher got down on the floor with the others and began trying to retrieve their charges. Finally, the usher was able to grab the collection plate and my father was able to grab his baby. The usher resumed his place in the aisle, and my father resumed his place in the pew. The money eventually quit rolling and chinking across the floor, and my brother eventually quit screaming.

By this time, half the congregation was embarrassed and trying to wish the whole thing out of existence. The other half of the congregation was snickering or outright laughing. My father wished he could just fall through the floor, and my mother wished he would.

Isn't giving like this today? We feel like we're letting go of the important things in life to take hold of the collection plate and put something in it. We feel embarrassed at some times, and we're made to feel guilty at other times. As a result, any sermon on giving is considered too much.

The way giving is approached, we can certainly see why. Sometimes we are made to feel like the man who announced the collection plate would now be passed with the warning, "And now brethren, let us give in accordance with what we reported on our Form 1040."

Oh Jesus, you went through so much for me. How could you? You dreaded it. The Father said it was the only way. You did it for him. For me. For love. How can I ever pay you for eternity with you, paid for with your agony and tears, your flesh and your blood?

Viewpoint of Outsiders

George Gallup wrote in *The People's Religion: American Faith in the '90s,* page 144, that the number-one reason given by people for having abandoned the church was "too much concern [1] for money." [2]

George Barna, another pollster, found the same thing and wrote of it in his *Never on a Sunday: The Challenge of the Unchurched.* [3] In both cases, half of the dropouts gave this as their primary reason for leaving the church.

A large portion of religious radio or TV programs, either before, during, or after, make at least one appeal for money "or else this ministry cannot go on." It is as though the public is required to support this man, when it was this man's idea to go on the air, not the public's.

Everyone is acquainted with the money scams of some media evangelists, bilking believers out of thousands of dollars, sometimes life savings. In fact, the book *The Day America Told the Truth* lists TV evangelists as 69th out of 71 professions Americans thought were dishonest. They were beaten out even by prostitutes.

[4]

In his book, *Inside the Minds of Unchurched Harry and Mary*, Lee Strobel, a former atheist, said, "When I first went to church, I suspected that the ministry's real goal was to fleece me. Actually, I was secretly hoping I would find the church was a scam because not only would I have a front-page story for *The Chicago Tribune*, but I could reject the church and its God along with it." [5]

Several years ago, *Time* magazine interviewed a well-known minister. The reporter's pre-listed questions centered on his salary, his vacations, his cars, his houses, whether he owned an airplane or boat, and what his benefit package was.

Jesus never asked for money. Never. Never, ever! Even though he traveled all over the "holy land" preaching during a period of three years, he never asked for money. He could have worked miracles to get money, but never did. Well he did one time in order to pay Peter's and his annual temple tax, which Peter got out of a fish's mouth (Matthew 17:24-27). We have no indication he continued to work at his carpentry trade once he began his ministry. There were people who voluntarily supported him (Luke 8:1-3), but he never asked for their money. [6]

How could that be?

But, before we get into what the church leadership has a right to expect of people and possible approaches, let us look at what the church does not have a right to.

God, I'd never drop out of church because of money. No matter how much they asked for, I wouldn't drop out. Well, I may go to another church, but I'd never drop out for good.

Old Testament Giving

TITHING WASN'T ALL

Tithing, that is, giving one-tenth of one's income, is mentioned only twelve times in the Old Testament. It is mentioned four times in the New Testament, and always in reference to Old Testament tithing. It is never mentioned in connection with Christianity.

The first mention is of Abraham who lived before the Law of Moses, but voluntarily gave one-tenth of everything to the priest of Salem (Genesis 14:20 and Hebrews 7:5-9).

According to the Law of Moses, the Jews had to tithe every crop and every animal (Leviticus 27:30-32; Deuteronomy 14:22-28). These tithes were used by the Levite tribe to live on, and the Levites in turn were to give a tenth of what they'd received for the priests to live on (Numbers 18:24-28). In Jesus' day, but still during the era of the Law of Moses, Jews tithed even spice seeds, and then bragged about how holy they were (Matthew 23:23, Luke 11:42; 18:11-14).

Only Levites and priests were allowed to collect the tithes, and they did this by going around to all the towns (Nehemiah 10:37-38). When people failed to pay their tithes, God said they were robbing him (Malachi 3:8-10).

But it didn't stop there. Over and above their tithes, Jews were required to give the first fruits of their crops, firstborn of their herds, and other gifts (2nd Chronicles 31:5-12).

But still the good Jew did not stop giving. Deuteronomy 12:6 refers to "your [1] tithes, [2] and special gifts, [3] what you have vowed to give, [4] and your free will offerings, [5] and the firstborn of your herds and flocks." Some people even got so they bragged about their freewill offerings which were over and above their tithing (Amos 4:4)!

Storerooms were set up in every town to store the special contributions, first fruits, and tithes (Nehemiah 12:44; 13:5).

Furthermore, every third year, all Jews were to set up a welfare program with an additional tithe for the Levites, aliens, fatherless, and widows in times of emergency. So, once every three years, Jews were to give 20% of their income.

PAYMENT FOR PRAYER REQUESTS

Special prayer requests involved what the Jews referred to as vows. They paid in "temple shekels" which, in today's buying power, is about $5. Examples of vows/prayer requests were....

for traveling mercies (Genesis 28:20)
to dedicate oneself or someone else for special service to God (Leviticus 27:2)
to dedicate oneself as a Nazarite (Numbers 6:2-18)
to be delivered from an enemy army (Numbers 21:2)
to have victory over an enemy army (Judges 11:30, 39)
to have a child (1st Samuel 1:11; Proverbs 31:2)
to return to one's home and be reconciled with family (2nd Samuel 15:7-8)
to be freed of troubles and desertion by friends (Psalm 22:11, 25; 66:13)
to thank God if prayer is answered (Psalm 50:14, 56:12; 65:1)
to prove allegiance to God before others (Psalm 76:11; Isaiah 19:21)
to thank God for a verdict of not guilty (Psalm 116:8, 14, 18-19)
to find the perfect place to build (Psalm 132:1-5)
to recover from illness (Job 22:27; Jonah 2:7-9)
to express fear of and acknowledge God's justice (Jonah 1:16)
to express peace (Nahum 1:15).

David, by the way, made vows every day (Pslam 61:8). These prayer requests were not free. Leviticus 27:2-7 lists the following money that had to be paid for vows/prayer requests:

Male 20-60 50 shekels $250
Female 20-60 30 shekels $150
Male 5-20 20 shekels $100
Female 5-20 10 shekels $ 50
Male birth-5 5 shekels $100
Female birt-5 3 shekels $ 15
Male 60+ 15 shekels $ 75
Female 60+ 10 shekels $ 50

ANIMAL/FOOD OFFERINGS

Leviticus 5:15 refers to "...a ram from the flock, one without defect and of the proper value in silver, according to the sanctuary shekel." One shekel of silver was worth about $25 dollars in today's values. Therefore, let us give a minimum value to every animal of $25. Below is a list of potential offerings:

$25   FIRSTBORN (Leviticus 3:45-47). Whenever an animal or person bore their firstborn, that child or animal had to be given to God's service. However, they could be redeemed or bought back for five shekels each.

$25   BURNT OFFERINGS (Leviticus 1:6, 8-13; 8:18-21; 16:24) could be a bull, ram, or male bird. It was voluntary for (1) atonement for unintentional sin in general, (2) expression of devotion, or (3) commitment and complete surrender to God's will.

$ 5   GRAIN OFFERINGS (Leviticus 2; 6:14-23) were grain, flour, oil, incense, bread, and salt. They were sometimes burned up with a burnt offering, and sometimes eaten with fellowship offerings. It was voluntary for (1) recognition of God's goodness and provisions, (2) devotion to God.

$10   FELLOWSHIP OFFERINGS (Leviticus 3; 7:11-34) could be any clean animal or a variety of breads. It was voluntary for (1) thanksgiving.

$20   SIN OFFERINGS (Leviticus 4:1 — 5:13; 6:24-30; 8:14-17; 16:3-22) had to be a goat or lamb, or perhaps a bird if poor, or of flour if extremely poor. It was mandatory for (1) atonement for specific unintentional sin, (2) confession of sin, (3) forgiveness of sin, (4) cleansing from defilement.

GUILT OFFERINGS (Leviticus 5:14 — 6:7; 7:1-6) had to be a ram or lamb, but were not offered very often. It was mandatory for unintentional sin requiring full restitution (such as killing someone else's animal) plus 20%. It was mandatory for cleansing from defilement.

Let us now make out a sample annual giving budget for a good male Jew.

$3,000/yr making one vow @ $250 Each Month
   500/yr sacrificing 20 firstborns in herd @ $ 25 Each Spring
 1,300/yr asking forgiveness for one unknown, unintentional sin @
       $ 25 Each Week
   250/yr reaffirming dedication to God @ $ 5 Each
   520/yr giving thanks to God for his goodness @ $ 10 Each Week
 1,040/yr asking forgiveness for one known, intentional sin @
       $ 20 Each Week

$6,610 TOTAL FOR MIDDLE-INCOME JEW
$3,000 PLUS TITHING OF AVERAGE INCOME OF $30,000
**$9,610 YEARLY TOTAL GIVING AVERAGE GOOD JEW —
32%**

So, we see that an average middle-income good Jew gave one-third of his income to God, not one-tenth. Plus, every third year, he was required to give an additional tenth ($3,000 in our example or $250/month) for the welfare program (Deuteronomy 26:12), which would take his total contribution to $1025 per month or $12,610. That's 42% of their annual income each third year!

Are we sure we want to get involved in the Jewish rules for giving? Anyone who tries to get people to tithe is being inconsistent.

First of all, tithing was part of the Law of Moses, and only represented one-third of what the average good Jew was expected to give. Yes, Abraham gave one-tenth, but he did it out of faith, not requirement. God never commanded him to do this.

Second, if people insist on tithing anyway, to be consistent, they must also offer animal sacrifices, which is part of the same law, go to the temple three times a year, etc. Actually, there are approximately 600 laws involved in the Law of Moses. People insisting on keeping the old law must keep it all. If they fail to obey any part of it, they are guilty of breaking the entire law (James 2:10).

Third, the Law of Moses was nailed to Jesus' cross, thus nullifying it in the Christian era (Colossians 2:14 and Hebrews 8:6, 13).

I thought I knew all about tithing, God, but now I see that was just the tip of the iceberg. Do our leaders know all this? This is really strange. I never heard of it before.

New Testament Giving

There are only five passages in the entire New Testament on

giving. Does this mean it is not important? No. It only takes God saying something one time to make it so.

However, it seems that some church leaders have so much to say about tithing and other variations of "giving," that they're indirectly chiding God for omitting so much discussion about it. However, God had it all figured out. It is man who has complicated it.

The first mention of giving is in Acts 4:32-35, right after the church began. It is a beautiful example of giving just because they wanted to, not because there was a thermometer on the wall, finance committee meetings, a campaign, pre-assigned envelopes, or even a church-owned business. Let's just quote it:

"All the believers were one in heart and mind. No one claimed that any of his possessions was his own, but they shared everything they had....There were no needy persons among them. For from time to time those who owned lands or houses sold them, brought the money from the sales and put it at the apostles' feet, and it was distributed to anyone as he had need."

Did all the early Christians sell all their real estate and donate the money to the church? No. It says that "from time to time" someone would sell something so the money could be used by other Christians who were in need.

Did the church go into a selling business? No. The individuals did the selling themselves and then brought the money to the church for distribution. Notice, they sold their possessions. That means valuables, or cookies, or whatever they had, individual Christians sold on their own.

In the account that follows, one couple brought money to the church, but lied about the amount by saying this was 100% of the sale price when it was not really. The amount was not as important as the lie.

Peter replied, "Didn't it belong to you before it was sold? And after it was sold, wasn't the money at your disposal?" Did Peter ever say the church owned anything? No. Did he say the church sold anything or received any of the money directly from the purchaser(s)? No. The church was not involved until after the selling transaction took place.

So, in the same way, if we are good at selling a particular commodity, we should sell it on our own in private, and consider the money from it as ours. Then we can take it to the church. We could tell others in our congregation about it to give them a chance to purchase, but we should follow their example and sell whatever we have as a private transaction.

Did it ever cross the minds of the early Christians for the church to go into a business? Probably. After all, selling things in the temple lobby and providing services (currency exchange and animals to sacrifice) in the temple lobby were accepted practices. But did the apostles allow it? Never. In fact, Jesus angrily condemned it.

Surely they understood just how effective free-will giving is. In Exodus 35:4-9, Moses asked the people if they would voluntarily donate whatever was necessary to build the tabernacle and the golden furniture in it. Did they grumble? No way. Exodus 36:2-7 says the people kept giving and giving and giving.

Someone went to Moses and complained, "The people are bringing more than enough for doing the work the Lord commanded to be done." As a result, "the people were restrained from bringing more" (Exodus 36:6).

God, for some reason this makes sense. People shouldn't be squeezing the money out of us. But does it work? It sounds like it could. I hope it does.

Free-Will Offerings

Paul is the only apostle to write down instructions about giving. Ninety percent was to the church in Corinth, the church he had so many problems with, and which required at least two letters to try to straighten them out. Because they were lazy? No. It was because their zeal was clouding what God wanted them to do.

He covered this same issue regarding the Jews when he said in Romans 10:2 and 17 "they are zealous for God, but their zeal is not based on knowledge." Their zeal had to be based on something besides the emotions or man's logic, for "faith comes from...the word."

In 1st Corinthians 9:13-14 Paul referred to the Jewish practice of feeding the priests and Levites from the sacrifices the people offered, which was allowed for in the Law of Moses. He said that practice could continue so as to provide support for various ministers of the church.

Reading Exodus through Deuteronomy in the Old Testament shows the large variety of work the Levites did around the temple, especially since no one else was allowed in the building itself. Therefore, today we can support any minister who preaches, evangelizes, oversees (elder), does secretary work, does janitor work, or whatever their ministry.

Notice, he did not include the practice of selling, although he had personally witnessed it upon many occasions on the temple property, having been raised and educated in Jerusalem. What he did allow was for the offerings of the worshippers be used to support the priests and Levites serving in the temple. That is all.

We do know that Paul did not accept the church's money except in dire emergency. Instead he sold tents (Acts 18:3). Did he take them to the church building to sell? No, he did it on his own.

Later in the book he told the Corinthians to take up a collection every Sunday of each member "in keeping with his income" and save it so that when he arrived, they'd be ready with their collective donation for the poor. Notice, the church was not to collect money any other day of the week. If we'd just keep this one rule, it would sure go a long way into convincing people "all the church wants is your money."

Much later, Paul wrote Timothy in Ephesus and told the church that any widow age sixty or above left alone with no family, and who dedicates herself to good works, should be supported by the church. However, he warned that if a widow has family — children or grandchildren — they are to support her or be considered worse than unbelievers. (See 1st Timothy 5:3-10.)

Thus far we have seen that the money can go to support people with various ministries in the church, and it can go to support Christian widows with no family. What else was their money used for?

God, I've always wondered whether being paid makes preachers like mercenaries. I guess not. You are wiser than I and you said it is okay. Thanks for the explanation.

Benevolent Program

Paul got involved in a large benevolent program for the Christians in Jerusalem, Judea. Why?

Most of the Christians at that time were in Judea. Christians there and everywhere were losing their jobs, their property was being taken from them, and breadwinners were being imprisoned (Hebrews 10:32-34). Christians in Jerusalem were doing the best they could, selling their possessions and lands to help out (Acts 4:32-37), but eventually that ran out. They needed outside help.

On Paul's second missionary trip, he told the Christians in Corinth, southern Greece, about the poor Christians in Judea in southern Palestine. They became the instigators of a campaign to send relief money to them (2nd Corinthians 8:10.) It would take time to collect all the money, so Paul went ahead and left Corinth without their donation.

He returned to Judea where he saw the poverty for himself. So, on Paul's third missionary trip, he went through the provinces of Galatia and Asia in today's Turkey, telling people about the needs of the poor Christians in Jerusalem and Judea (1st Corinthians 16:1).

He told the church in Ephesus also (1st Corinthians 16:1). While in Ephesus, he wrote the church in Corinth in southern Greece that he was going to visit them. Toward the end of his letter he said,

"Now about the collection for God's people: Do what I told the Galatians [Turkish] churches to do. On the first day of every week, each one of you should set aside a sum of money in keeping with his income, saving it up, so that when I come no collections will have to be made" (1st Corinthians 16:1-2).

He further provided for fiscal responsibility with his next statements: "Then, when I arrive, I will give letters of introduction to the men you approve and send them with your gift to Jerusalem. If it seems advisable for me to go also, they will accompany me [to Jerusalem]" (1st Corinthians 16:3-4).

Next he went back to Northern Greece, called Macedonia, where he returned to the city of Philippi (Acts 19:21 – 20:2). There, he told them about the financial problems of the Christians in Jerusalem and Judea. He also bragged to them about the congregation in Corinth, Greece, just south of them, saying they'd decided to send a sizeable contribution to Judea (2nd Corinthians 9:1-2).

The Philippians were fairly poor Christians themselves. Yet, "out of the most severe trial, their overflowing joy and their extreme poverty welled up in rich generosity...they urgently pleaded with us for the privilege of sharing in this service to the saints" (2nd Corinthians 8:2, 4).

Just before Paul went to Corinth down in Achaia, the southern province of Greece, he wrote to them a second letter telling them he was not commanding them to give (2nd Corinthians 8:8), but since they had decided the previous year to make a donation, "now finish the work, so that your eager willingness to do it may be matched by your completion of it, according to your means" (2nd Corinthians 8:11).

He went on to say that they should give "according to what one has, not according to what he does not have. Our desire is not that others might be relieved while you are hard pressed, but that there might be equality" (2nd Corinthians 8:13).

Once more Paul was fiscally responsible with the donation of the Christians. He sent this letter to the Corinthians by Titus and "we are sending along with him the brother who is praised by all the churches for his service to the gospel. What is more, he was chosen by the churches to accompany us as we carry the offering....We want to avoid any criticism of the way we administer this liberal gift" (2nd Corinthians 8:18-20).

He concluded his discussion of the benevolent campaign

requests to various congregations by urging them to "finish the arrangements for the generous gift you had promised [a year earlier]. Then it will be ready as a generous gift, not as one grudgingly given....Each man should give what he has decided in his heart to give, not reluctantly or under compulsion, for God loves a cheerful giver" (2nd Corinthians 9:7).

Paul went on to Corinth in southern Greece (Achaia) and stayed three months (Acts 20:3). While there, he wrote the church in Rome that he wanted to go there soon to impart spiritual gifts to them (Romans 1:11). Near the end of his letter, he asked the Christians to pray for the benevolence campaign with this explanation.

"Now, however, I am on my way to Jerusalem in the service of the saints there. For Macedonia [northern Greece] and Achaia [southern Greece] were pleased to make a contribution for the poor among the saints in Jerusalem" (Romans 15:25-27). Paul further asked the Christians in Rome to pray that the Jewish Christians in Jerusalem will accept such a gift from Gentile Christians (Romans 15:31).

Some of those who accompanied him later on the way back to Jerusalem were three Christians from the province of Asia where Ephesus is and one from the province of Galatia (Acts 20:4), both in Turkey.

Soon thereafter, Paul arrived in Jerusalem "to bring my people gifts for the poor and to present offerings" (Acts 24:17).

God, I always thought benevolence was pretty straight forward. If someone knocks on the church door, give him some food. I never thought of coordinating with other churches like this. And they all trusted Paul with their money. They knew he loved you.

Fund Raisers

But, if we are on a tight budget, where are we going to get the money to give others?

In some denominations, it is standard to hold bazaars in the church basement or out in the parking lot at least once a year and advertise it to the general public.

Did the Jews sell things on temple grounds? Yes, they did. They sold animals to people who had traveled such long distances to offer sacrifices, it was more practical to purchase the equivalent of what they would have brought with them. Or they were made available to people who did not own any herds of their own. In fact, the priests arranged for merchants to set up their booths in the temple courtyard where the women and Gentiles were allowed to worship.

Further, since the temple only dealt with temple currency — the temple shekel — people exchanged their Roman currency and currency from other parts of the world for temple currency right there on temple grounds.

But Jesus strenuously objected to this practice once at the beginning of his ministry and once near the end. They were buying and selling on temple grounds. All through Leviticus, the book explaining temple worship in detail, it says that offerings were to be BROUGHT to the entrance tabernacle/temple to be offered there. The courtyards were considered the entrance since the temple structure itself was a much smaller building in the center.

Wasn't the courtyard an okay place to assist the worshippers? The temple complex was made up of five sections. In the innermost section was the actual temple building itself. Only priests and Levites could enter it. Around that was a courtyard that only men could enter. Around that was a courtyard that only women and Gentiles could enter. Around that were the walls to the temple complex which also contained storage rooms, apartments, and so on.

Jesus was upset that the animal sales and currency exchanges were being made in the courtyard. (The courtyard was the size of several football fields.) So he drove them all from the temple area and declared, "How dare you turn my Father's house into a market!" (John 2:14-16).

Then, three years later right after his triumphal entry into Jerusalem, Jesus once more entered the temple complex, and once more drove out the merchants and currency exchangers shouting, "It is written, 'My house will be called a house of prayer,' but you are making it a 'den of robbers' " (Matthew 21:12-13).

The first time he objected to them being there. The second time he objected that they were not only there, but they were robbing the people, probably with exorbitant prices.

Well, what if the church bizarre were moved away from the church building with easier access by the general public, people who do not attend that church? The apostle John in his old age probably 60 years later said, "It was for the sake of the Name that they went out, receiving no help from the pagans" (3rd John 7).

Who are the pagans? Basically, they non-Christians. And how are we to judge who is a Christian and non-Christian when they file up to give us their money? Often, we can't.

Well, what about the church going into some kind of business anonymously? Large denominations sometimes do that. Many business leaders were converted in the early church, but we have no evidence they used their expertise to develop a business for the church to run and raise money for it.

"But what if I have some property I want to sell and give the proceeds to the church?" someone asks. That is provided for. Other situations are too. Read on.

God, I never thought of it that way. I guess it gives me an idea of how outsiders must think of us — always thinking of ways to make money. At least, when we advertise it, it must seem that way to them. No wonder they think all churches want is their money. Forgive me.

Creating Heaven

So, the question remains: If we are on a tight budget, where are we going to get the money to give others? If our personal outgo is that close to our income, it may take time to adjust. it.

The most helpful book I have run into was apparently written by a Buddhist, Timothy Miller: *How to Want What You Have.*

Some people play sports with the attitude that they have to win every time. We look down on this type of attitude, but most of us have the same attitude toward money. We must always be the winner; otherwise we're considered failures.

We are trying to meet spiritual starvation with material things. We go to work so we can come home so we can eat so we can sleep so we can go back to work. We buy bigger houses, nicer cars, send our children to college so they can get a good job, and come home to eat and sleep and go back to work. The author concludes that it is "like a macabre marathon dance that can only be escaped by dying. [6]

What is this emptiness we are so driven to fill but which is never filled? We long, in the midst of all our treading water, to feel some sense of significance. Each one of us is just one in a world of millions, a world that hardly even and hardly ever notices us. We want to feel like we did not live life in vain.

We humans, who live in a material world, are naturally drawn to material things as proof to others and to ourselves that we are significant. And we use mathematics to prove it. We count our paycheck, the number of times we went out to eat, the number of shoes or shirts in our closet, the number of cars in our driveway, the height of our house.

Isn't it strange that, with such a strong instinct for more, humans do not have an instinct that tells us when we've accumulated enough. Enough always eludes us. We are self-driven to believe that enough is just around the corner—one more promotion, one more raise, one more award, one more car.

The brilliant author of this book went on to explain that we must retrain our instincts for more material things and develop drives to show people compassion, savor each moment as a fulfilling experience, express gratitude for what we do have, and finally to meditate.

These are all good. But, let's take this deeper in the direction of Christianity. What does God say we live on this earth for? Our foremost purpose in being born is to die (Psalm 22:29, LBV). [7] Is that morbid? Not to Christians. Are we Christians?

The psalmist said, "But as for me, my contentment is not in

wealth but in seeing you and knowing all is well between us. And when I AWAKE IN HEAVEN, I will be fully satisfied, for I will see you FACE TO FACE" (Psalm 17:15 LBV). [8]

Just before Paul's death, he said, "I have fought the good fight, I have finished the race, I have kept the faith. Now there is in store for me the CROWN OF RIGHTEOUSNESS! which the Lord, the righteous Judge, will award to me on that day" (2nd Timothy 4:8).

Earth is just the corridor to heaven. We've got to travel through earth to get to heaven. Heaven is so indescribable that God uses earthly terms to try to describe it. Which terms? Those used to describe the wealth we so irresistibly crave and cannot get enough of here on earth.

Yes, in our frantic rushing here and there and everywhere, seldom resting, never able to get rid of the addiction for more, we are frustrated because deep down we know we cannot have it all. Oh, but that's wrong. We CAN have it all. But not here. Once we realize it is heaven we are frantically seeking, we can put things into perspective.

I guess, God, that I have tried to purchase heaven on earth. I always knew money couldn't buy true happiness, but always made a joke out of it. It's not a joke, is it, God? Money can rule me, can't it? Help me look at myself as I really am.

Give and You Will Receive

Do we want heaven? Do we want others to have heaven? That's what it all boils down to. Giving is one way to help both ourselves and others.

People have no problem giving when they see a true need. But they must be convinced in their own hearts it is a true need. It isn't something church leaders need to be harping after them about.

As we saw above, Paul never insisted that the church at

Corinth lead a congregational campaign of giving for the poor Christians in Jerusalem and Judea. It was originally their idea (2nd Corinthians 8:10), then he took that same idea to other congregations and told them about it. They all liked the idea and began saving for the poor. But by then, the Corinthians had gotten bored with the idea.

Paul simply told them [this is a paraphrase], "I bragged to others about you, and now you're backing out. You're embarrassing yourselves and me" (2nd Corinthians 9:2-5).

So, what caused them to give in the first place? The Philippians in Macedonia expressed it best. They were poor, and Paul did not expect anyone to give so much they ended up poorer than the ones they were helping (2nd Corinthians 8:13-15). Even though they were poor, they gave out of "overflowing JOY" that "welled up" within them. "Entirely ON THEIR OWN, they urgently pleaded with us for the PRIVILEGE of sharing in this service to the saints" (2nd Corinthians 8:2-4).

Three things were involved: Joy, self-motivation, attitude of honor and privilege.

Yes, God, that is true. I've experienced it myself. I've given to people who didn't even ask, because I saw their need. It does work, doesn't it? Just show me the need.

The Nitty Gritty

Perhaps much more time needs to be devoted in our Sunday meetings to the needs for which the congregation gives. In fact, it may be that seldom are the needs even mentioned. As far as the members are concerned, a cold plate is passed into which cold cash is placed.

If the leadership seems to be dragging the money out of people, perhaps the people don't see it as a need, then perhaps the congregation shouldn't be involved in it. So, how should it be done?

BUILDING

Ninety-nine percent of congregations are giving toward their building, whether mortgage payments, or rent payments; also insurance, utilities and upkeep. We need to get past those cold and impersonal bricks and light bulbs and carpet cleaner. What is the building being used for?

Is it being used for Sunday worship and occasional potlucks, and sitting empty the rest of the time? Perhaps the congregation should be renting a school somewhere instead.

Is the building being used during the week, but only by the members? In that case, its cost is not going to save the lost. James 5:20 tells us, "Remember this: Whoever turns a sinner from the error of his way will save him from death and cover over a multitude of sins."

If we were born to die so we can go to heaven, then others were too, and need to be helped to learn how. Just as Jesus attracted people's attention before his sermons by performing miracles that helped people, we can use our buildings to do things that help people.

People in the community need our building. And, since the church is not to have a business, we should not be charging for it, other than deposits to cover possible damage. When we charge for the use of our building, we're no better than any other worldly organization.

Our building can be used for dependency and co-dependency groups, for scouts, for the elderly, for weddings and funerals, for service organizations such as the Lion's Club, and so on. Instead of asking for payment, we can ask one of us be allowed to go through a 20-minute session with their group explaining why our congregation exists and how to become Christians. That's pretty cheap payment.

As a result, the community will see the church as being there for their benefit without being money-grubbing. Also, it will give an opportunity to explain salvation to people who might have never listened to us. And last, it is a way of getting people through the physical and psychological barrier of the front door, in order to get them feeling at ease and possibly interested in returning on Sunday.

There are other uses for the building. Just use your imagination and think of your congregation's interests and talents. On Sundays, before the collection plate is passed around, something should be said about how the building was used that week. If we have nothing to report, perhaps we need to look again at our spiritual motives for having the building.

SALARIES

People know the preacher and his family have to live decently. Also anyone else on the payroll of the church. But what is the church getting in return for their investment?

People on the payroll should be able and willing to tell about what they accomplished on behalf of the congregation that week or month. They should, however, never be made to feel the congregation is checking up on them. We are lucky to be able to have people more talented than we are to do part of our work for us.

As for the secretary, what are we giving the secretary to include in the church bulletin? Is it exclusively for inspirational articles? Is there anything in it that talks about the needs of the congregation's sick or elderly? Is there anything in it about the needs in the community that individual members might be able to help with in the name of the church? (More on this in the chapter on announcements.)

And the missionaries we support. We need to get a monthly report from them, and parts of it shared with the congregation each Sunday.

Does all this take time? You bet. But it is the way to motivate people to keep giving and keep wanting to give.

BENEVOLENT WORK

What benevolent work did "we" do the previous week

through our cold cash in that cold collection plate? If we did not help anyone in need at all, perhaps there is something wrong. Nearly every week, most ministers are approached by drifters coming to the building for a handout. The congregation seldom if ever hears about it. Perhaps we should.

Do you know that when we were told in the Bible to give alms, we were never told to make sure the people we were helping were worthy or would use the money wisely? True, there are ways to help them where they do not get cash, such as giving them food out of the congregation's supply, or putting them up in a motel, or paying their bus fare or utility bill. Jesus said, "It is more blessed to give than to receive" (Acts 20:35).

As far as people deserving our benevolence, are we worthy or do we use our blessings wisely that God gives us? God "causes his sun to rise on the evil and the good, and sends rain on the righteous and the unrighteous. If you love those who love you, what reward will you get....And if you greet only your brothers, what are you doing more than others? Do not even pagans do that?" (Matthew 5:45-47).

Was there anything in the newspaper last week about a person or family needing help? A member should feel free to bring it to the attention of the congregation. If the treasurer says there isn't enough in the treasury for this worthy cause, perhaps some of the members will want to give a little extra that week.

Has your congregation purchased any Bibles or songbooks or Bible school material to be used in teaching publicly or in private? The congregation has a right to know about it. It's their money.

Cold hard cash in a cold hard collection plate while someone sings or during a lull in the worship is murder on the giving of a congregation. When people see a need, they will give, especially when they can identify with something.

If leaders bring up a program and no one is giving toward it, perhaps it needs to be stopped. There are hundreds of programs that congregations could be involved in. It just depends on the interests of the members and the needs of the church and community.

Paul said, "Each man should give what he has decided in his heart to give, not reluctantly or under compulsion, for God loves a cheerful giver" (2nd Corinthians 9:7).

When we give, we must keep in mind, not the cold plate and cold cash, but that fact that "this service that you perform is not only supplying the needs of God's people but is also overflowing in many expressions of THANKS TO GOD. Because of the service by which you have proved yourselves, MEN WILL PRAISE GOD" (2nd Corinthians 9:12-13).

Thank you, God, for explaining this in your word. I don't guess I ever understood it. You don't ask for money, you ask for food. You don't ask for dollars, you ask for clothes. You don't ask for coins, you ask for Bibles. I'm catching on, God. I'm catching on.

The Gift of Giving

How can we honestly tell whether we have given from our heart? This is an individual thing. Probably the best barometer is to ask ourselves this: When I give to that cause, do I really want to give more? If the answer is yes, then you are giving enough within your ability and from your heart. The cheerless giver will resent any amount that they give.

But, is it fair to the people who do give a lot, to be in a congregation where there are those who give just a dollar bill? There will always be people within a congregation who have very little to give. They may be retired and on a low fixed income. They may be single parents who have to work day and night to keep their family clothed and fed and in decent shelter.

It is an equality thing. For everyone is given a different gift. Romans 12:6-8 describes it beautifully.

"We have different gifts according to the grace given us. If a man's gift is PROPHESYING [knowing God's word], let him use it in proportion to his faith. If it is SERVING, let him serve; if it is TEACHING, let him teach; if it is ENCOURAGING, let him encourage; if it is CONTRIBUTING to the needs of others, let him give generously; if it is LEADERSHIP, let him govern diligently; if it is showing MERCY, let him do it cheerfully."

Being in a position to give monetarily toward the material programs of the church is a gift. It should be used with as much faith and sincerity as someone who has the gift of teaching classes, or encouraging the depressed, or serving the sick. All are equal in God's eyes.

If there is no one around who wants to know what is in God's word, the Bible, the gift of prophesying is not going to be used. If there is no one around who has physical needs, the gift of serving is not going to be used. If there is no one around who needs to understand God's word, the gift of teaching is not going to be used. When there is no one around who is depressed, the gift of encouraging is not going to be used. When there is no one around who has monetary needs, the gift of contributing is not going to be used.

Givers must be shown a reason to give. Then they will give generously and not grudgingly or out of obligation.

This helps me, too, God, because I can't give as much as I want to. I have felt so guilty about it. But that's just not my talent. You've given that talent to someone else, and given me a talent to encourage people. Thank you.

Second-Generation Church Accounts

Justin, who lived about 150 AD, wrote this in Apology I, 67: "We always remember one another. Those who have, provide for all those in want....Those who have means and are willing, each according to his own choice, gives what he wills, and what is collected is deposited with the president. He provides for the orphans and widows, those who are in want on account of sickness or some other cause, those who are in bonds [jail] and strangers who are sojourning, and in a word he becomes the protector of all who are in need." [9]

Justin, in Apology I, 14: "We who loved more than anything else ways of acquiring wealth and possessions now bring what we have into a common treasury and share with everyone who is in need." [10]

Tertullian, who lived about 170 AD, wrote this in Apology xxxix:1-5: "Although we have a kind of money-chest, it is not gathered from the fees of our leaders as if religion were a matter of purchase. Every individual puts in a small contribution on the monthly day, or when he wishes and only if he wishes and is able. For no one is compelled, but he contributes voluntarily. These contributions are trust funds of piety.

"They are not spent on banquets...or drinking clubs; but for feeding and burying the poor, for boys and girls destitute of property and parents; and further for old people confined to the house, and victims of shipwreck; and any who are in the mines, who are exiled to an island, or who are in prison merely on account of God's church....So great a work of love burns a brand upon us in regarding to some. 'See,' they say, 'how they love one another.' " [11]

Dionysus of Corinth wrote about 170, and quoted in Eusebius Church History IV.xxiii.10: "For this practice has prevailed with you from the very beginning, to do good to all the brethren in every way, and to send contributions to many churches in every city. Thus refreshing the needy in their want, and furnishing to the brethren condemned to the mines." [12]

Irenaeus of Lyons in Gaul (France), wrote about 180 Against Heresies IV,xiv.3: "And instead of the tithes which the law commanded, the Lord said to divide everything we have with the poor. And he said to love not only our neighbors but also our enemies, and to be givers and sharers not only with the good but also to be liberal givers toward those who take away our possessions." [13]

Clement of Alexandria wrote about 200 AD Who Is the Rich Man that is Saved? 33: "Do not judge who is worthy and who unworthy, for it is possible for you to be mistaken in your opinion. In the uncertainty of ignorance it is better to do good to the unworthy for the sake of the worthy than by guarding against those who are less good not to encounter the good. For by being sparing and trying to test those who are well-deserving or not, it is possible for you to neglect some who are loved by God." [14]

7. SPIRITUALITY OR RELIGIOUS FIX

But when his heart was **lifted up**,
And his spirit was hardened in pride,
He was deposed....and they took his glory from him.
Daniel 5:20 (NKJV)

Famous Theologians

About 450, AUGUSTINE—PRE-CATHOLIC: "Suppose we advise all our brethren not to teach their children [to speak their native language by example] because on the outpouring of the Holy Spirit the apostles immediately began to speak the languages of every race; and warn everyone who has not had a like experience [to learn their own language] that he need not consider himself a Christian, or may at least doubt whether he has yet received the Holy Spirit? No." (On Christian Doctrine, Preface, Point 5)

About 1270, THOMAS AQUINAS—CATHOLIC: "Both Paul and the other apostles were divinely instructed in the languages of all nations sufficiently for the requirements of the teaching of the faith." (Summa Theologica, Secunda Secundae Partis)

About 1536 and 1543, JOHN CALVIN—REFORMED CHURCHES: "Those who, rejecting scripture, imagine that they have some peculiar way of penetrating to God, are to be deemed not so much under the influence of error as madness. For certain giddy men have lately appeared who, while they make a great display of the superiority of the spirit....The office of the Spirit promised to us is not to form new and unheard-of revelations....What can be plainer than this prohibition— 'let not prayers or thanksgivings be offered up in public except in the vernacular tongue'....We see, then, how Satan sports among them with impunity" (Institutes of the Christian Religion, Book I, 9:1; and Commentary on the Epistles of Paul the Apostle, I Corinthians 14:16).

1674, JOHN BUNYAN—BAPTIST: "But the devil, that he might...render the scriptures also odious and low, telling them of the 'scriptures' within; which Christ never taught, nor yet his disciples: But they...have given themselves over rather to follow the suggestions of the devil than the holy scriptures....But this design the devil carries on by pretending to show them a more excellent way which they may attain to...from the light within them." (The Works of John Bunyan, Vol. II, pg. 136, "Some Gospel Truths Opened According to scriptures").

1861 and 1866, CHARLES SPURGEON—BAPTIST: "But do you know the effect of an experimental [experiential] minister?...This is their style: 'Except thou art daily feeling the utter rottenness of thine heart....Except thou abidest on the dunghill...thou art no child of God.' Who told you that?....Those who pray unintelligible prayers, prayers in a foreign tongue, prayers which they do not understand: we know without a moment's discussion...the prayer which is not even understood cannot be a prayer in the Spirit, for even the man's own spirit does not enter into it, how then can the Spirit of God be there?" (Sermons in the Metropolitan Pulpit, pg. 173, and pg. 615.)

I lift up the arms of my heart to you, oh God. I reach for you with the hands of my spirit and I touch you. You are so delightful, grand as the glowing morning sun. Even when it is red before a brewing storm, you say, "It's just me. I'm still shining. I'll be back right after the storm." You are my forever God.

My brother-in-law, a Maxwell, used to brag in his youth that he was descended from Sir Maxwellus, the noble Brit with Roman citizenship. The family has yet to find any evidence of a historic figure who even carried that name.

So it was that a few years ago, when he went to Scotland determined to find the Maxwell castle, the family all replied, "Sure, Jim. Yeah. Right," in no uncertain derogatory terms. Then the unbelievable happened. He found it! The Maxwell castle! It was triangular in shape and built of red stone. It no longer had a roof, and trees were growing inside it. Nevertheless, it was the Maxwell castle.

My sister said that when he went "inside" of "his" castle, he wandered around kind of in a trance as though he was having "a religious experience," as she termed it.

The reference that my sister made to the "religious experience" actually does express what people today seem to be searching for in their religion: An experience. Being able to reach the unreachable. Being able to experience the unbelievable. A term has been coined to explain it: "experiential religion."

Society in industrial and information-age countries feel it has experienced about as much as it can accomplish for now. But it wants more. Having triumphed over nature, electronics, and the mind, today's society now strains to triumph over the spirit. This triumph, they call "spiritualism" which is reached through the "religious experience."

Many people go from church to church searching, and feel they all lack spiritual dimension, an intimate relationship with the divine, and an intimate relationship with the congregation.

Further, in our world of instant everything, they want it right now. Some finally give up searching the churches and just stay home to try finding spirituality in solitude.

In 1997, the *Vancouver Sun* in an article regarding spirituality, quoted someone as saying, "One must 'die before you die' by replacing human qualities with divine ones....emphasis on spiritual experiences....not afraid of spiritual ecstasy... visions...while whirling in mystical dance."

This is a description of Sufism where, among other things, worshippers "dance in exaltation while pointing one hand to heaven and one to earth." Followers also believe "music carries one's soul into the divine presence," and chanting the 99 names of God melodiously, "brings peace to anybody who listens." It was their effort to reach spirituality. [1]

The same year, the Associated Press carried an article about people who "jump up and down, stomp the dirt and throw themselves to the ground. Delirious with religious fervor, they shout, 'God!'....The chants become louder and faster....It is worship....the idea is to prepare oneself for God." It was a description of Muslim worship. This was their effort to reach spirituality. [2]

The Hindu religion that is permeating much of North American thinking, suggests meditating on the syllable OM. *The Upanishads*, the chapter on "Prasna" says:

"The syllable OM...when it is fully understood and meditation is therefore rightly directed...whether he be awake, dreaming, or sleeping the dreamless sleep, and attains to Brahman. By virtue of a greater understanding he attains to the celestial sphere....The sage, with the help of OM, reaches Brahman, the fearless, the undecaying, the immortal!" This was the Hindu effort to reach spirituality. [3]

In *The Teachings of the Compassionate Buddha*, the chapter on becoming a monk says this: "With the pure Heavenly Eye...he sees beings as they pass away from one form of existence and take shape in another....To him, thus knowing, thus seeing, the heart is set free from the deadly taint of lusts, is set free from the deadly taint of becomings....Rebirth has been destroyed. The higher life has been fulfilled." This was the Buddhist effort to reach spirituality. [4]

The *Encyclopedia Britannica* states, "references to ecstatic speech and oracular pronouncements can be found, for example, in the classical writers; and in the [ancient] Greek language...the phrase *lalein heterais glossais* referred to *glossolalia*. The utterances of the Pythian priestess of Apollo at Delphi may be considered examples of it. Various observations of the phenomenon have also been made in peoples of primitive cultures." This was the Greek effort to reach spirituality. [5]

The early church historian, Eusebius, reported that late in the second century, a man named Montanus claimed to be so spiritualistic that some even called him the Holy Spirit incarnate. In Boo*k V, chapter XVI*, Eusebius reported that Montanus...

"...was carried away in spirit, and wrought up into a certain kind of frenzy and irregular ecstasy, raving, and speaking, and uttering strange things....he excited two others, females, and filled them with the spirit of delusion, so that they also spake like the former, in a kind of ecstatic frenzy, out of all season, and in a manner strange and novel....

"Theodotus, one of the first that was carried away by their prophecy, as it was called....as if he should at some time be taken up and received into the heavens, and who falling into trances, gave himself up to the spirit of deception." [6]

In *chapter XVII*, Eusebius also reported what the historian Miltiades, a contemporary of Montanus, wrote about this supposed spiritual phenomenon:

"But the false prophet is carried away by a vehement ecstasy, accompanied by want of all shame and fear. Beginning, indeed, with a designed ignorance, and terminating, as beforesaid, in involuntary madness.

"They will never be able to show that any of the Old or any of the New Testament, were thus violently agitated and carried away in spirit. Neither will they be able to boast that Agabus, or Judas, or Silas, or the daughters of Philip, or Ammias in Philadelphia, or Quandratus, or others that do not belong to them, ever acted in this way." This was a "Christian" effort to reach spirituality. [7]

In addition to the Montanists mentioned above who were disfellowshipped from the church about 175 AD, speaking in tongues revived in Christian advocates among mendicant friars in the 1200s, the little prophets of Cevennes, the Camisards, the Jansenists and the Irvingites. It was revived again in the 1600s among both Catholics and protestants, and again in the 1900s. All were efforts to reach spirituality.

I once read a book written in praise of "tongues" in which the author struggled to touch God. He finally prayed that he needed another language in which to praise him and say he loved him. In fact, he needed a thousand tongues with which to worship God. Later in his book he said that, as people grow in their worship of God, "sooner or later" they will speak in tongues. [8]

At this point, we will look at spirituality as an act of public worship within a congregational assembly. First, because it appeared in other world religions, we will investigate the phenomenon of "tongues."

God, I had no idea that other religions spoke in tongues. This is confusing. I thought it was only a Christian thing. And I certainly never heard the early church didn't like it. No one ever told me that. I do want to please you, God. Please be patient with me while I learn.

First Occurrence in the Early Church

In fairness, we will cover every verse in the New Testament on tongues. The first is a reference by Jesus himself just before he returned to heaven. This is what was said in Mark 16:15-16 in Jesus' own words:

" 'Go into all the world and preach the good news to all creation. Whoever believes and is baptized will be saved, but whoever does not believe will be condemned. And these signs will accompany those who believe: In my name they will drive out demons, they will speak in new tongues; they will pick up snakes with their hands; and when they drink deadly poison, it will not hurt them at all; they will place their hands on sick people, and they will get well.' "

We know from 1st Corinthians 12:7-11 that not everyone who became a Christian performed all the signs listed above. This phenomenon of tongues was given equality with picking up poisonous snakes and drinking deadly poison without being killed. Therefore, there was as much a predominance of these latter two signs as speaking in tongues.

Further, Jesus did not say "unknown" tongues; he said "new" tongues. In every instance of the word "tongues" occurring in the New Testament, it is from a Greek word, "*glossa*," meaning "languages."

The first time this occurred is recorded in Acts 2. Verse 4 says, "All of them were filled with the Holy Spirit and began to speak in other [not unknown] tongues as the Spirit enabled them."

Who were the "them" who began to speak in other tongues? Acts 1:15 says there had been 120 present—both men and women—when a replacement was made for Judas' office as apostle (1:13-15). Have you ever heard anyone claim there were 120 people present, and therefore 120 received the gift of tongues because it says "all" of them?

Yet, Acts 2:1 says, "When the day of Pentecost came...." This was clearly another day. Otherwise the day would have been placed at the beginning of the account of the 120, not at the beginning of the account of the apostles. Further reading will give other evidence as to who was there.

In verse 3, the word "they" occurs, but still with no identification. Verse 4 refers to "them," still with no identification. Verse 7 gets more specific, for it refers to "they" and "them" as "these MEN who are speaking" and as "Galileans." Verse 14 narrows down "they" and "them" and "these men" even more, referring to Peter with the Eleven. Then Peter specifically tells what "these men" were doing.

What were the tongues they were speaking? Verse 8 says "Then how is it that each of us hears them in his own native language?" There we have it in plain black and white.

We must realize that Peter was not the only apostle who preached that day. His sermon was recorded, but the other apostles preached too. Everyone heard "all these men speaking in their own language, not just Peter. Peter stood up with the Eleven (verse 14), and in verse 37 the people "said to Peter and the other apostles."

Since we know 3,000 were baptized that day, they surely preached to anywhere from 10,000 to perhaps even 100,000. For one apostle's voice to carry to even 1,000 without a sound system like we have today would be a great feat.

How many languages were represented in the audience that day? The regions represented were 15 if you count them in verses 9-11. This gives one of three possibilities for the languages spoken that day.

1.The simplest is that each apostle spoke one of twelve languages, and three others repeated their sermon in the other languages.

2.Or, some of the regions mentioned had languages that were similar. For instance, Parthia, Media, Elam and Mesopotamia were at various times parts of the same empire: The Babylonian Empire, then the Persian Empire, then the Grecian Empire, and finally the Roman Empire. Also, Phrygia and Pamphylia were very small provinces next to each other in one corner of southern Turkey.

3.Or, we know that the apostle Peter wrote to the churches in Capadocia, Pontus and Asia (all in Turkey) in the Greek language. The Apostle Paul wrote to the church in Rome in the Greek language. Paul also wrote to Titus on the isle of Crete in the Mediterranean in the Greek language. Both Paul and the apostle John wrote several churches in the province of Asia in the Greek language.

This first instance of tongues occurred when the first Jews were baptized into Christ in Jerusalem. The next time tongues is mentioned is in Caesarea on the coast of the Mediterranean Sea when the first Gentiles were baptized into Christ in (see Acts 10).

Second Occurrence in the Early Church

This occurrence began when a Gentile named Cornelius, who was morally good but still not saved, was told by an angel in a vision that he should send for a Jew named Peter. The next day, Peter had a vision where God told him to break a specific Jewish law — to eat certain forbidden meat. Right after that Cornelius' messengers accompanied Peter to Cornelius' house. Jews back then were forbidden to enter a Gentile's house.

But before Peter began preaching the gospel, he said, " 'I now realize how true it is that God does not show favoritism but accepts men from every nation who fear him and do what is right. You know the message God sent to the people of Israel, telling the good news of peace through Jesus Christ, who is Lord of all' " (10:34-36).

At the end of his sermon, "while Peter was still speaking these words, the Holy Spirit came on all who heard the message. The circumcised believers [JEWS] who had come with Peter were ASTONISHED that the gift of the Holy Spirit had been poured out EVEN ON THE GENTILES" (10:44-45).

How did they know this? Because the Jews "heard them [GENTILES] speaking in tongues and praising God" (10:46). The word "heard" is from the Greek *akouo* which means to harken with understanding. This *akouo* is the same word used in John 8:26 and 40 referring to Jesus harkening to Jehovah's words, and in 2nd Timothy 2:2, referring to Timothy harkening to Paul's words.

So, the Jews not only heard a sound coming from the Gentiles' mouths, but they understood the sound — recognizable words. They knew that they were words of praise. Back when the apostles preached on the Day of Pentecost in Acts 2, their words were condemnation for crucifying Jesus, and exhortation to repent. They were not words praising God other than honoring his will.

Furthermore, after this second occurrence when Peter went to the other apostles to explain himself for baptizing people who the Jews considered "untouchables," he said, "As I began to speak, the Holy Spirit came on them, as he HAD ON US AT THE

BEGINNING" (Acts 11:15).

When was the only other time tongues occurred? Acts 2 says it was at the beginning of the church. And who had the gift of speaking in tongues? The apostles. Therefore, these Gentiles had the same ability — to speak in the native languages of other people.

Interestingly, they were still lacking something important that they had to do. The apostle Peter announced to his Jewish friends, " 'Can anyone keep these people [Gentiles] from being baptized with water? They have received the Holy Spirit just as we [Jews] have.' So he ORDERED that they be baptized in the name of Jesus Christ."

Why would they need the gift of languages? So the Gentiles could go to their own people and preach the gospel. That was part of Jesus' command. "Go into ALL the world and preach the Gospel to ALL creation" (Mark 16:15).

Third & Fourth Occurrences
in the Early Church

The third time tongues is mentioned is in Acts 19 in Ephesus. Ephesus was a city in today's Turkey, across the Aegean Sea from Greece. Acts 18:24-28 explains how a Jew named Apollos was there preaching only the baptism of John. Priscilla and Aquilla taught him "the way of God more adequately." Then, instead of correcting what he had taught in Ephesus, Apollos rushed on to Achaia in southern Greece.

So Paul went to Ephesus. When he arrived and found these believers, Paul asked them, " 'Did you receive the Holy Spirit when you believed?' They answered, 'No, we have not even heard that there is a Holy Spirit' " (19:2). They went on to explain that they had only been baptized into John's baptism. Paul replied, "'John's baptism was a baptism of repentance' " (19:4). Were they saved yet?

"On hearing this, they were baptized into the name of the Lord Jesus" (19:5). Why didn't Paul baptize them into the name of the Father, the Son and the Holy Spirit like Jesus commanded in Mark 16:15? Because they had no idea who the Holy Spirit was. So

Paul gave them the Holy Spirit separately. Then they received the proof they had because "they spoke in tongues and prophesied" (19:6). The word "spoke" here is from the Greek word *laleo* meaning to tell something as in a conversation. Now these Ephesians understood the Holy Spirit. (More on the relationship of tongues with prophesying later.)

Could just anyone receive the Holy Spirit separately? No. Apostles had to be present. Back in Acts 8, a deacon named Philip went to Samaria, a province in the middle of Palestine, to preach. He even performed some miracles. But, keep in mind, the church was probably only a couple years old. None of the New Testament had been written yet. Preachers were having to hear the apostles and then go on and teach what they remembered. Sometimes even the well-meaning were not getting everything straight, just as Apollos above hadn't.

When the apostles in Jerusalem heard that even Samaritans [half-Jews, half-Gentiles] had believed in Jesus, these apostles "sent Peter and John to them. When they [apostles Peter and John] arrived, they prayed for them that they might receive the Holy Spirit, because the Holy Spirit had not yet come upon any of them; they had simply been baptized into the name of the Lord Jesus. Then Peter and John placed their hands on them, and they received the Holy Spirit" (8:14-17).

Even Simon the sorcerer recognized that the apostles had to be present for this to occur. Acts 8:18 says "Simon saw that the Spirit was given at the laying on of the APOSTLES' hands."

Note, also, that Jesus told his "apostles he had chosen" (Acts 1:2), "John baptized with water, but in a few days you [the apostles] will be baptized with the Holy Spirit." Baptism of the Holy Spirit only occurred two times in the New Testament, to the first Jews — the apostles on the Day of Pentecost (Acts 2) and to the first Gentiles — the household of Cornelius (Acts 11:15-18).

God, I didn't know the gifts of the Holy Spirit were so intermingled with the work for the apostles. There's so much more for me to learn. I'm trying, God. I'm trying.

General References in the New Testament

The word translated "tongues" is from the Greek word *glossa*. We are investigating every scripture in the New Testament which uses this word *glossa*. We must keep in mind that *glossa* refers to words the tongue forms that are both good and bad.

Here are the scriptures which refer to *glossa* as being bad. Romans 3:13-14 says, " 'Their throats are open graves; their tongues practice deceit. The poison of vipers is on their lips. Their mouths are full of cursing and bitterness.' " If tongues is unknown, how would anyone know the words were deceitful, bitter, and cursing?

James, Jesus' brother, said in his letter that if anyone considers himself religious and doesn't control his tongue (*glossa*), he deceives himself and his religion is worthless (James 1:26). Elsewhere he said the tongue (*glossa*) is evil full of boasting that, like a spark in a dry forest, can create a destructive fire. The tongue is restless and deadly poison and can corrupt a person (James 3:5-8). If tongues is unknown, how could anyone know someone was boasting, and how could it corrupt anyone?

The apostle Peter said in I Peter 3:10 that the tongue was evil and deceitful, and if we expect to live very long, we must learn to control it and not insult even our enemies. If tongues is unknown, how could our enemies know they were being insulted?

The apostle John warned that we are not to just tell people we love them with our tongue (*glossa*), but to prove it by our actions and telling the truth (1st John 3:18). If tongues is unknown, how could people know someone was a hypocrite if they didn't know their words were about love, and how could they know they were lying? John said we were not to just love "with words." This term is from the Greek *logos* which means logic and reason. If tongues is unknown, how could they be spoken with logic and reason?

Some people have said that tongues is gibberish. The Bible covers this under the word "babble." In Acts 17:18 Paul tried to get the Greeks in Athens to believe in the one true God. The philosophers who heard him said he was babbling as he seemed to be advocating some foreign god or gods. If tongue (*glossa*) is babbling, how could these philosophers draw any conclusion about what Paul was saying?

Paul wrote to his protégé, "Timothy, guard what has been entrusted to your care. Turn away from godless chatter, and the opposing ideas of what is falsely called knowledge, which some have professed and in so doing have wandered from the faith" (1st Timothy 6:20). He wrote him a second time with this same warning: "Avoid godless chatter, because they who indulge in it will become more and more ungodly" (2nd Timothy 2:16). The word "godless chatter" is translated "vain babblings" in the King James Version, and is from the Greek word *keno-phonia* which means empty sounds.

Others will say that tongues refers to groanings, and cite Romans 8:26, "In the same way, the Spirit helps us in our weakness. We do not know what we ought to pray for, but the Spirit himself intercedes for us with groans that words cannot express." But the word translated "groans" is from the Greek *stenagmos* which means to sigh. Sighs are not words.

God, I never connected the gift of tongues with other uses of the tongue in the Bible. There's really a connection. I had no idea. Keep being patient, God. I'm trying. I really do want to please you.

Apostle's Letter to the Corinthian Church

INTRODUCTORY MESSAGE

The reason this first letter of Paul to the church at Corinth was written is pivotal to understanding. This was not a nice letter. It was not fun for the Christians in this congregation to read. Why?

Some people from Corinth reported to Paul both by letter and in person that the church there was quarreling (1:10-11). Paul said they were acting like babies (3:1), were still worldly, (3:3), and one man was taking pride over another (4:6).

Paul said he had to write to them to "shame them as children because some had become arrogant" (4:14, 18). People in the congregation were being boastful (5:6) which was, of course, hurting others. Although they were now Christians, their lives were still full of malice and wickedness (5:8). They were even being enslaved by otherwise permissible things (6:12).

This congregation was "in the middle of a crisis" (7:26). Why? Because people were seeking their own good instead of the good of others. They were acting like the word of God had originated with them (14:36). As a result, their meetings were doing more harm than good (11:17)!

Paul wrote this letter to avoid making a painful visit to them (2nd Corinthians 2:1). He was greatly distressed and anguished in heart, and had shed many tears over them (2nd Corinthians 2:4).

His letter is divided up by subject. He wrote about church harmony first. Then in 7:1 he said, "Now for the matters you wrote about." They realized things were terribly wrong, and some of them wrote to Paul out of desperation.

Paul's reply to their letter is divided into two major parts. Chapters 7—11:16 covers their private Christian lives. In 7:1 he talks about marriage, beginning 8:1 he talks about eating meat offered to idols, beginning 9:1 he talks about supporting himself so he didn't have to take payment from them, beginning 10:1 he talks about purchasing meat at the market that had been offered to idols.

Finally, beginning 11:1 Paul talks about women praying and prophesying "because of the [example of] the angels" (11:10). Since angels delivered their prophecies to individuals and not to groups, Paul is talking about the woman's relationship to her husband and others in the home.

(Keep in mind that Paul did not number his sentences or write his letters with chapter divisions. This was done over a millennium later by an uninspired man.) So finally, in verse 11:17 Paul begins talking about their public meetings. He introduces the subject thusly: "In the FOLLOWING directives I have no praise for you, for your MEETINGS do more harm than good. In the FIRST place...."

In fact, all the following verses refer to their meetings. Besides the one above, 11:33 says, "when you come together...." 12:28 says, "in the church, God has appointed...." 14:6 says, "If I come to you and speak.... 14:23 says, "So if the whole church comes together...." 4:26 says, "When you come together...." 14:33 says, "As in all the congregations...." 15:12 says "but if it is preached.... and 16:1 says "Now about the collection...."

So beginning here to the end of the letter, Paul talks about what Christians should do in their meetings, not in private. Beginning 11:17 he talks about keeping the Lord's Supper in the assembly, beginning 12:1 he talks about spiritual gifts used in the assembly ("message of wisdom...message of knowledge...healing...prophecy...tongues...interpretation" (12:8-10).

Beginning 13:1 he talks about love being superior to tongues, beginning 14:1 he talks about tongues in the assembly, beginning 14:26 he talks about orderliness in the assembly, beginning 15:1 he talks about what they must preach regarding the resurrection of the dead "But if it is preached...." 15:12). He closes his letter talking about collections in the assembly (16:1).

God, I adore you. You are my life and light. You are my reason for living. I long to see you someday face to face. I just wish I could express what I feel.

ALL MENTIONS OF TONGUES

Tongues is mentioned several times in both chapters 12 and 13. First, where did they get their spiritual gifts? We learned earlier the apostles had to be present to give them. In 1:6 Paul says "Our testimony about Christ was confirmed in you. Therefore you do not lack any spiritual gift."

Paul's testimony had to be confirmed or proven to be true. He could have come from anywhere claiming to have been inspired by God. How did he confirm his words? The same way Jesus did. He did many miraculous signs "that you may believe."

In fact, in Paul's second letter to the Corinthians he referred to "the things that mark an apostle — signs, wonders and miracles" done among them. Therefore, when Paul was with them to start the congregation in Corinth he gave them spiritual gifts.

In chapter 12, verse 10 Paul said some had received miraculous powers, some prophecy, some distinguishing between spirits, some speaking in "different kinds of tongues." The word translated "kinds of" is the Greek word *genos* which means race, nationality.

One other gift was the interpretation of tongues. This word translated "interpretation" is from the Greek word *hermeneia* which means an explanation, a commentary. It is the same word used in Luke 24:27 where, after Jesus' resurrection from the dead he appeared to some men and, "beginning with Moses and all the Prophets, he explained to them what was said in all the scriptures concerning himself."

It is also the same word used in the *Septuagint*, the Greek translation of the Old Testament centuries earlier, where the Law of Moses was read to the Jews, with the Levites "making it clear and giving the meaning so that the people could understand what was being read" (Nehemiah 8:8). More on this later.

In 12:28, Paul listed various gifts. As he began his list he said, "first of all...." The last gift he listed was tongues. The term "first of all" is from the Greek *proton* which refers to order in rank or order of importance. The least important gift was "different kinds of tongues." This term is from the Greek *genos* indicating race or nationality, not babbling or gibberish.

In 12:30, Paul asked, "Do all speak in tongues?" The word translated "speak" is from the Greek *laleo* which means to tell something. How could they tell something to people if they were speaking in an unknown language?

Chapter 13 only mentions tongues twice. Verse one is critical and almost always misapplied. "If I speak in the tongues of men and of angels, but have not love, I am only a resounding gong or a clanging cymbal."

What are the tongues of angels? Many people say it is gibberish, babbling. But what does the Bible say the tongues of angels is? Just what language do angels speak in? Below are all the times in the Bible an angel spoke on earth.

Genesis 16:7-12 an angel spoke to Hagar and was understood by her. Genesis 16:3 says Hagar was **Egyptian.**

Genesis 19:10-21 an angel spoke to Lot's family and was understood. Genesis 11:31 says they were Chaldean (**Babylonian**).

Genesis 21:14-18 an angel spoke to Hagar again and was understood. Genesis 16:3 says Hagar was **Egyptian**.

Genesis 22:1-12 an angel spoke to Abraham and was understood. Genesis 11:31 says Abraham was Chaldean (**Babylonian**).

Exodus 3:1-3 an angel spoke to Moses and was understood. Exodus 1:15, 2:9-10 says Moses was raised as an Egyptian.

Judges 13:2-17 an angel spoke to Samson's parents and was understood. Judges 13:1 says they were Israelites (who spoke **Hebrew**).

2 Kings 1:3-4 an angel spoke to Elijah and was understood. 1 Kings 17:1 says Elijah was an Israelite (who spoke **Hebrew**).

Daniel 8:16-25; 9:21-27 an angel spoke to Daniel and was understood. Daniel 1:1-4 says Daniel learned the **Babylonian** language.

Luke 1:8-20 an angel spoke to Zechariah and was understood. Luke 1:4 says Zechariah was an Israelite (who now spoke Aramaic).

Luke 1:28-38 an angel spoke to Mary and was understood. Luke 3:24f and other places say Mary was an Israelite (who now spoke Aramaic).

Luke 2:8-12 angels spoke to shepherds and were understood. Luke 2:4 says the shepherds were Israelites (who now spoke **Aramaic**).

Matthew 28:1-7 an angel spoke to Mary Magdalene and others and was understood. A map reveals that Magdala was in the province of Galilee in Palestine where the Jews lived (who now spoke **Aramaic**).

Acts 10:1-8 an angel spoke to Cornelius and was understood. Acts 10:1 says Cornelius was an Italian officer, so probably spoke **Latin**.

Acts 12:5-10 an angel spoke to Peter and was understood. John 1:44 says Peter was from Capernaum in the province of Galilee in Palestine where the Jews lived (who now spoke **Aramaic**).

Revelation 5:2, etc. an angel spoke to John and was understood. Matthew 4:18-21 says John was from the province of Galilee in Palestine where the Jews lived (who now spoke Aramaic). However, he wrote about the vision in **Greek.**

So, what language do angels speak in? Our examples give us Egyptian, Chaldean, Hebrew, Babylonian, Aramaic, Latin, and Greek. Therefore, angels speak in the language of whoever they are speaking to. They do not speak in unintelligible gibberish.

Finally, 13:8 says love will go on forever, but prophecies will cease and tongues will be stilled. The word translated "stilled" is from the Greek word *pauomai* which means to stop, to make an end. In Luke 8:24, for instance, it was used by Jesus causing the storm to cease.

God, I always wanted to talk angelically. It never occurred to me angels speak the languages already spoken on earth. Isn't there some special language I can speak to you with?

CHAPTER 14

Now for chapter 14. We will cover every verse in order to get a proper perspective. Paul had listed the gifts most important as those involving messages. Here and in 12:28-30 he listed spiritual gifts and gave tongues as the least in importance. He had already told them in 13:1 that love was superior to tongues, and in 14:1 that prophecy was superior to tongues.

Remember, Paul was not explaining the wonderful experience of tongues. He was bawling them out for misusing this gift. This is not so much a chapter on what to do as it is what not to do. Over and over, beginning with **verse 1**, Paul tells them prophecy was much superior. It seems they weren't getting it through their stubborn heads.

There is something very revealing in **verse 2**. Readers with the King James Version will readily see it. The word "unknown" is not in the Greek!

The King James Version italicizes all words that are not in the original language. Another example of this is in Ecclesiastes 12:13 (KJV): "Let us hear the conclusion of the whole matter: Fear God, and keep his commandments: for this is the whole [duty] of man."

As to the meaning of this verse, keep in mind Paul is not talking about private behavior but public worship. Therefore, anyone who speaks in the public assembly in a language foreign to the others is not speaking to men. God understands him, but no one else does. It's a mystery to the others because they do not understand him. This is apparently what Paul was referring to back in chapters 4 and 5, saying some people were taking pride over others, they were arrogant, and they were boasting.

I have personally heard people who speak in unintelligible sounds tell those who did not that they couldn't because Satan was in those other people and interfering with them. It was as though those who spoke in what they considered tongues were boasting that they were more holy than people who did not. Does this do anything to encourage those who do not? Does it build them up? No, they are led to feel inferior and to question their own faith.

In contrast, Paul says in **verses 3 and 4** that everyone who prophecies in the public assembly encourages and comforts the others because they can understand what is being said. People insisting on speaking in a foreign language in the assemblies were making themselves look good, but it did nothing to encourage the church. Paul basically said, "Stop doing that!"

Paul wished in **verse 5** that everyone in their congregation could speak in foreign languages if that was their desire. But he said that they were selling themselves, others, and God short. He said he wished they'd rather long to be able to prophesy.

Just what is prophecy? The word in Hebrew means to pour out. Thus, a prophet pours out the mind of God. In Greek it means to publicly expound. Expound comes from the Greek *exponere* which means to expose, to express point by point in detail.

For example, Amos explained prophecy in 3:7-12 and on through the book. "Hear this word the Lord has spoken....Surely the Sovereign Lord does nothing without revealing his plan to his servants the prophets.... Proclaim....Therefore this is what the Sovereign Lord says....This is what the Lord says...."

Amos explained it further in 7:15-17: "But the Lord took me...and said to me, 'Go, prophesy to my people Israel.' Now then, hear the word of the Lord....Therefore this is what the Lord says."

Ezekiel was told in 4:7 to prophecy, and also what to wear and so on while he did. Then in 5:5,7,8,17 he prophesied: "This is what the Sovereign Lord says....Therefore this is what the

Sovereign Lord says....Therefore this is what the Sovereign Lord says....I the Lord have spoken."

Later Ezekiel was told by God to prophecy to bones scattered throughout a battlefield. "Then he [God] said to me, 'Prophesy to these bones and say to them, "Dry bones, hear the word of the Lord!" This is what the Sovereign Lord says to these bones:

'I will make breath enter you and you will come to life. I will attach tendons to you and make flesh come upon you and cover you with skin; I will put breath in you, and you will come to life. Then you will know that I am the Lord.' So I prophesied as I was commanded. And as I was prophesying, there was a noise, a rattling sound, and the bones came together, bone to bone" (Ezekiel 37:4-7).

Finally, 2nd Peter is about "prophecy of scripture". In other words, prophecy is scripture. From these examples, we see, then, that prophecy is the exact words of God. But, especially in the example from Ezekiel, we may not feel like we understand completely the implications of this prophecy. We may feel we need someone to explain its meaning as it applies to our own lives. This is where interpreters are needed.

Paul said they who prophesied in the assembly were greater than those who spoke in foreign languages among them. The only exception would be someone who would interpret what was said, both into the prevailing language and into a sense that could be applied to their lives.

Interpretation as it is commonly used regarding unintelligible words is strictly translating. Even if this were all the word meant, first of all, in most congregations where gibberish is said in the name of tongues, people do it from their seats, and no one stands up and interprets for them.

A sure way to see if someone really knows how to interpret in the sense of translating into English, is to ask someone to speak in tongues and record it. Then play the recording to someone who claims the gift of interpretation and have them either write down or record their interpretation. Then play the tongues to someone else claiming the gift of interpretation and have them write it down or record their interpretation. Do it at least twice; but if possible, more.

One of the problems with this experiment is that interpretation of tongues today is not considered very spiritual. Therefore it is difficult to find anyone claiming this gift. But if you can do it, do you think the interpretations will be the same? If they are truly inspired by God they will be. The few I know about who have consented to do this have failed.

Now in **verse 6**, Paul gets into the PURPOSE of speaking in foreign languages. He said that the foreign language must be used to bring a revelation, a word of knowledge, prophecy or a word of instruction direct from God. They should not be talking just to be talking. They are instructing. Paul did not say to use tongues to just pray and praise God. He told them to use it to TEACH UNBELIEVERS.

Remember, the New Testament was not yet written. People had to rely on the apostles to know just what God wanted them to do. The apostles proved they were giving God's truth by performing some miracles. But sometimes the apostles were not around. So, in that case, people were given special knowledge of the truth through the gifts of prophecy, etc. Otherwise, they would have had to guess what God wanted them to do.

In **verses 7-9** Paul compares speaking a foreign language that no one in the congregation understood to playing an instrument in such a jumbled manner there is not really any tune. Also it was like a trumpet being sounded for an army, but in such a jumbled way that no one knew whether it was advance or retreat, taps or reverie.

In **verses 10 and 11**, he says there were all kinds of languages in the world, but none of them were without meaning. None of them was gibberish. But, if someone speaks a foreign language in the assembly no one knows or can grasp, they may as well be speaking into the air.

Did Paul say here that if we do not grasp the meaning of the person speaking the tongue we are not as spiritual as the speaker? No. Did Paul say that if we do not grasp the meaning, we're unsaved sinners? No. Did Paul say if we do not grasp the meaning, we simply do not know that language? Yes.

Once more Paul says it again in verse **12.** Since they were so eager to have spiritual gifts, they should be asking for those which build up the assembly. Remember, Paul is talking to the Corinthians church about their assembly.

Therefore, Paul says that if they insist on wanting to speak in foreign languages while praying, they should at least include the interpretation in their prayer (**verse 13**). Why? Because if they pray in the assembly in a foreign language, their mind is unfruitful (**verse 14**).

Let's look at the use of the word "mind" here. First, it means understanding (Luke 24:45). Second, it means knowledge (Romans 1:28). Third, it means conviction (Romans 14:5). Fourth, it means insight (Revelation 13:18).

Now let's look at the use of the word "unfruitful." This same word appears in Matthew 13:22 where the Word of God was "choked" out of hearts, in Ephesians 5:3-4 where evil put us in darkness away from God, in Titus 3:14 where people do not devote themselves to good, in 2 Peter 1:5-8 where people are ineffective and unproductive with their knowledge of God, and in Jude 10 and 12 where church leaders speak about things they don't understand and are spiritually dead.

Therefore, in a nutshell, the unfruitful mind does not understand the Word of God enough to apply it to their lives. Speaking or praying in a language in a church assembly that no one knows causes this.

Therefore, Paul said in **verses 15-17**, they were to pray in the assembly with both their spirit and understanding mind, and sing that way too. They were not to talk or pray or sing in a foreign language no one understood.

If they praise God in prayer or song in a foreign language, "how can one who finds himself among those who do not understand say 'Amen' "? After all, they don't understand what they're saying. Paul didn't say the rest of the congregation was freed from saying "amen" to a song or prayer, but that they could do it correctly only if they understood what was being said. What does "amen" mean? It means "so be it" or "I agree." Giving thanks in a foreign language does not edify the others. It's that simple.

Was Paul against speaking in foreign languages? No. Paul did it all the time (**verse 18**). He traveled all over preaching and needed this gift. So did the other apostles. After all, Jesus told them in Mark 16:15-16 that they were supposed to preach the gospel to the whole world. How effective would they have been if they'd had to stop and learn the language of each area they went to?

Acts 17:6 says "These men who have caused trouble ALL OVER THE WORLD have now come here." Romans 1:8 says, "...your faith is being reported ALL OVER THE WORLD." Romans 10:18 says, "Their voice has gone out into ALL THE EARTH, their words to the ENDS OF THE WORLD." Colossians 1:23 says, "This is the gospel that you heard and that HAS BEEN PROCLAIMED TO EVERY CREATURE UNDER HEAVEN, and of which I, Paul, have become a servant."

According to secular history, Andrew went to Greece, Peter stayed in the Middle East and southern Europe, Thaddeus went to Russia, Thomas went to India, Philip went to Turkey, Nathaniel went to Russia, Matthew went to Ethiopia and Egypt, and Simon went to Great Britain

But, Paul said in **verse 19** that he did not abuse this gift and speak the language of one foreign land to people of another foreign land. He said he would rather speak five intelligible words that instructed the church than ten thousand in a foreign language the people didn't understand.

Now Paul really lets them have it. "STOP THINKING LIKE CHILDREN!" he says in **verse 20**. They had become childish in the way they had insisted on speaking a foreign language to their congregation that their congregation didn't understand. They just wanted to show off.

Then he spells out the whole issue to them in **verses 21 and 22**: "Tongues, then, are a sign, not for believers but for unbelievers; prophecy, however, is for believers, not for unbelievers." What is the difference in tongues and prophecy?

Obviously, the gift of tongues was supposed to be used to give the INITIAL GOSPEL MESSAGE to people in a new territory that did not know about it as they went "into all the world to preach the gospel." It was used by missionaries to explain to unbelievers Jesus and how to become Christians.

On the other hand, after they became Christians, the gift of prophecy was used by Christians among believers before the New Testament was written to explain God's will for the rest of their lives.

Still in the nitty-gritty, Paul goes on to say in **verses 23-25** that unbelievers visiting their worship service will think they're all crazy, or as he expresses it, "OUT OF YOUR MIND!" if people are speaking in a language no one else knows. But, if in the assembly people are prophesying, that is explaining God's will for their lives — the visiting unbeliever will understand his sinful condition and be convicted. The visiting unbeliever will then say, "God is really among you! How do I become one of you?"

How do unbelieving visitors feel when they come into your worship?

The worship services of the church at Corinth seemed to be bordering on mass egotism. Many were jockeying for position and demanding to be noticed. Paul told them to at least take turns (**verses 26**). If the assembly doesn't encourage the entire congregation, something is terribly wrong.

And with one last encouragement, he brought up tongues again. If they insist on being childish and speaking a language no one else knows, someone MUST interpret both into the known language and into words where they can apply it to their lives. Otherwise, they're just talking to themselves and to God (**verse 27 and 28**).

Actually, if they wanted to speak in tongues so badly, perhaps they should have gotten out on the circuit and spread the gospel in other places with their gift.

Oh God, I never connected tongues with converting the world before. Is that what it is for? I'm trying to understand so I can please you more. I want to be truly spiritual in your sight.

God's Definition of Spirituality

The Bible never uses the actual word spirituality. The closest it comes is "spiritually" and "spiritual." The word spirit is a translation of the Greek word *pneuma* which means breathing or blowing. We know that people breathe by its results, but we cannot see breath. We know that the wind blows by its results, but we cannot see the wind.

Jesus explained it this way: " '...no one can enter the kingdom of God unless he is born of water AND the Spirit. Flesh gives birth to flesh, but the Spirit gives birth to spirit....The wind blows wherever it pleases. You hear its sound, but you cannot tell where it comes from or where it is going. So it is with everyone born of the Spirit' " (John 3:5-8).

Spirituality is the same. We cannot see spirituality. We know someone has it by the results. Romans 8:6 says we should "be spiritually minded" (KJV). So from this we know that spirituality has to do with the mind. What else does it have to do with?

The written law of God (Romans 7:6, 14)
The gift of salvation (Romans 15:27 & Acts 10:36, 18)
Truth, mind of Christ, the Word of God (1st Corinthians 2:2:13-16, John 17:17)
Food of God, the Word of God (1st Corinthians 3:1 & Hebrews 5:12-14)
Seed, the Word of God (1st Corinthians 9:11 & Matthew 13:19)
Drink of Christ, water of eternal life (1st Corinthians 10:3-4 & John 7:38)
Miraculous powers that confirmed the Word were really from God (1st Corinthians 12:1, 12; 14:37; John 20:30-31)
Our heavenly body (1 Corinthians 15:44-46)
Sinlessness (Galatians 5:19-6:1)
Salvation, the blessings of heavenly realms (Ephesians 1:3; 2:6- 7)
Worship (Ephesians 5:19 & Colossians 3:16)
Satan's forces of evil (Ephesians 6:12)
Knowledge of God's will (Colossians 1:9)
People in the church (1 Pet. 2:5 & 1 Timothy 3:15)

In a nutshell, we see that spirituality is linked to the Word of God which is called the law of God, the mind of God, truth, knowledge of God's will. It was also the miracles that confirmed the Word of God. Therefore, we cannot have spirituality out of our imaginations. Spirituality comes from the Bible.

Spirituality is also linked to sinlessness, salvation, worship, the church. Of course, we do not know what things are sin unless we check with the Bible. We do not know how to be saved unless we check with the Bible. We do not know if we are in the church unless we check with the Bible.

There is no scripture listed above regarding spirituality as an emotion. It all deals with the Word of God, the *Logos*. "In the beginning was the Word, and the Word was with God, and the Word was God....The Word became flesh and made his dwelling among us" (John 1:1, 14). The term "word" is from the Greek "logos" from which we get another word, logic.

What many people today define as "spirituality" is an emotionalism akin to someone on a drug "high." Interestingly, the sin of sorcery condemned by God comes from the Greek word *pharmakeia* from whence our word for pharmacy or drugs. It is a sin to act like we are on a drug high in the name of Jehovah God. It is frightful, it is confusing, it is non-productive, and it is wrong (Revelation 21:8; 22:15).

Spirituality, then, is not emotionalism. Spirituality also is not what comes out of our imaginations. Spirituality is knowing and following the Word of God.

There is a parallel to understanding spirituality with understanding — fasting. Jesus said in Matthew 6:16-18, "When you fast, do not look somber as the hypocrites do, for they disfigure their faces to show men they are fasting. I tell you the truth, they have received their reward in full. But when you fast, put oil on your head and wash your face, so that it will not be obvious to men that you are fasting, but only to your Father, who is unseen; and your Father, who sees what is done in secret, will reward you."

In an era when fasting was practiced frequently (we modern Christians miss a blessing by not fasting), Jesus said people were going out of their way to look the part of holy people so others would admire them. Today, in our worship services, especially where it comes to emotionalism, we are trying to look the part of holy people. An unknown poet explained,

> Let us keep our fast within,
> Till heaven and we are quite alone;
> Then let the grief, the shame, the sin
> Before the mercy-seat be thrown

Fasting is an act of self-restraint. It belongs to the sphere of self-discipline. It is strictly a personal and private matter. What is public is the results of fasting, the results of self-discipline. But we cannot show the actual process of self-discipline. In fact, we would spoil the process by attempting to show it, like wearing a "humble" button.

Just as a plant must begin its growth in the darkness of the soil, we begin our spiritual growth in the darkness of our own inner thoughts and prayer to God. And just as we can never safely expose the roots of a plant, we can never show the exact process by which we develop and protect our own spiritual roots. All moral and bodily restraint, all humbleness of body and spirit are represented by fasting, and it is a complete failure of self-restraint to want to show others our self-restraint.

It is the same with spirituality. Spirituality (salvation) comes from reading the Mind of God, the Word of God (Romans 10:1-3, 17). No one else can absorb the Mind of God, the Word of God into our minds for us. We have to do it for ourselves. It is a personal thing. A private thing. Developing faith from it all is something that cannot really be expressed in words. It happens within our own minds. And faith that comes from the Word of God and following it leads to salvation (Romans 10:3, 17).

We should be grateful that salvation does not rely on emotions. If it did, we'd be very confused about our salvation. David understood the tug-of-war that occurs between emotions and logic. Look at Psalm 42 where he struggled with his faith.

Here David begins a debate between his emotions (his soul)

and his logic. Let's look in on the drama as David has a talk with himself:

SCENE: His soul is panting for God, thirsting for God, trying to meet with God. He's been crying day and night asking where God is.

EMOTIONS: Where is your God? Remember how I used to go with the multitude, leading the procession to the house of God with shouts of joy and thanksgiving among the festive throng?

LOGIC: Why are you downcast, O my soul? Why so disturbed within me? Put your hope in God, for I will yet praise him, my Savior and my God.

EMOTIONS: My soul is downcast within me.

LOGIC: Therefore I will remember you from the land of Jordan....

EMOTIONS: Deep calls to deep in the roar of your waterfalls; all your waves and breakers have swept over me.

LOGIC: By day the Lord directs his love, at night his song is with me—a prayer to the God of my life.

EMOTIONS: I say to God my Rock, "Why have you forgotten me? Why must I go about mourning, oppressed by the enemy?" My bones suffer mortal agony as my foes taunt me, saying to me all day long, "Where is your God?"

LOGIC: Why are you downcast, O my soul? Why so disturbed within me? Put your hope in God, for I will yet praise him, my Savior and my God.

Isn't it wonderful that our salvation doesn't depend on how spiritual we feel? If it did, we'd be in and out of salvation, depending on how we felt.

I have known people who did gauge their salvation by their emotions. They'd say something like, "I cried and cried all one day because of my sins and asked God to forgive me. Then I felt such release, and knew I was now saved." Then they'd say a few years later, "I thought I was saved, but I wasn't really. This time I cried and cried for several days because of my sins and asked God to forgive me. Then I felt so good that this time I knew he'd saved me."

Then a few years later the rise in emotions would happen again, only this time more intensely. On and on the cycle went for them. Thinking they knew for sure they were saved, then wondering, then doubting, then in hopelessness once again.

Salvation does not depend on our emotions. Salvation depends on what we logically believe about what Jesus did for us. Is remorse, love and gratitude involved in our salvation? Of course. Many emotions are involved. But they are the result of our logically reading God's word, and then logically accepting it and following it.

Why are we given the spiritual gift of salvation? There is more than one reason. The obvious one is so we can go to heaven. But there is another reason. Ephesians 2:8-10 explains, "For it is by grace you have been saved, through faith—and this not from yourselves, it is the gift of God—not by works, so that no one can boast. For we are God's workmanship, CREATED in Christ Jesus TO DO GOOD WORKS, which God prepared in advance for us to do."

Well, God, I think this is good news and bad news. I thought there was a higher emotional plain I could reach with you. But since it is so hard — actually impossible — to reach the emotional plain I wish to reach with you, it relieves me of the burden of trying to reach it. I have sometimes felt so spiritually inadequate.

Spirituality and Touching Jesus

The Spirit cannot be seen any more than breath or wind can

be seen. But the results of breath and wind can be seen. So too, spirituality cannot be seen. Only the results of spirituality can be seen. The results are in our attitudes and deeds.

For instance, Galatians 5:22-25 explains clearly, "But the fruit [result] of the Spirit [spirituality] is love, joy, peace, patience, kindness, goodness, faithfulness, gentleness and self-control. Against such things there is no law. Those who belong to Christ Jesus have crucified the sinful nature with its passions and desires. Since we live by the Spirit, let us keep in step with the Spirit."

Furthermore, James, the brother of Jesus said, "What good is it, my brothers, if a man claims to have faith but has no deeds? Can such faith save him? Suppose a brother or sister is without clothes and daily food. If one of you says to him, 'God, I wish you well; keep warm and well fed,' but does nothing about his physical needs, what good is it? In the same way, faith by itself, if it is not accompanied by action, is dead" (James 2:14-17).

Do we want to touch Jesus? Jesus told us how. " 'For I was hungry and you gave me something to eat, I was thirsty and you gave me something to drink, I was a stranger and you invited me in, "I needed clothes and you clothed me, I was sick and you looked after me, I was in prison and you came to visit me....whatever you did for one of the least of these brothers of mine, you did for me' " (Matthew 25:35-36, 40).

Therefore, everything In this book about applying God's Word in worship and in service is spirituality.

Do we want to touch Jesus? Every time the announcements are made and someone responds, "I'll take some food over to them on Monday," that is spirituality.

Do we want to touch Jesus? Every time we enter into prayer together after getting into each other's hearts and lives and asking them, "What do you need prayer for?" that is spirituality.

Do we want to touch Jesus? Every time we partake of the Lord's Supper and compare our imperfection and being deserving of death and hell with Jesus' perfection and taking our punishment for us, as explained in God's Word, that is spirituality.

Do we want to touch Jesus? Every time we give money to help support evangelism, purchase Bibles, send food to the needy, that is spirituality.

Do we want to touch Jesus? Every time we sing praises to God in faltering voices but from deep within our soul, playing on the strings of our heart, that is spirituality.

Do we want to touch Jesus? Every time we read the Bible in order to know the Mind of God, so we can live the way he wants us to rather than what our imaginations think he wants, that is spirituality.

All we need to feel spiritual and special is to know God loves us. No matter how many times we sin, he loves us. No matter how many times we fall, God loves us.

We are not special to God because of how good we are, but because how good God is. Not because of anything we are, but because of who God is. We're not special because we are so loving, but because God is love. Not because we are so full of life, but because God is life. Not because we're so intelligent and spiritual, but because God is.

If we want to speak in a special language, let us speak in the language of love. Spirituality is sitting with a friend and telling them God loves them when they're good and bad, and will help them overcome the bad.

Spirituality is going with a friend who wants to join a self-help group like Alcoholics Anonymous. It's telling them how much God will help them. Then proving it with scriptures. Spirituality is going to an enemy gossiping against you and saying God loves you both, and there's nothing they can say or do to get you to stop loving them!

That's spirituality! That's high!

Thank you, God, for allowing me to be close to you through your word, through prayer, and through other people who are seeking to be close to you too — the church. I could never do it alone. Now I understand spirituality. It was a hidden treasure I hardly knew I had — and so precious. I fall at your feet and whisper once more Thank You.

Second-Generation *Church Accounts*

Clement of Rome, a friend of both Peter and Paul, wrote in AD 96, in his First Epistle 1:2-2:7 and his Genuine Epistle to the Corinthians 45: "What visitor among you is there who has not proved your most excellent and firm faith, who has not marvelled at your prudent and gentle piety in Christ, who has not proclaimed your magnificent practice of hospitality, and who has not blessed your perfect and sure knowledge?...There was an insatiable desire to do good, and a full outpouring of the Holy Spirit came upon all. You were full of holy counsel.... You have searched the scriptures, which are true, which were given through the Holy Ghost; and you know that nothing unrighteous or counterfeit is written in them." [8]

In the Epistle to Diognetus 5, about AD 140: "For Christians are not distinguished from the rest of men neither by country, language, nor customs. They do not dwell in cities of their own, nor do they use some strange language, nor practice a peculiar kind of life. Their teaching indeed has not been discovered by any speculation or consideration of men full of curiosity, nor do they busy themselves with human doctrine as some do." [9]

Irenaeus, about 180, wrote in Against Heresies I.x.1; and **Refutation and Overthrow of False Doctrine**, Bk. 2: "For the church, although dispersed throughout the whole world as far as the ends of the earth, received from the apostles and their disciples the faith...in the Holy Spirit, who has proclaimed through the prophets the plans of God and the comings of Christ....So far are they from raising the dead, as the Lord raised, and as the apostles by means of prayer, for even among the brethren frequently in a case of necessity when a whole church united in much fasting and prayer, the spirit has returned to the ex-animated body, and the man was granted to the prayers of the saints....

"Wherefore, also, those that were truly his disciples, receiving grace from him, in his name performed these things for the benefit of men, as everyone received the free gift from him. Some, indeed, most certainly and truly cast out demons, so that frequently these persons themselves that were cleansed from wicked spirits believed and were received into the church. Others have the knowledge of things to come, as also visions and prophetic communications; others heal the sick by the imposition of hands, and restore them to health. And, moreover, as we said above, even the dead have been raised and continued with us many years.

"As we hear many of the brethren in the church who have prophetic gifts, and who speak in all tongues through the spirit, and who also, bring to light the secret things of men for their benefit, and who expound the mysteries of God." [10]

8. MUSIC AND THE MASK

Your heart was lifted up because of your beauty;
You corrupted your wisdom for the sake of your splendor.
I cast you to the ground.
Ezekiel 28:17 (NKJV)

Famous Theologians

About 450 — AUGUSTINE — PRE-CATHOLIC: "Nor must we keep back the mystical meaning of the 'timbrel and psaltery.' On the timbrel leather is stretched, on the psaltery gut is stretched; on either instrument the flesh is crucified. How well did he 'sing a psalm on timbrel and psaltery' who said, 'the world is crucified unto me, and I unto the world'? This psaltery or timbrel He wishes thee to take up, who loveth a new song, who teacheth thee saying to thee, 'Whosoever willeth to be My disciple, let him deny himself and take up his cross and follow me.' Let him not set down his psaltery, let him not set down his timbrel, let him stretch himself out on the wood, and be dried from the lust of the flesh. the more the strings are stretched, the more sharply do they sound." (Expositions on the Psalms, Psalm CXLIX)

About 1270 — THOMAS AQUINAS — CATHOLIC: "Our church does not use musical instruments as harps and psaltries, to praise God withal, that she may not seem to Judaize" "It is pernicious to make use of the ceremonies of the Old Law." (Bingham's Ant., Vol. 3, pg. 137; Summa Theologica, Secunda Secundae Partis).

About 1525 — ULRICH ZWINGLY, REFORMED CHURCHES: Influenced the following events: "On Sunday the 19th of January [1528], the day on which the doctrine of the Mass was attacked....some men, excited by the passion of the moment, fell upon his beloved organ, an accomplice in their eyes of so many superstitious rites, and violently broke it to pieces. No more mass, no more organ, no more anthems!" (History of the Reformation of the Sixteenth Century, J. H. Merle D'Augigne, 1835, Translated by H. White B.A. of Canterbury, M.A. and Ph.D. of Heidelberg, 1844, Vol. XIII, pg. 606).

About 1540, MARTIN LUTHER — LUTHERAN: "...organs are ensigns of Baal" (Eckhard, Proponent of Instruments, in argument with John Calvin.)

About 1550 — JOHN CALVIN — REFORMED CHURCHES: "Music instruments in celebrating the praises of God would be no more suitable than the burning of incense, the lighting of lamps, and the restoration of the other shadows of the law. The Papists therefore have foolishly borrowed this, as well as many other things, from the Jews. Men who are fond of outward pomp may delight in that noise; but the simplicity which God recommends to us by the apostles is far more pleasing to Him....In Popery there was a ridiculous and unsuitable imitation [of the Jews]. while they adorned their temples and valued themselves as having made the worship of God more splendid and inviting, they employed organs and many other such ludicrous things, by which the Word and worship of God are exceedingly profaned, the people being much more attached to those rites than to the understanding of the divine Word....Musical instruments were among the legal ceremonies which Christ at his coming abolished; and, therefore we, under the Gospel, must maintain a greater simplicity" (Commentary on Psalm xxxiii, Commentary on 1 Samuel 18:1-9 and Four Last Books of Moses I:263).

ABOUT 1550—JOHN KNOX—PRESBYTERIAN: "This principle not only purified the church of human inventions and popish corruptions, but restored plain singing of psalms, unaccompanied by instrumental music." (Adam Clark, Commentary on Amos 6:5)

About 1775—JOHN WESLEY, METHODIST: "I have no objection to instruments of music in our chapels provided they are neither seen nor heard." (Adam Clark, Commentary on Amos 6:5)

About 1800—ADAM CLARK—METHODIST: "I have never known instrumental music to be productive of any good in the worship of God and I have reason to believe that it has been productive of much evil. Music as a science I esteem and admire, but instruments of music in the house of God I abominate and abhor. This is the abuse of music and I here register my protest against all such corruption in the worship of that Infinite Spirit who requires his followers to worship him in spirit and in truth" (Commentary on Amos 6:5).

1861, 1870, 1881, CHARLES SPURGEON—BAPTIST: "In many of our dissenting congregations, some five or six who are the choir, sing to the praise and glory of themselves, and the people sit still and listen, not daring to spoil music so magnificent....In many other places it is thought most seemly to delegate the work of human hearts and tongues and lips to some instrument which shall praise the Lord. May that never be the case here....If you and your choir wish to show off your excellent voices, you can meet at home...but the...church of God must not be desecrated to so poor an end....The institution of singers as a separate order is an evil, a growing evil, and ought to be abated and abolished....We should like to see all the pipes of the organs in our nonconformist places of worship either ripped open or compactly filled with concrete. The human voice is so transcendently superior to all that wind or strings can accomplish that it is a shame to degrade its harmonies by association with blowing and scraping" (Sermons in the Metropolitan Pulpit, London, 1861 pg. 218, 1870 pg. 353, 1881 pg. 474).

1888, JOHN GIRARDEAU—PRESBYTERIAN: "The church of Scotland....for centuries knew nothing of instrumental music in her public services....But...some who clamored for a more artistic 'celebration' of worship....The floodgates are up, and the result is by no means uncertain: the experience of the American Presbyterian church will be that of the Scottish." (*Instrumental Music in Public Worship*, Richmond: Whittet & Shepperson, Printers, 1888).

My heart sings to you, God. The strings of my heart tremble in lowliness, resonate in hope, and arise in echoes of love. From earth to heaven. From my heart to yours. From spirit to Spirit. Transcending worlds, my song spreads your laughter, calms my tears, and rests in you.

He wondered if she really loved him. He certainly did love her. But the way she responded to him was rather unusual, and at first left him wondering.

Whenever he went to pick her up at her house, she would fling open the door, sweep her arms upward, and—with a CD playing in the background—begin to sing her greeting to him:

With loving effervescence
I come into your presence!

Furthermore, every time he took her home, she would tell him to wait a moment and then fling open the front door, turn on the CD player again, and sing out her appreciation for their lovely evening together:

I love your words; they touch my heart
Even when we are far apart.

Well, he decided this was just her way. And, after all, one of the things he had liked about her from the beginning was that she wasn't shy about expressing her feelings toward him. He even got so he bragged to his friends about her. As a result, she was so pleased that he was pleased, she began singing while with him even more.

Eventually he began writing her love letters. When he would see her later, sometimes he would want to talk to her about the letters. When he'd ask her how she felt about his words, she would burst out in song:

When with you my heart can sing and chime.
When apart I relive that precious time.

To her amazement, he was a little annoyed. He tried not to show it because he loved her so, and appreciated her talent. But all he wanted to do was for them to talk one on one with each other. She'd talk to him some, but then burst out in another refrain:

How assuring it is to firmly know
You'd protect me from my every foe.

It was obvious she adored him. This he knew without all doubt. Who else would spend so much time writing such lovely lyrics and composing such magical melodies? So they continued their relationship.

One time while on one of their dates, she stepped out in front of a car; he saw it just in time to push her out of its path. But in the process, he was hit and hospitalized in a distant city where she could not go. He nearly lost his life. When he finally got well and returned, it was like receiving him back from the dead. She had no doubts how much he loved her.

In fact, when she finally saw him again, she could not control her emotions. He felt the same way and expected a hug and a quiet and intimate moment of just being reunited again. Instead, she burst out in another song:

Your life you willingly gave for me.
Your love is of measureless degree.

When other people heard her sing to him in public, they thought how lucky he was to have such a talented woman who adored him so. Indeed on the surface it seemed obvious she loved him.

But the singing became so incessant, more and more substituting their talks together, their quiet moments together, he finally began to seriously wonder who she was more interested in—him or herself. It was as though she were wearing a mask all the time. It was as though she was performing rather than face talking directly to him and allowing him to talk directly to her. It was as though she was always on stage.

This story is a parable. Do you see the parallels? God the Son—Jesus—is the groom awaiting the wedding day at the end of time on earth. His bride is the church. The time spent together is our worship.

Intimacy is avoided. Although there is mutual love, the woman is insisting on "pleasing" the man in her own way, regardless of what really pleases him.

Oh God, may I never do anything that displeases you. Help me understand more perfectly what does please you and not take for granted what people claim pleases you.

Hypocrites

Our word hypocrite comes from the Greek word, *hypocrites,* which originally meant pretender, but later came to mean an actor on the stage.

We usually think of hypocrites as doing something morally wrong in their life away from the church building, despite their declarations on Sunday morning of how much they love God. But we can have hypocrisy in our worship. There are examples in the Bible of hypocritic worshippers doing what pleased them instead of God, even though it seemed so right.

Cain and Abel both worshipped God. Cain and Abel both made valuable sacrifices to God. Both sacrificed their time to acknowledge God. Both sacrificed part of their livelihood, part of their income. How righteous of them both.

But Abel's worship was accepted by God and Cain's was not. Cain did not offer his gift with faith. Then why did he do it in the first place? Perhaps just to show off and make people think he was really religious when he wasn't. Abel, on the other hand, had offered his sacrifice with faith and love in his heart. (See Genesis

4:2-5).

How could God be displeased with Cain's worship? After all, Cain chose to worship God and not some idol. Cain wanted to please God. Cain sacrificed time and things of monetary value for God. Cain gave liberally. But what Cain did was not what God wanted him to do. Call it legalism if you want, but God calls it pleasing our Creator.

Then there were Nadab and Abihu. They were priests under their father, Aaron, the high priest. Nadab was in line to be the next high priest, in fact. One day they went into the tabernacle and burned incense to God. How beautiful a ceremony it must have been. This was their worship.

How did God reward them for this beautiful ceremony? The fire they used to light the incense blazed out and burned them. How could God do such a thing?

Nadab and Abihu both went to "church" regularly. Nadab and Abihu held high office in the "church." Nadab and Abihu worshipped God, not just weekly, but every day. How dedicated to the Lord these "clergymen" were.

So how could God have punished them? Because these men took fire from outside the Tabernacle against God's regulation for worship. Because what Nadab and Abihu did was not what God wanted them to do. (See Leviticus 10:1-3). Call it legalism if you want, but God calls it pleasing our Creator.

Then there was King Saul. He had just been to battle against the enemies of God and had captured all their sheep which he, in turn, planned to sacrifice *en masse* to Jehovah God. What a grand and holy event this was to be. Thousands and thousands of sacrifices to God! Nothing is too much for God. Nothing is too costly for God. Nothing withheld from God. What pageantry!

How did God reward King Saul for this grand ceremony in his name? God took the kingdom from Saul.

But King Saul had seemed to love God so much. After all, he took the chance of losing his own life in order to fight idol worshippers. Then he took the plunder and prepared a worship service like none had ever seen before! How grand it would be! How impressed the people would be. And God.

How could God have punished him for all this? Because Saul was told to destroy all the animals of these people who worshipped gods of their imagination. Because what King Saul did was not what God wanted him to do. (See 1st Samuel 15:3, 20-24.) Call it legalism if you want, but God calls it pleasing our Creator.

We will talk more later about what pleases God. Let us discuss for a moment first about what pleases our visitors, especially the lonely, unfulfilled, empty entitled people.

Like it or not, in "thinking of the visitors" we are often justifying what we want to do instead of what God wants us to do. It's not a matter of what is pleasing to God, we illogically surmise. It is popular today to have a lot of hype in our "seeker services." I suppose if no one is lonely or unfulfilled or empty, that would be effective on a permanent basis.

But does a grand musical presentation fill the hearts of the lonely or unfulfilled or empty? The music is important. It is part of the public worship. But, after the hype becomes old hat, so often people leave our congregations because ultimately they feel on a gut level that no one really cares how they feel.

Proverbs 14:13 says that, even though there may be a lot of laughter, people with heartache will still have their heartache. Does our congregation have a revolving door? Does it draw people temporarily; that is, until the heartache and loneliness resurfaces?

Ultimately, having more people on Sunday is what we want to do so we can convert more people. And that ultimately glorifies our Creator. We have to look at the big picture, we contend. Okay. Let's look at the big picture.

Jehovah God, we're doing everything we know how to glorify you to those who do not know you. You understand that, don't you, God?

Music In Jesus' Day

According to *Time Life Book: Rome,* music was as much a part of people's lives in Jesus' day as it is today. Indeed, they had background music during their entertainment, just as we do during movies.

According to the mosaic of the *Dar Buc Ammera* from Zliten, 2nd century A.D., while gladiators fought in the amphitheater to entertain the people, they were accompanied by a band of musicians playing such instruments as bronze horns, trumpets, and the water organ. [2]

Plautus wrote of "rollicking musical comedies" for the commoner. [3]

As depicted on a wall painting from Stabia, probably lst century A.D., *Museo Nazionale*, Naples, at Roman banquets a single performer might play two instruments at the same time, such as plucking a cithara with one hand and a harp with the other. [4]

They had their military bands too. Sometimes they played in front of the procession just before entering battle. And they always played after they won and as they re-entered their home cities in triumph. These triumphal processions after winning wars included a band of flute, horn and trumpet players.[5]

So, it wasn't as though music was uncommon or unpopular in Jesus' day. On the contrary, music was expected at just about all occasions of pomp and ceremony or entertainment.

It is striking then, that when Jesus traveled about for some three years spreading the news of the impending Kingdom of God, never was music even mentioned other than for children playing games and funerals (Matthew 11:16-17).

Even for his own triumphal procession into Jerusalem, there is no mention of music (see Matthew 21:21:9; Mark 11:9; Luke 19:37; John 12:13).

Only when Jesus instituted the Lord's Supper was religious music finally mentioned. Did he organize great pomp and ceremony for this grand historic occasion? No. Did he organize choirs and dramas and costumes and decorations? No. He held it in private. He held it quietly. And when he was through leading them in their first communion, they sang one hymn (Matthew 26:30). That's all.

How amazing it is to our modern minds to think of this auspicious ceremony including only one quiet hymn. Or of the entire ceremony itself being so quiet.

Was it foreign in Jesus' mind to have a lot of singing and playing which he could call upon for his newly instituted religious ceremony? No. He was used to it. After all, the Jewish religion guided by the Law of Moses under which Jesus lived his entire life, included many rules about their use of music in their services. They are quite interesting.

God, I just want to praise you in my songs. Show me how. I'm trying, God. I'm really trying. Don't let me get discouraged.

Choirs in Judaism

There are always ads on the religious page, in the church listings section in the newspaper, or on radio or TV about special religious singing groups or performances various evenings of the week. They are meant to draw visitors. And, of course, they are usually wonderful in their own way. Do they draw visitors?

Usually they draw people who are already religious and already attending church somewhere. However, let's consider what it would take to draw the unchurched.

Our reasoning is that we have to compete with TV, rock concerts or other kinds of performances professionally done get them to come to church. Therefore, we have to draw them on their level, whether or not it is a spiritual level.

Of course, it all makes sense. And in their own way, they accomplish some good. I remember going to hear Christian college choruses sing at special programs; and since I loved to sing, I decided I wanted to go to a Christian college and be able to sing like that. Yes, they accomplish some good at their special programs set aside just for that. But I was already religious.

Well, what about drawing people to come to church on Sunday? In order to have such high-quality music, we would have to have a special singing group or choir every Sunday.

Did the church always have special singing groups and choirs? According to the *New Catholic Encyclopedia*, the entire

congregation sang until around the sixth century when only men were permitted to sing in church. Soon that, too, was limited, and only the Catholic clergy could sing. Up until then it was unison singing, the only kind that civilization knew about.

Gradually during the Middle Ages, the idea of singing in harmony came into being, and there became a demand for trained singers. These singers were usually monks who had been trained in their monasteries. In a nutshell, then, choirs were introduced by the Roman Catholic church around the sixth century. [6]

Is there anything in the Bible about choirs during the regular worship attended by everyone? Let's look it up and find out.

The Bible does not usually say the word choir, but often refers to singers singing together. Obviously, they were choirs.

The first mention is in 1st Chronicles 6:31-46. It says King David, around 1000 BC, put certain men in charge of the music in the house of God after the ark was put inside. There was still no temple in David's day, so it explains they "performed their duties according to the regulations" in front of the tabernacle. The tabernacle, which was actually a tent, was too small to hold a choir in addition to all the other things that had to be accomplished in it. Besides, they couldn't be heard as well inside.

Back in verse 1, it says Levi, one of the twelve patriarchs whose descendants became one of the twelve tribes of Israel, had three sons: Gershon, Kohath and Merari. Then in verse 33, it lists the head musician — the choir director. His name was Heman, and he was a descendant of Kohath. Heman was a grandson of the prophet Samuel, the last and probably most famous judge of Israel. What a legacy!

Verse 39 says Heman's associate at his right hand was Asaph, who was a descendant of Gershon. And verse 44 says Ethan, a descendant of Merari, was at Heman's left hand.

The next mention is in 1st Chronicles 9:33. By this time, the temple had been built. This scripture relates that the musicians — still all Levites — stayed in apartments provided for them at the temple, and they were exempt from other duties because they were responsible for providing music both day and night. Being a "church" musician was a full-time job!

By now there were a lot of men in these choirs—470 to be exact (1st Chronicles 15:5-10). Heman later appointed someone to be in charge of all the choirs. So he appointed Kenaniah to be in charge of the singing "because he was skillful at it." You will find this in 1st Chronicles 15:22 and 27. Kenaniah was musically talented, a God-given gift. How pleased he must have been to be able to use his talent for the Lord.

The next mention of choirs is under the reign of King Solomon, David's son, when the brand-new permanent temple was dedicated. After the choir sang, according to 2nd Chronicles 5:13-14, the glory of God filled the temple. This, of course, was a sign from God that he was well pleased with what was going on.

The mention of choirs is not made again for several centuries. Finally, when King Josiah restored scriptural Mosaic worship, they had a Passover feast at the temple, the first in many years, and the greatest since the days of Samuel. Here is the first mention of God's direct authorization of the use of choirs. It says the musicians, descendants of Asaph, "were in the places prescribed by David, Asaph, Heman and Jeduthun the king's seer [prophet]" (2nd Chronicles 35:15).

Once more there is silence in the history of the Jews, much of which was due to the Jews forsaking worship to Jehovah in favor of idols, and their eventual exile to Babylon. They returned to Palestine to rebuild the temple under the leadership of Ezra around 540 BC. Singers were listed as the returnees in Ezra 2:41 & 70; 7:7, and 10:24, still all Levites.

A few years later, Nehemiah returned to Jerusalem to rebuild the walls. Nehemiah 7:1, 44, 73 lists the fact that singers, descendants of Levi, returned with him and were appointed to do their jobs at the temple. Nehemiah 10:28-39 says these singers, along with the gatekeepers, stayed at the temple, and declared, "We will not neglect the house of our God."

So, after all these years, how often were the choirs performing? Nehemiah 11:22-23 says they performed every day as other Levites offered sacrifices or whatever they were to do daily.

By this time, there were so many singers (see above), plus

the 4000 orchestra members (1st Chronicles 23:5), they built entire villages just for them and their families (Nehemiah 12:28-29)! What a grand idea! They could get together and practice any time they wanted! Is it any wonder, then, that when they all got together to sing in Jerusalem under their choir director, Jezrahiah, "the sound of rejoicing in Jerusalem could be heard far away"?

Nehemiah now points out the continuity of having choirs at the temple. "For long ago, in the days of David and Asaph, there had been directors for the singers and for the songs of praise and thanksgiving to God. So in the days of Zerubbabel and of Nehemiah, all Israel contributed the daily portions for the singers and gatekeepers. They also set aside the portion for the other Levites" (Nehemiah 12:45-47). Yes, the singers were even supported by the "church."

Later, Nehemiah became quite disturbed when he learned the apartments had been taken away from the singers, also the rooms used to store their equipment, and they were no longer getting paid. All of them had just gone home to their villages (Nehemiah 13:5 & 10). After he restored them, Nehemiah prayed, "Remember me for this, O my God, and do not blot out what I have so faithfully done for the house of my God and its services."

So, there you have it. **Choirs in the Bible.**

Where did they perform? In the temple.
When did they perform? Every day and into the night.
How did they make a living? By being paid to sing.
Who were they? Male Levites.

Jehovah God, I knew that there were choirs in the Bible. That's why we have them where I attend church. They are exactly what you wanted. I'm so glad we are pleasing you.

Choirs in the Church

Did God through his prophets say they could have choirs if they wanted to? No. **He insisted on it.** He designated what they were to do, when they were to do it, that they were to be paid, and that they were to be only males from the Levite tribe.

Does that mean we should have choirs now during our Christian worship? If God made so many specifications in the Old Testament, he would have repeated them in the New Testament. God did not just leave it up to our discretion. He was specific in the Old Testament with what he wanted. **Did he forget in the New Testament? He didn't in the Old Testament.** There is no mention of choirs in the New Testament.

If we choose to copy the Old Testament pattern, then our choirs must be only men, only from the Levite tribe, they must sing all day every day at the church building, and they must be paid.

But, of course, Jesus nailed the Old Law written down by Moses to the cross (Colossians 2:14).

By the time of Martin Luther in the late 1400s and early 1500s, there was no longer any such thing as congregational singing. It had gradually been taken over by choirs and the clergy. J. H. M. D'AuBigne in the early 1800s explained in his book, *History of the Reformation of the Sixteenth Century*, that the congregations which broke away from the Roman Catholic church no longer had monks and priests; therefore the chanting of the clergy was to be succeeded by the singing of the entire congregation.

Martin Luther, therefore, translated many of the Psalms into the language of the people and set them to tunes to be sung by the congregation. [7]

Baptist leader, Charles Spurgeon, said this in his sermon entitled, "Singing in the Ways of the Lord" preached in 1881:

"Oh, brethren, let us take care that all our songs are to the honour and praise of God, for if we ever sing to our own praise it will be idolatry. I fear much public worship is thus marred. We heard of a man in Boston, in America, praying such a grand prayer that the newspapers said on the next day that it was 'the finest prayer that had ever been offered to a Boston audience.'

"Why, we hear of churches where four people are hired to do the praise of God, and all the people sit still and listen to them. And that is according to the New Testament, is it? It must be a very 'revised version,' surely. I find nothing of that sort in the book I have been accustomed to use.

"Let all the people of God praise him. Singing should be congregational, but it should never be performed for the credit of the congregation. 'Such very remarkable singing! The place is quite renowned for its musical performance.' This is poor..." [8]

Henry Halley said, "....even at best, it is better that the people sing than that they listen to singing. Why not turn the whole congregation into a choir? Under proper leadership, the hymns of a vast congregation could be made to rise like the swell of an ocean's roar, and cause angels in heaven to lean over and listen.

"....It was the public singing of Luther's hymns that bore his preaching over central Europe, and shook the world into the Reformation. It was singing that made the great Welsh revival. Was there ever a revival without it?

"....Sing the same hymns often. Only as they are sung often can the people become familiar with them. It is the hymns that we know that are the ones we love. And we never tire of the hymns we love, never. Sing the old hymns. Sing them over and over. A church that would do this would not have to beg people to come to church. It could not keep them away.

"Memorize hymns. A congregation should be taught to memorize the hymns they sing most often, at least some of the verses. They will sing better, and feel deeper, the spirit and power of what they sing. It will give power to the service. Train children to sing hymns and to memorize them. It is the best religious education. It will develop their spiritual growth, and tend to tie them to the church for life." [9]

Well then, if it is indeed possible that we cannot have trained choirs, we have to have something. What about all those people who can't keep a tune? At least an instrument of some kind would keep everyone on key, and hopefully drown out the bad singers among us who are just as embarrassed for themselves as the rest of us are for them.

Yes, we know that God loves bad singers as well as good singers. We understand that God hears a perfect voice when we raise puny imperfect voices to him. But what about the visitors? Certainly, they're not going to want to come back if the singing is bad, are they? . Furthermore, we might lose what members we have if the singing gets to be too insufferable. Surely God wouldn't want that.

Before we enter into the next phase of music in worship, let us look at some surprising historical facts about church music. For in it we find out that what we in our century take for granted was always acceptable in the church was not widely accepted at all until the sixteenth century. First, review all the quotes of famous theologians of past centuries on the subject at the beginning of our chapter.

Oh, God, I want so much to please you in song. We all thought you'd be more pleased the better the singers were. We all thought it would glorify you, God.

Instruments in Judaism

Pianos and organs were not invented for well over 600 years after the time of Christ, and not very well developed until about the 1700s, and therefore 2700 years after the time of David, and about 4000 years after the time of Moses. So, research on instruments used during worship must be done in the Bible concordance using the keywords "play" instrument," "musician," and even "singer."

The first mention of instruments used in worship is 1st Chronicles 15:16-22 which goes into some detail. In addition to the Levite singers, they were to be accompanied by musical instruments. The instruments were not left to chance or personal discretion. The selection of instruments was specified: **Lyres (psaltries), harps and cymbals.**

A trio—Heman, Asaph and Ethan, the head musicians—were to sound the bronze cymbals. An octet was to play the **lyres.** And a sextet was to play the **harps.** It must have sounded very angelic—the strings of the lyres played with a pick, the strings of the harps played with fingers, and the **cymbals** keeping the tempo. Try to imagine it. So beautiful!

When King David brought the ark of the covenant made under the direction of Moses to Jerusalem where he had erected a new tabernacle (tent of worship) there was a grand procession. Rams' horns and trumpets sounded out to call people's attention to it. And what instruments were played? **Cymbals, lyres and harps** were played while the singers sang (1st Chronicles 15:25-28).

From then on, Levites were appointed to perform various duties "before the ark of the Lord" by playing, yes, the **lyres, harps and cymbals**, and to "blow the trumpets regularly" (1st Chronicles 16:4-6, 41-42).

By the time David was old, he had quite an orchestra for worship. There were 4,000 Levites appointed to "praise the Lord with the musical instruments" (1st Chronicles 23:5)!

After King Solomon built the permanent temple and the golden ark of the covenant had been placed in the Most Holy Place of the temple, "all the Levites who were musicians...stood on the east side of the altar, dressed in fine linen and playing **cymbals, harps and lyres.** They were accompanied by 120 priests sounding trumpets. The trumpeters and singers joined in unison, as with one voice, to give praise and thanks to the Lord. Accompanied by trumpets, cymbals, and other instruments, they raised their voices in praise to the Lord and sang" (2nd Chronicles 5:12-13).

Was God pleased with the use of these instruments? You bet he was. In the next verse it says that God's glory filled the temple. Later, after Solomon's prayer of dedication, the Levites took "the Lord's musical instruments which King David had made for praising the Lord." Then the priests blew their trumpets. So could instruments be used to praise God? You bet.

Then, when the temple was dedicated, 2nd Chronicles 7:6 says the priests took their positions ready to offer sacrifices, as did the Levites "with the Lord's musical instruments, which King David had made for praising the Lord and which were used when he gave thanks." Opposite the Levites the priests blew their trumpets.

Some may say that this was David's idea and not endorsed by God. Not so. These instruments were commanded by God.

Some 500 years later, one of the last kings of Israel,

Hezekiah, had the temple repaired, it having been closed in favor of idol worship. When it was rededicated, Levites were stationed in the temple with the usual **cymbals, harps and lyres** "IN THE WAY PRESCRIBED BY DAVID AND GAD THE KING'S SEER AND NATHAN THE PROPHET; THIS WAS COMMANDED BY THE LORD THROUGH HIS PROPHETS." As soon as the burnt offerings began to be sacrificed, the singers began to sing, accompanied by trumpets and the instruments. (See 2nd Chronicles 29:25-30).

Notice what instruments were still being played: **Cymbals, harps and lyres.** But then, that's what God had designated.

Shortly after that, the first Passover was celebrated in many years. For seven days the Levites and priests sang in the temple every day accompanied by the Lord's instruments of praise (2nd Chronicles 30:21).

After Hezekiah, temple worship was neglected again. But when King Josiah became king, they once more repaired the temple, and would you believe all Levites "skilled in playing musical instruments" were made supervisors over the repairmen (2nd Chronicles 34:12-13).

About a hundred years later, after the Jews were taken exile to Babylon and then returned, Nehemiah led them to rebuild the walls of Jerusalem that had been destroyed in their capture years earlier. These walls were dedicated with songs of thanksgiving and instruments. Which instruments? **Cymbals, harps and lyres** (Nehemiah 12:27-28 & 36).

There are many references to individuals singing to God accompanied by a musical instrument, most of them being in the Psalms.

Okay, we see that God commanded instruments to accompany the singers. But they weren't just any instruments. They were **cymbals, harps and lyres**. Trumpets (and sometimes rams' horns) were used to call attention to what was going on, but apparently seldom played songs. And this was all done during the days that the Law of Moses was in effect.

Heavenly Father, I love you and worship you. The instruments do too.

It is just one more way to worship you. I'm eternally grateful you made instruments available to us all.

Plucking Strings to the Lord

Well, what about New Testament and Christian worship? No instruments are mentioned except in connection with funerals and children playing. None were mentioned in connection with worship after the time of Christ and the end of the Law of Moses.

Was this an accident? Did God forget to mention the instruments, or did he leave it up to our discretion? He didn't forget in the Old Testament. He didn't leave it up to the worshippers' discretion in Old Testament Jewish worship. Why would he forget in New Testament Christian worship?

We may say that we choose to copy the Old Testament where instruments were used. In that case, we can only play the cymbal, lyre (psaltry), and harp. Furthermore, the only ones who can play them are Levites. Seen any Levites lately? Further, they are required to play while the Levite priests offer their daily animal sacrifices. Slaughtered any animals in the name of the Lord at church lately?

Others may concede that instruments should not be part of worship, but one can play hymns on the piano or guitar in other places and sing them, because that is not worship. When is it worship and when is it not? It is not worship if a person is not paying attention to the words, such as when trying to learn a tune. Are there other exceptions?

If we're in a building with stained-glass windows, that's worship, but if we're in a building with curtains, that's not worship? If we're sitting on a seat thirty feet long, that's worship, but if we're sitting on a short seat, that's not worship? If we're wearing street clothes, that's worship, but if we're wearing costumes, that's not worship? If we're with a group, that's worship, but if we're alone, that's not worship?

We have examples in the Bible of people worshipping informally in small groups on a hill (Genesis 22:4f), on a road

(Joshua 5:13f), at a camp site (Judges 7:13-15), in a yard (Job 1:20), in a house, (Matthew 2:11), in a boat (Matthew 14:33), in a garden (Matthew 28:9), in a cemetery (Mark 5:3,6), on a river bank (Acts 16:13f).

Further, we have examples in the Old Testament of worshipping with song completely alone, and yet honoring the commandment given by God by using only those instruments He authorized in public worship. See Psalm 71:22 which says, I will praise with the lyre, psaltry and harp; Psalm 92:1-4 mentions singing praises with an instrument of ten strings, psaltry and harp, for God made ME; and Psalm 144:9 says I will sing upon the psaltry and instrument of ten strings to praise God.

H. G. Wells in his famous history of the world published in 1920, said that by the mid-500s, "The music of the early Christian centuries was devout and enthusiastic rather than elaborate....'A Christian maiden,' said St. Jerome, 'ought not to know what a lyre or a flute is.' Psalm singing and instrumentation were taken over by the Christians from the Jewish services" [10]

The *New Catholic Encyclopedia* states that the early church prohibited musical instruments because they were paganistic. It also states that "the organ has never been prescribed for use in the Roman Catholic church by church law; it has apparently been used in the church consistently since the 9th century. By the 13th century the organ was certainly in general use." [11]

However, in 1903, Pope Pius X opposed the use of instruments in worship, although he approved of the organ. Pope Pius XI later followed this same determination. "In 1939, Pope Pius XII relaxed this prohibition, allowing instrumental music that was executed artistically."

In his book, *Early Christians Speak: Faith and Life in the First Three Centuries*, by Everett Ferguson, he wrote this:

"Until the latter part of the fourth century the psalms were performed responsorially. That is, the main content was sung as a solo by a cantor (psalter he was called in the church) with the congregation repeating the last words or responding with a refrain or acclamation [because they had no song books]....

"In Christian hymnography the words were the important

things and melodies were adapted to the words. This was possible where the words were chanted and so were not bound to a rigid form of meter. The priority of the words and the form of rendition ensured that the singing was done without instrumental accompaniment. Indeed, an instrument had no function in these simple chants with their emphasis on the content of praise.

"There is no certain evidence of the use of instruments in the Christian liturgy until the later Middle Ages. Because of the associations of musical instruments with immorality in the pagan world, the church fathers took a very dim view of them in any setting. [12]

The *Catholic Cyclopedia*, considered one of the most accurate sources of church history, says this in Volume 10: "For almost a thousand years Gregorian chant, without an instrumental or harmonic addition, was the only music used in connection with the liturgy....While all this development [of music instruments] had up to the first half of the sixteenth century, served mainly secular purposes, it was through Ludovico Grossi da Viadana (1564-1627) that the use of instruments became more common in churches."

Holy Father, I never thought of these things before. I have been pleasing you all these years. Surely this cannot be wrong. God, I just want to please you.

Heavenly Harps

Instruments are mentioned in Revelation and that's part of the New Testament. Definitely they are. So are choirs. Let's look at those passages.

In Revelation chapters 8-11, trumpets are mentioned. Did they play tunes? Actually, they were used to draw attention to important events, just as they were used to draw the attention of armies and also of worshippers in the Old Testament temple (Numbers 10:1-10). The sound of the trumpets is described in the Hebrew as *taqa* also used for clap, smite, strike and not associated with music. In fact, Paul said in 1st Corinthians 14:8, "If the trumpet does not sound a clear call, who will get ready for battle?"

The temple was not just a building. It was a whole complex

the size of nearly four football fields. (A football field is 160' x 360'.) The main temple building was 90' x 30'. But around it were two courtyards. The inner court was 150' x 300' and all around that was an outer court 300' x 600'. And attached to the walls were many rooms used for various purposes. Therefore, trumpets had to be used to call attention to important happenings.

Cymbals are not mentioned in Revelation. Neither are lyres (psaltries). But harps are. Let's look at them.

Revelation 5:8-14 says four living creatures and twenty-four elders fell down to worship the Lamb [Jesus]. Each one — the 28 — held a harp and a golden bowl full of incense. Then this ensemble began to sing as though they were choir directors. For immediately they were joined by millions of angels, and finally by every creature in heaven and on earth. At the end of the great musicale, involving all of heaven and all of earth, the four creatures shouted "Amen!" and the twenty-four elders fell back down to worship again. Wow!

Revelation 14:1-4 tells us that 144,000 from earth who had been redeemed sang before the throne of God, the four living creatures, and the 24 elders. Here, the earthly choir is singing to the heavenly ensemble! Their singing sounded like harpists playing their harps.

Revelation 15:2-8 tells us that in front of the throne of God (identified by the sea of glass) were the saved holding harps given them by God. They were singing about all nations of earth coming to worship God. Then one of the four living creatures gave seven angels seven golden bowls.

First, who were the creatures? Without going into a separate study, most people agree that four represent the earth — four corners, four winds, etc. The word "creature" is *zoon* in Greek, from the root word *zoe* meaning life. They seem to be life forms in heaven (not angels) always found in scripture associated with created life on earth and its atonement. We might call these cherubim the guardians of life, both physical and eternal.

Who were the 24 elders? Again, without going into a long study, it seems that 12 would represent the Twelve Tribes of Israel and therefore all Jews in Old Testament times. The other 12 would represent the Twelve Apostles and therefore all Christians in the New Testament.

Who were the 144,000? We must see Revelation as entirely symbolic or entirely literal. We cannot pick and choose according to our own desires. If we take the 144,000 literally, Revelation 7:1-8 says there were 12,000 saved from each Jewish tribe. That would mean, literally, that no Christians can be saved.

But, taken symbolically, they would represent all the saved of the Old Testament/Jewish era (12 Tribes of Israel and followers) and all the saved of the New Testament/Christian era (12 Apostles and followers). Multiplying 12 x 12 gives us 144. Ten generally represents all-inclusiveness. Thus, we end with all the saved of the O.T. (12), times all the saved of the N.T. (12), times all-inclusiveness (10), times all-inclusiveness (10), times all-inclusiveness (10) = 144,000. In other words, none of the saved will be left out of heaven! What reassurance!

And what were they holding?

Revelation 5:8 explains the cherubim and elders held bowls of incense which represented the prayers of Christians on earth. Revelation 15:7 explains that one of the cherubim handed the seven angels bowls representing the wrath of God.

However, the harps are not explained. If the bowls were symbolic, the harps would have to be also. We look elsewhere for an explanation of harps when used symbolically, for the Bible always explains itself. Literal Instrument: *Kithara* Greek for 10-stringed harp: The New Testament Greek word *kithara* is translated in Revelation as harp. Josephus described a kithara as having 10 strings and being played with a pick.

KINNOR: Hebrew for 10-STRINGED HARP, aka VOICE OR HEART: An Old Testament Hebrew word for harp is "*kinnor.*" In Job 30:27-31, Job complains about his stomach, his skin, his fever, and his voice. His voice is described as a harp. In Isaiah 16:11, Isaiah says his heart and inmost being are like a harp.

Literal Instrument: "*Asor*" Hebrew for 10-stringed instrument: This Old Testament word is found in Psalm 33:2 and 92:3, literally translated the "ten-stringed instrument," and in Psalm 144:9 translated the "ten-stringed lyre" [psaltry].

PSALO: Greek for SONG SUNG WITH A STRINGED INSTRUMENT, aka HEART: This New Testament word refers back to the psalms which David sang with his lyre or psaltry. It is used in connection with Christian worship in 1st Corinthians 14:26, Ephesians 5:19, Colossians 3:16, and James 5:13.

What is interesting is Ephesians 5:19 which specifies — AT LAST! — the instrument to be played while singing psalms: "Speak to one another with psalms, hymns and spiritual songs. Sing and MAKE MUSIC IN YOUR HEART to the Lord." That is, play on the strings of your heart! How beautiful and intimate!

The word translated psalms is the Greek *psalmos*. The word translated "make music" is *psallo*. Once more, then, we see that the 10-stringed instrument sometimes translated harp and sometimes lyre or psaltry, represents the believer's heart.

So now, back to Revelation, we see that the four cherubim and the 24 elders are **holding the prayers and the hearts of saints** on earth. What a beautiful symbol that incense and harps come to mean in heaven!

Before the end of the first century, the temple in Jerusalem was forever destroyed. And with it the possibility of accurately worshipping the Old Testament way. With it the literal alters of incense, the literal place of sacrifice, the literal harps.

The alter of incense, the altar of sacrifice, and the harps are all stored up in heaven now. For now the temple is our bodies. The incense is our prayers, the sacrifice is our daily life, and the harps are our hearts. Why would we want to make literal again such beautiful symbolism?

God, this is all new to me. I always thought music was music, worship was worship, and it was all the same to you. I never knew about the symbolism to spiritual things. Music spiritual? What a thought!

The Pattern: A Shadow of Things to Come

The book of Hebrews in the New Testament is full of

descriptions of Jewish worship and what it came to symbolize later in Christian worship.

Hebrews 7:26—8:1—A high priest was appointed to offer sacrifices for the sins of the people of the Old Testament once a year. Jesus became our high priest and sacrificed his own body for the sins once and for all.

Hebrews 8:5—The sanctuary/tabernacle/temple served as "a copy and shadow of what is in heaven. That is why Moses was warned when he was about to build the tabernacle: 'See to it that you make everything according to the pattern.' "

Hebrews 9:1-5; 12, 24—The Most Holy Place was where the golden ark of God's presence, watched over by the cherubim, was placed. For the Christian, the Most Holy Place is now in heaven where the very throne of God is.

Hebrews 9:21-28—Without the shedding of blood, there was no temporary forgiveness. Therefore, under the Old Testament regulation, lambs were sacrificed; in the New Testament era, Jesus was the Lamb of God who paid the price for us.

Hebrews 10:19-20—A curtain hid the Most Holy Place from the worshipper's view in the Old Testament. Jesus became that curtain and tore it so the saved could all enter the Most Holy Place in heaven.

What if the believers had not followed God's regulations in the Old Testament Jewish era? The pattern would have been flawed. We would have been unable to quite understand Jesus' sacrifice for us, and the significance of God's presence available to us all in heaven.

We would have been unable to quite understand that the choirs limited to only Levites in the Old Testament era were to include all Christians in the New Testament era. Every Christian is a choir member.

We would have been unable to quite understand that the instruments played by these Levites in the Old Testament era were to represent the hearts of all Christians in the New Testament era.

And what if we believers do not follow God's regulations (the few there are) in the New Testament Christian era? The pattern will be flawed. If we do not all sing, as spiritual priests (yes, all Christians are priests — 1st Peter 2:5, 9; Revelation 1:6, 5:10, 20:6) in the choir, we cannot quite understand the magnitude of the choirs in heaven. If we do not play on the strings of our heart, we cannot understand the hearts that are being played before God in heaven.

Is it worth it? Hiding our voices and hiring someone to do our singing for us like the Jews did? Is it worth it? Hiding our hearts and playing on temporal instruments like the Jews did?

Holy Father, the symbols are beautiful. Why didn't anyone ever show this to me from the Bible? Why didn't anyone ever help me make the connection? It's beautiful! And I missed it, God.

The Unmasking

Dr. Greg L. Bahnsen, who has many blogs on the internet (but who is now deceased) spoke in one of his blogs on the death of many things in the church. Here is what he said about church music: "So far, this means that my attending 'church' is just a matter of taste. I don't particularly like what goes on in most 'church services.' If 'church' were billed as a 'concert' instead, in which the 'worship team' or the 'music ministry' were a well-known Christian group on tour, and the concert featured 'a special message' by Pastor So-and-So, I wouldn't want to go."

In Acts 3:6, Peter told a beggar he was about to heal, "Silver or gold I do not have, but what I have I give you." And so, in a similar way, would it ever be possible for Christians to say, "Choirs and instruments have I none, but the puny voice I have I give you"?

Courage? Would that take courage? You bet! The kind of courage that, when we all get down to it, perhaps we do not have. What would it mean to our Sunday worship? Really, on the gut level, what would it mean? It would mean facing a part of ourselves that would unmask us.

It would mean songs sometimes stumbled through because we didn't know the tune or words. It would mean songs sometimes dragged because we're not very good at keeping good tempo. It would mean sometimes making a fool of ourselves.

Fools? Do we really want to look like fools? Could we endure the embarrassment? Do we dare take off our mask among each other?

Paul said in 2nd Corinthians 12:9-10, "I will boast all the more gladly about my weaknesses, so that Christ's power may rest on me. That is why, for Christ's sake, I delight in weaknesses, in insults, in hardships, in persecutions, in difficulties. For when I am weak, then I am strong."

The story is told of an American university student visiting the home of Beethoven at Bonne. She asked permission to play on his piano. After playing a few bars of the "Moonlight Sonata," she turned to the guard and said, "I suppose all of the great pianists have played during visits here." "No, miss," the guard replied. "Paderewski was here two years ago but said he was not worthy to touch it."

One day in London, a preacher got all dressed up in his finest and started walking down a busy street. People walking in the opposite direction toward him often laughed in obvious derision as they read the words he had attached to his hat in large letters: The words were A FOOL FOR CHRIST'S SAKE. But those who passed by and then turned back to deride this religious fanatic even more, saw another card attached to the back of his hat. It read: WHOSE FOOL ARE YOU?

A professor of Greek in the 1800s was impressed by one of his students who turned in assigned translations in fine Greek prose. The professor asked the student about it and he confessed that he received help from his uncle, W. Kelly. The professor wished to meet him.

At the arranged time, the two Greek scholars met. The professor asked Mr. Kelly what his vocation was. To his surprise, Mr. Kelly replied, "I am a preacher and travel here and there all over the country ministering the Word of God to groups of Christians." Aghast at such a waste, the professor replied, "Man, you're a fool!" To that, Mr. Kelly replied, "For which world?"

Poet Edward Rowland Sill wrote "The Fool's Prayer" around 1865:

The royal feast was done; the King sought some new sport to banish care,
So to his jester cried, "Sir Fool, kneel now and make for us a prayer!"

The jester bowed and bent his knee upon the monarch's silken stool.
His pleading voice arose, "O Lord, be merciful to me, a fool.

"Earth bears no balsam for mistakes; men crown the knave and scourge the tool
That did his will; but Thou, O Lord, be merciful to me, a fool."

The room was hushed; in silence rose the King, and sought his gardens cool,
And walked apart, and murmured low, "Be merciful to me, a fool." [14]

We interrupted our discussion of motives at the beginning of this chapter to discover some facts. Now let us return to our motives.

Is our church music for the right reason? When we are through singing and playing a beautiful song with all the right notes, or watching others do so, do we want to say, "Aren't we good"? or "Isn't God good"?

But, someone says, we must give our best to God. Indeed we must. But, deep down, what is the best?

Should all of us who feel we do not have good enough voices worthy of God pay a soloist to take our place? If our motive is to give God with the best, technically we would have to go out and find a better soloist than we already have in our congregation.

So, we run a newspaper ad and hire the best soloist in the city. But there's still a soloist out there better than this one. So, if we're going to give God the best, we need to continue our search. Surely there is an opera singer or folk singer somewhere with the best voice in the world.

We would then feel obligated to hire that singer to give God the best. But what if there is an unknown out there with the voice "of an angel" who is not generally known? We still would not be able to offer God the best voice there is.

The same thing could be said of choirs and orchestras. If our motive is to offer the best we can, we have a problem. Even if we found the best soloist, the best choir and the best band in the world, they wouldn't be able to take the place of every Christian in the world. There would be churches all over the world with no one singing at all because they couldn't come up with the best for God.

Let's back up now. What is it that God wants us to give him? The best that each of us has. That means that, when there is singing, we all sing, and in the process we all "teach and admonish one another with all wisdom" (Colossians 3:16) through our songs. Does this say we all entertain and admonish one another?

But we still can't get rid of the nagging problem that, without professional help, our song service would sound unbelievably terrible.

It's hard to take off our masks of perfection, isn't it? Here we are with good jobs, houses, lawns with the proper amount of mulch, computers, cars, motorcycles, cell phones, and the respect of our peers. Does God expect us to strip all that off in front of other people? We could do it alone, but not in front of others. Please, God! Not that!

Perhaps now we are at the crux of the entire problem. We do not want anyone to see our frailties. So we keep our mask on and hire others to take our place so we look good.

It is time to take off our masks. It is time to humble ourselves and show ourselves as we really are—frail human beings with weaknesses. And in the process, to reveal that, not only do we not always sing with complete perfection, but we don't live with complete perfection either.

Holy Father, I want to look good in front of my friends. I protect all my private sins from their knowledge. I'd be mortified if they knew my weaknesses, even the horrible way I sing.

Resetting Our Priorities

But, back to the weak Christians and the visitors. We have to compete with TV, professional concerts, and so on. Who said? Well, they won't come back if our song service isn't perfect and entertaining like they're used to seeing. Who said?

Did we ever stop to think that perhaps it is our very perfection that turns them off and we never see them again?

How many times have we heard the expression, "Holier than thou"? Is that what we're portraying in our music during worship?

What does such superiority complexes do to others? It either makes others feel even more inferior, or provides so much entertainment "in the name of the Lord, of course," that we and they forget we worship God, not ourselves.

The Associated Press published an article in July 2000 on "Sacred Harp" singing; that is, singing without any accompanying instruments. "Now Sacred Harp singing is attracting a new following on college campuses and in urban areas."

Many of their favorite songs were composed in the 1700s and 1800s. The latest version of their Sacred Harp songbook is published by the Sacred Harp Publishing Co. in Bremen, Georgia. Over the past thirty years, it has sold about 90,000 songbooks.

It is appearing in large cities such as Los Angeles, San Diego and Seattle, and it is the younger people pushing it. Twenty-three states host Sacred Harp conventions attended by people of all denominations and ages. They even have a web site here: http://fasola.org

"Come on, now!" someone may still be objecting. You're expecting too much. What about our dignity?

What about Jesus' dignity? Hebrews 5:7 says Jesus begged God with loud cries all his life not to have to go through the crucifixion and everything associated with it. Remember the Garden of Gethsemane? I just don't believe he was quietly praying. Jesus was meek, but he was not quiet. There were times when he was in the temple and called out in a loud voice (see John 12:44, for instance).

So here he was in the garden just before his arrest, probably crying his heart out and begging God not to make him go through with the crucifixion. His anguish was so bad, in fact, that an angel had to come to help give him courage (Luke 22:39-44). And do you think his apostles could hear him? Of course they could. He wore no mask. He begged right in the hearing of his friends.

What about Jesus' dignity? Though he was God in the form of a man, he allowed himself to be beaten and tortured. Then he allowed himself to be stripped naked in front of a crowd and put on display on a cross for the whole world to see. Yes, what about Jesus?

Do you think most visitors are motivated to come to service because they heard about your choir or organist and want to be entertained, or because they want to make a connection with a Jesus who understands them? Which group is more able to understand Jesus?

Holy Father, it's hard to trust you in this. I still don't see how being so humble would attract visitors. Well, it worked for Jesus. But Jesus was different.

Time Taken From the Empty Entitled

Some may still object, that it would kill enthusiasm to spend twenty minutes to a half hour singing off-key. Could be. But do we have to sing that long?

Most modern books on worship emphasize the music and proclaim it is the central part of worship. But is it? Do we now have too much of a good thing?

Singing has taken over our worship to the detriment of time for Bible reading, prayer, the communion and soul sharing! Let's repeat that: Singing has taken over our worship to the detriment of time for Bible reading, prayer, the communion, and soul sharing! We've become unbalanced.

When Jesus instituted the Lord's Supper, explaining that the bread and wine would now represent his lacerated body and shed blood, did they have a long song service? Mark 14:26 says they sang one hymn.

Later, when Paul was trying to straighten things out with the sincere but mixed-up church in Corinth, he said things were not being done in order. He didn't say they were doing the wrong things, but they weren't in order. What things?

He said whenever they came together, "everyone has A HYMN, a word of instruction, a revelation, a tongue [language] or an interpretation [interpolation;" same word used in Luke 24:27 as explained]. He didn't say to add more and more of these, but have a little less.

He talked elsewhere about their priorities. Did he ever say they were to sing more? In 1st Corinthians 14:24-25 and elsewhere, he said they were to prophecy more, which in our day would mean to read the Bible more. What percent of the time do we spend reading right out of the Bible in our worship, compared with the percent of time we spend singing?

In 14:27-31 Paul talked about "anyone" who speaks in a language, "someone" must interpret, "two or three" prophets, and a revelation comes to "someone." But regarding prophecy (the Word of God) he said, "You can ALL prophecy in turn so that EVERYONE may be instructed and encouraged." (Remember, prophecy was relied on then before the Word was written and assembled.) But Paul never said to sing more.

Where in the Bible is there reference to a "music ministry?" There are references to preaching and teaching ministries, benevolent ministries, prayer ministries, but never music ministries.

If Paul were to write to us today, what would he say? Would he say our singing had turned into performances to each other rather than the intended revealing of our innermost self, imperfections and all? Would he say spend more time reading what God has to say to us? Would he say spend more time in prayer? Would he say spend more time remembering Jesus' death and resurrection? Our music program has taken over.

Sunday is the day God set aside specifically for the Lord's Supper, the day Jesus conquered death. We must center our worship on his sacrifice and our sins that caused it, and in telling others the story of our Lord's suffering in our place. It is a sin to take that time away to do something the New Testament hardly says anything about.

If our congregation has a lot of gifted singers and the congregational singing is wonderful, we may say, "But our people won't come to worship if we don't sing a lot. They love to sing too much."

Perhaps we're being inconsistent. Look at our Bible classes? Do we take up half the Bible class time singing and leave only half for Bible study because people wouldn't come if we didn't sing a lot? What about our small groups? Do we take up half the sharing time singing and leave only half for sharing?

Perhaps much of the arguing between generations today about the types of music is just a symptom of a greater problem: We have placed music on too high of a pedestal, and it is choking out the rest of our worship. It started 150 years ago when instruments began to be generally accepted in all denominations, putting high enough priority on the music service to spend hundreds or thousands of dollars on instruments to the detriment of the needy, lonely and untaught. Now it has nearly taken over everything else.

Someone says, "But I've had a music ministry all my life." By that they mean they perform solos in front of the congregation. Well, we can make ourselves look good by singing alone in front of the congregation in our perfection. Or we can make the entire congregation sound good by sitting among them and singing along with them, the imperfect ones.

Where's our humility? Let us take off our masks. And after our songs, rather than say, "We sure were good," let us say, "God sure is good."

Shall we completely abandon all the magnificent compositions and choirs? Perhaps when we come together for Sunday worship we should. People are being entertained and then going home still lonely and unfulfilled and empty and lost.

One man went to a John Fogarty concert, and the next day wrote this about his experience:

"But concerts are not about concerts. It's an introspective experience masquerading as a demonstrative one... and if you pay close attention to the audience (where the real show is found) there is a tangible sadness laced into it....

"I studied and eavesdropped on as many of the thousands who had made a pilgrimage to hear the music they love as I could. All around me people spoke frankly of their real-world struggles between songs. Behind me during a 30-second lull, a woman shared with a girlfriend about her mother's cancer. I heard stories of heartbreaking tragedies within earshot....You could watch struggling relationships in full-on overcompensation mode hoping to reignite... [19]

As long as singing is allowed to take the highest priority in our worship time, there is little or no time left for the other just-as-important parts of worship. Perhaps that is why our worship services today are not taken too seriously. People come in, spend a lot of time singing, have a good time, have a brief prayer, a brief sermon, a Bible verse (maybe), probably not the Lord's Supper, then go home. Lonely once again.

Singing is wonderful. But do we have to rely on people SINGING to us that Jesus loves us when we long so desperately to hear people SAYING Jesus loves us? Has our singing monopolized our worship to the determent of the other important things? Has the music become a god unto itself?

Let us take time, not just to sing it, but to tell people sitting next to us, "Jesus loves you." Let us take time, not just to sing vague prayers, but to say specific prayers. Let us take time, not just to sing "To the Work," but to find out how we—the hands, feet and mouth of Jesus—can minister to the loneliness of those among us.

There are countries in the world today where converting to Christianity is illegal. Being illegal, if caught, they face prison and even death. Most of the people in these countries have never even seen a printed Bible. So, when they convert to Christianity, they meet and worship in secret. In secret they study the Bible from a flash drive on their computer because it is illegal in such countries to even possess a Bible. In secret they pray. In secret they whisper their songs. Who do you think is closer to God in their song service?

Oh God, I love the people I worship with. I love our visitors. I had no idea our performances were taking time away from them that they needed to personally learn of your love. I'm so sorry, God. Forgive me.

Second-Generation *Church Accounts*

Pliny, who wrote about 100 AD said in his Letters [to the Emperor Trajan] Book X.xcvi: "....they sang in alternative verses a hymn to Christ.... [notice, ONE hymn]" [15]

Tertullian, who lived about 155 to 222 AD, wrote from Carthage in On the Soul 9:4: "....the psalms are chanted...." [16]

Clement of Alexandria wrote about 190 AD in Miscellanies VI.xiv.113:3: "....praising, hymning, blessing, singing...." and in Instructor III.xi.80.4: "Those who sing such and sing in response are those who before hymned immortality...." [17] He further said, "We make use of only one organ or instrument, even the peaceful word, with which we honor God; no longer with the old psaltry, trumpet, drum or pipe." [18]

9. BAPTISM: WHAT IN THE WORLD FOR?

Keep back your servant also from presumptuous sins;
Let them not have dominion over me.
Then I shall be blameless
And I shall be innocent of great transgression.
Psalm 19:13 (NKJV)

Famous Theologians

About 1270, THOMAS AQUINAS—CATHOLIC: "As the Apostle says (Rm. 6:3), 'all we, who are baptized in Christ Jesus, are baptized in His death.' And further on he concludes (Rm. 6:11): 'So do you also reckon that you are dead to sin, but alive unto God in Christ Jesus our Lord.' Hence it is clear that by Baptism man dies unto the oldness of sin, and begins to live unto the newness of grace. But every sin belongs to the primitive oldness. Consequently every sin is taken away by Baptism." (Summa Theologica, Tertia Pars)

About 1550, JOHN CALVIN—REFORMED CHURCHES: "Baptism resembles a legal instrument...for he commands all who believe to be baptized for the remission of their sins. Therefore, those who have imagined that baptism is nothing more than a mark or sign by which we profess our religion before men...have not considered that which was the principal thing in baptism—which is, that we ought to receive it with this promise, 'He that believeth and is baptized shall be saved' (Institutions, Book 4, Chap. 15, paragraph 1).

About 1700, MATTHEW HENRY—PRESBYTERIAN: "First, they must admit disciples by the sacred rite of baptism....Baptism is an oath of abjuration, by which we renounce the world and the flesh as rivals with God for the throne in our hearts....In baptism we take Christ to be our Prophet, Priest and King, and give up ourselves to be taught and saved and ruled by him....Disciples, all baptized Christians....In the latter clause baptism is omitted because it is not simply the want of baptism, but the contemptuous neglect of it which makes men guilty of damnation" (Commentary, Matthew 28:19; Mark 16:16).

About 1750—GEORGE WHITEFIELD—METHODIST (Commentary, John 3:5, Vol. 4, pg. 302, 355). ...."He who persists in this act of rebellion against the authority of Christ will never belong to his kingdom....Does not this verse urge the absolute necessity of water baptism? Yes: when it may be had. But how God will deal with persons unbaptized we cannot tell" [1]

About 1775—JOHN WESLEY—METHODIST: "Buried with him in baptism...alluding to the ancient manner of baptizing by immersion...." [2] By baptism we enter into covenant with God....made members of Christ; made the Children of God. By water, as the means, the water of baptism, we are regenerated or born again" (Commentary on the New Testament, pg. 350 and

Preservative, pg. 146-150). [3]

About 1800 — ADAM CLARK — METHODIST — "Undoubtedly the Apostle here means baptism...Baptism is only a sign, and therefore should never be separated from the thing signified....It is a rite commanded by God himself and therefore the thing signified should never be expected without it" (Commentary, John 3:5 and Titus 3:5). [4]

1864 and 1881, CHARLES SPURGEON — BAPTIST [Note changes in outlook between those 17 years]: **[1864]** "Do we who baptize in the name of the sacred Trinity as others do, do we find that baptism regenerates? We do not....Baptism does not save the soul....the preaching of it has a wrong and evil influence upon men....most atrocious that in a Protestant church there should be found those who swear that baptism saves the soul....He has no right to be baptized until he is saved.... " **[1881]** "They had faith, and a glimmer of knowledge sufficient to make them right recipients of baptism....He who has been baptized into Christ sees Christ in baptism....our representative union with Christ....we were thus buried with him....Baptism is an acknowledgment of our own death in Christ....You are brought up again from the pit of corruption unto newness of life....now you have been dead and buried and have come forth into newness of life....baptism represents resurrection....this life is entirely new" (Sermons in the Metropolitan Pulpit, London, Sermon No. 573 1864, Sermon No. 1627 in 1881).

Thank you, Jesus, for all you did to save me. You left heaven for earth. You left protection to walk alone. Finally you left life for death. Sin causes a chain reaction that only a miracle can stop. So you came back to life.

It happened in Korea sometime between the Korean War and the Viet Nam War.

The men involved were in the American Air Force on a military base near Seoul and near the DMZ (Demilitarized Zone, aka no-man's-land) with its northern border on atheist and Communist North Korea. The men had just been confined to the base because the Koreans had just started rioting and the Korean government wanted to get it under control themselves.

Coincidentally, when this happened these men had already gathered with missionaries from all over Korea for a religious retreat. It certainly was a retreat — in more ways than one. In fact, they retreated longer than they had intended. So they took advantage of the time. They just had more sessions of talking about the Bible and what God meant to their lives in a foreign country and away from their families.

It had an impact on all of them. After a few days it had an especially powerful impact on one of the men. He decided he wanted to be baptized.

Well, they had a predicament. In order to immerse the man, they had to find something on the base large enough to immerse him into. No bathtubs anywhere. No water troughs either. They couldn't think of anything.

Then it hit one of them. The well. There was an old well on base. Full of anticipation, these hardened military men scouted out the well, threw some pebbles down it to confirm it still had water in it, then lowered some long objects into it to determine how deep the water was. Their conclusion was that it was over six feet deep. Plenty enough.

But how to get the man down there? This man's Air Force was not full of a bunch of dummies. It didn't take them long to figure it out. They would lower the man down into the well.

Was he out of his mind? It was just a baptism. Couldn't it wait? But he insisted he did not want to wait. Well, then, why didn't he just let them pour some water on his head? No, it had to be immersion.

At first they considered lowering him by a rope, but he didn't want to go down there alone—not for obvious reasons, but for reasons that will be apparent in a moment.

Okay. So how far was it down to the water's surface? They estimated 15 feet, maybe more. They needed volunteers. And got them.

Then the man desiring baptism sat on the side of the well, took hold of the hands of the man who would be baptizing him, the latter kneeling by the well. When they had stretched as far down into the well as they could, a third man took hold of the second man's ankles. Then the second man started slowly down into the well. No water yet. So a fourth man took hold of the ankles of the third man.

Someone yelled from down in the dark well. "I've reached the water! It's up to my waist!"

Then something holy happened. From down in the old well, the men could hear the words, "I believe Jesus is the Son of God!"

It echoed up through the well, swirled around the hearts of the men, and then rushed beyond to the soul of Jesus.

A pause. Then the echo again. "I now baptize you...." Baptize you? In a well?

"....in the name of the Father, the Son, and the Holy Spirit!"

That was it. Now for the final moment.

The man still on the ground above bent slowly down, estimating about three feet, then pulled himself back up with the aid of his buddies. One by one, then, each man was pulled to the top of the well and light. Finally they saw their new Christian friend.

Grins. Tears. Laughter. Handshakes. Bear hugs.

It was over. But as they walked back toward their barracks to change clothes, they knew it wasn't over. They knew everything had just begun.

God, not that again. I wish you'd made them leave this chapter out. I get so tired of it.

Form and Substance

Wasn't all that much ado about nothing? Surely God wouldn't want people to be humiliated like this. It's bad enough for people to be baptized in a church baptistery. It's a little embarrassing. Actually, not just a little embarrassing. It's extremely embarrassing. Mortifying.

Just think about it. We'd have to actually allow someone else to push us underwater. It's like handing our lives over to them. What if they held us under?

Then, when we came back up out of the water, we'd be a mess. Our clothes wet and clinging, water in our eyes, hair a holy mess. Not a professional look at all. Not a distinguished look. Not a look of dignity. All that just so someone can dunk us. We'd look like fools.

Is it all just a lot of legalism?

Did you know that in our English Bibles, the word "baptism" was never translated from the original Greek? Never. It was transliterated. It was anglicized. The Greek word is *baptizo* or variations of it, depending on the sentence structure.

The word is found in the ancient Greek writings of Homer about 900 BC, Plato about 400 BC, Polybius about 100 BC, Diodorus about 40 BC, Strabo between 50 BC and 25 AD, Josephus about 75 AD, Plutarch about 120 AD, and others. For example, Homer used it in his *Iliad* numerous times to describe dipping or sinking. Polybius used it to describe the sinking of a ship. Diodorus used it to describe animals going into water. [5]

After baptism was introduced as part of Christianity, historical records still bear this out. *The Catholic Encyclopedia* states explicitly that the word baptism is derived from the Greek word *bapto* or *baptiso*, to wash or to immerse. It goes on to say:

"The most ancient form usually employed was unquestionably immersion. This is not only evident from the writings of the Fathers and the early rituals of both the Latin and Oriental churches, but it can also be gathered from the Epistles of St. Paul, who speaks of baptism as a bath. In the Latin church [Rome], immersion seems to have prevailed until the 12th century. After that time it is found in some places even as late as the sixteenth century." [6]

The earliest archaeological evidence of a baptismal font was found at a house at Dura Europos which was remodeled as a place of Christian meeting around 233 AD and destroyed about twenty years later. One room was set aside for baptisms. At one end of this room was a basin under a canopy. The basin was 5'4" long and 3'4" deep. [7]

Anyone observing Medieval coats of armor and lengths of beds realizes that people were not nearly as tall then as modern people are. This is borne out in historical documents also. Therefore, a baptismal font 5'4" would be plenty long enough to lay a person down in the water. And the depth would be plenty for a person to stoop until underwater also.

There seems to have been no church buildings as such until the time of Constantine in the early 300s. Constantine had originally been named Emperor/Caesar of Gaul, which we today call France. But he wanted more, so he invaded and obtained control of other parts of Europe, concentrating most on Italy. In Rome he built a palace with attached chapel and baptistery, considered to be the first ever church building. They are today called the Lateran (papal) Palace, the Basilica Constantiniana, and the Fons Constantini.

There is an interesting history of the baptistery architecturally, "baptistery" originally referring to a building where baptisms occurred. With Constantine setting the prototype, until the 11th century, baptisteries were frequently buildings separate from but next to church buildings, and often large and ornately decorated.

Beginning about the 4th century, the entire baptistery was dome roofed. The dome symbolized death to sin and opening up of the heavenly realm. This led to the baptistery being built in octagon shape. Seven was considered the number of completeness (3 + 4, heaven plus earth), and eight meaning new beginnings, "as the sacrament of baptism marks the beginning of the Christian life." The actual font was also octagonal.

The baptismal fonts themselves were pools or cisterns with edges at floor level, or built up with sides above floor level. During the 4th and 5th centuries, fonts were large enough to accommodate several people at the same time.

Between the 6th and 9th centuries baptisteries were reduced to small chapels inside larger church buildings or cathedrals. According to the *Encyclopedia Britannica,* these chapels were small rectangular rooms with an apse (semi-circular extension) at one end which contained the actual font. [8] (In earlier temples to the gods, the apse was where the statue to a particular god or goddess was placed. Also, the apse sometimes appeared in palaces where the king would sit and pronounce judgment.)

During the Middle Ages, the outside walls of the baptismal pools and basins were very ornate with symbolic and geometric motifs of imbedded marble.

Baptismal fonts large enough to baptize by immersion were built until the 13th century when pouring and sprinkling began to be pushed by the Catholic church. Then commonly the font was just a small basin on a pedestal. [9]

God, that's okay for those people. I'm happy for them. But it had nothing to do with me.

Gradual Changes In Form

Writings of first-century Christians regarding baptism are at the end of this chapter. In the second century we have the following, with approximate dates, and capitalizations mine:

120 AD, Egypt, *Barnabas*, 11:1,8,11 — "Let us inquire if the Lord was careful to make a revelation in advance concerning the water and the cross....Blessed are those who placed their hope in his cross and DESCENDED into the water....We DESCEND into the water full of sins and uncleanness, and we ascend bearing reverence in our heart and having hope in Jesus in our spirit." [10]

130 AD, Rome, Italy, *Shepherd of Hermas*, Vision III.iii.3; Mandate IV.iii.1; Similitudes IX.xvi.3-6 — "Your life was saved and will be saved through water....there is no other repentance except that one when we DESCENDED into the water and received the forgiveness of our former sins....Before a man bears the name of the Son of God he is dead, but whenever he receives the seal, he puts away mortality and receives life. The seal then is the water. They DESCEND then into the water dead and they ASCEND alive. The seal itself, then, was preached to them also, and they made use of it in order that they might 'enter into the kingdom of God.'...They DESCENDED therefore with them into the water and ASCENDED again. The former went down alive and came up alive, but the latter who had fallen asleep previously went down dead but came up alive." [11]

150 AD, Rome, Italy, Justin Martyr, *Apology* I,61 — "As many as are persuaded and believe that the things taught and said by us are true and promise to be able to live accordingly are taught to fast, pray, and ask God for the forgiveness of past sins, while we pray and fast with them. Then they are led by us to where there is water, and in the manner of the regeneration by which we ourselves were regenerated they are regenerated.

"For at that time they obtain for themselves the washing IN water in the name of God the Master of all and Father, and of our Savior Jesus Christ, and of the Holy Spirit. For Christ also said, 'Unless you are regenerated, you cannot enter the kingdom of heaven.' " [12]

170 AD, Sardis, Turkey, Melito, *On Baptism*, fragment— "Are not gold, silver, copper, and iron, after being fired, baptized with water? One in order that it may be cleansed in appearance, another in order that it may be strengthened by the DIPPING....why is Christ also not washed in the Jordan?" [See Bible account below] [13]

180 AD, Antioch, Turkey, Theophilus, *To Autolycus* II.xvi— "Moreover, the things which CAME FROM the waters [at creation of earth] were blessed by God, in order that this might be a sign that men were going to receive repentance and forgiveness of sins through water and the 'washing of regeneration,' namely all those who come to the truth and are born again, and receive blessing from God." [14]

190 AD Carthage, Africa, Tertullian, *On Baptism* 1, 7, 4, 12— "We as little fishes, in accordance with our 'ichthys' Jesus Christ, are born IN water....Baptism itself is a bodily act, because we are baptized IN water, but it has a spiritual effect, because we are set free from sins. There is no difference whether one is washed IN the sea or IN a pool, IN a river or a fountain, IN a reservoir or a tub, nor is there any distinction between those whom John DIPPED in the Jordan and those whom Peter DIPPED in the Tiber, unless that eunuch whom Philip DIPPED in the chance water found on their journey obtained more or less of salvation....It has assuredly been ordained that no one can attain knowledge of salvation without IMMERSION. This comes especially from the pronouncement of the Lord, who says, 'except one be born of water he does not have life.' " [15]

195 AD Alexandria, Egypt, Origen, *Homilies on Exodus* V:5— [in commenting on the crossing of the Red Sea speaks of

Christian baptism] "The evil spirits seek to overtake you, but you DESCEND INTO the water and you escape safely; having washed away the filth of sin, you COME UP a 'new man,' ready to sing the 'new song.' " [16]

In the same century that Constantine who built the first known separate baptistery and font, these early Christians wrote describing baptism as an immersion.

350 AD Jerusalem, Palestine, Cyril, *Catechetical Lectures* **XCVII:14** — "For as he who PLUNGES into the waters and is baptized is SURROUNDED on all sides by the waters, so were they also baptized completely by the Spirit. The water, however, flows around the OUTSIDE, but the Spirit baptizes also the soul within completely." [17]

350 AD Caesarea, Palestine, Basil, *On the Holy Spirit* **XV:35** — "How then do we become in the likeness of his death? We were BURIED with him through baptism....How then do we accomplish the DESCENT into Hades? We imitate the BURIAL of Christ through baptism. For the bodies of those being baptized are as it were BURIED in water." [18]

380 AD Milan, Italy, Ambrose, *On the Sacraments* **III.i.1,2** — "We discoursed yesterday on the font, the appearance of which in shape is like a TOMB, into which we are received, believing in the Father and the Son and the Holy Spirit, and we are PLUNGED and we LIFT ourselves UP, that is we are RESURRECTED....So therefore also in baptism, since it is a likeness of death, without doubt when you DIP and RISE UP there is made a likeness of the RESURRECTION." [19]

390 AD, Antioch, Turkey, John Chrysostom, *Baptismal Instructions* **II;26; Homilies on John XXV:2, on John 3:5** — "When the priest pronounces, 'So-and-so is baptized into the name of the Father and of the Son and of the Holy Spirit,' he three times puts the head DOWN and RAISES it UP, preparing you to receive the DESCENT of the Spirit by this mystical initiation....Exactly as in some tomb, when we SINK our heads in water, the old man is BURIED, and as he is SUBMERGED BELOW, he is absolutely and entirely HIDDEN. Then when we LIFT our heads UP, the new man again COMES UP." [20]

Only once in the 2nd century is anything preserved of writings saying baptism did not have to be immersion, only once in the 3rd century, and only once in the 4th century. They are as follows:

100 AD, Syria, *Didache* 7 — "Concerning baptism, baptize in this way. After you have spoken all these things, 'baptize in the name of the Father, and of the Son, and of the Holy Spirit,' IN running water. If you do not have running water, baptized in other water. If you are not able in cold, then in warm. If you do not have either, pour out water three times on the head 'in the name of the Father, and of the Son, and of the Holy Spirit.' Before the baptism the one baptizing and the one being baptized are to fast, and any others who are able. Command the one being baptized to fast beforehand a day or two" [Notice the person is standing IN water and then water is poured over the head.] [21]

250 AD Carthage, Africa, Cyprian, *Epistle* 75 [69]:12 — "You have asked also, what I thought concerning those who obtain God's grace in sickness and weakness, whether they are to be accounted legitimate Christians, because they are not washed with the water of salvation but have it poured on them....In the sacraments of salvation, when necessity compels, and God bestows his mercy, the divine abridgments confer the whole benefit on believers, nor ought anyone to be troubled that sick persons seem to be sprinkled or poured upon when they obtain the Lord's grace....Whence it appears that the sprinkling also of water holds equally with the washing of salvation." [Notice this was in case of "sickness and weakness." [22]

320 AD Caesarea, Palestine, Eusebius, *Church History* VI.xliii.14, quoting a letter from Cornelius of Rome, Italy, 251-253 — "[Novatian] fell seriously ill and was thought to be about to die. In the bed itself on which he was lying he received grace by water being poured around over him, if it is proper to say that such a one received it." [Notice, this was one instance when someone was ill. The text goes on to state that immediately Novatian was then made a bishop of the church. Neither was approved by the writer, Cornelius.] [23]

It is obvious, then, from history that the views of pouring

and sprinkling were not generally acceptable or accepted.

God, they are entitled to their opinion and I'm entitled to mine. I wish this chapter would hurry up and end.

Biblical Evidence

Ultimately, however, it does not matter what people did through history. These are given to show the slowness in a substitute form of "baptism" being developed, it being contrary to what Christians were originally taught in the scriptures by the apostles. Ultimately, God's opinion and directions are the only ones that matter. We are not being saved by our fellow man, but by God. So, we do what he asks us to, grateful for the opportunity.

Below are the scriptures which indicate that the person was immersed:

JOHN THE BAPTIST'S FOLLOWERS, Matthew 3:6 — "Confessing their sins, they were baptized by him IN the Jordan RIVER." Mark 1:5 — "Confessing their sins, they were baptized by him IN the Jordan RIVER." John 3:23 — "Now John also was baptizing at Aenon near Salim, because there was PLENTY of WATER, and people were constantly coming to be baptized."

JESUS' BAPTISM, Matthew 3:15-16 — "Jesus replied, 'Let it be so now; it is proper for us to do this to fulfill all righteousness.' As soon as Jesus was baptized, he went UP OUT of the water. At that moment heaven was opened, and he saw the spirit of God descending like a dove and lighting on him." Mark 1:9-10 — "At that time Jesus came from Nazareth in Galilee and was baptized by John IN the Jordan [River]. As Jesus was coming UP OUT of the WATER, he saw heaven being torn open and the Spirit descending on him like a dove."

ETHIOPIAN'S BAPTISM, Acts 8:38-39 — "And he gave orders to stop the chariot. Then both Philip and the eunuch went DOWN INTO the WATER, and Philip baptized him. When they came UP OUT of the WATER...."

APOSTLE PAUL & "ALL OF US", Romans 6:3-5 — "Or

don't you know that all of us who were baptized into Christ Jesus were baptized into his death? We were therefore BURIED with him through baptism into death in order that, just as Christ was RAISED from the dead through the glory of the Father, we too may live a new life. If we have been united with him like this in his death, we will certainly also be united with him in his RESURRECTION."

How important was it to the first Christians? The first four books of the New Testament are the life of Christ. The fifth book is the Acts of the Apostles which tells how they started the church and how people became Christians.

Let's make a chart itemizing what each scripture says people did to be saved under the direction of Jesus' Apostles.

Scripture	People	Heard/ Read	Be- lieved	Re- pented	Con- fessed	Sent for a crowd	Baptized	Prayed Sinner's Prayer
Acts 2:37-41,47	3000 Jews Jerusalem							
Acts 8:5-6,12	People in Samaria							
Acts 8:30-39	Ethiopian							
Acts 9:3-6, 17-19	Saul/Paul** (future Apostle)							
Acts 10:1-2, 48	Cornelius & Household							
Acts 16:14-15	Lydia & Household							
Acts 18:1,8	Corinthians							
Acts 19:1-6	Ephesians							
Acts 22:7-16	Saul/Paul** (future Apostle)							

*Receiving Holy Spirit is another study. Notice, even though he was morally upright, he still had to do something else.

**Notice, even though he had seen a vision of Jesus, he still had to do something else.

Now, on your chart next to each convert's name, list only those acts actually mentioned in the passage. In other words, even though we assume they all believed, if it is not listed in the passage, do not put it on your chart.

Done? Now look at your chart. Something stands out. Only one thing is listed that they all did to be saved. The writer of Acts assumed the reader would take for granted certain things were done (such as believe), so didn't always mention them. But the writer always emphasized one thing so that people would never take it for granted. They were all baptized! Isn't that amazing?

God, I don't like the direction this whole thing is going in. No one is ever going to convince me to get dunked.

Even Denominational Creeds Agree

LUTHERAN:

Martin Luther's Small Catechism, Part Four, Articles I-IV: "Baptism is not simply water, but it is the water comprehended in God's command [Matthew 28:19-20]....It worketh forgiveness of sins, delivers from death and the devil, and confers everlasting salvation on all who believe....the water without the Word of God is simply water and no baptism....a gracious water of life and a washing of regeneration in the Holy Ghost; as St. Paul says to Titus in the third chapter verses 5-8....It signifies that the old Adam in us is to be drowned....St. Paul, in the Epistle to the Romans, chapter 6, verse 4 says: 'We are buried with Christ by baptism into death'. "

CALVINISM:

***Institutions,* c. xvi:** "Baptism resembles a legal instrument properly attested, by which he assures us that all our sins are canceled, effaced and obliterated so that they will never appear in his sight, or come into his remembrance, or be imputed to us. For he commands all who believe to be baptized for the remission of their sins."

PRESBYTERIAN:

Confession of Faith, **Chapter xxviii, Sec. i:** "Baptism is a sacrament of the New Testament, ordained by Jesus Christ, not only for the solemn admission of the party baptized into the visible church, but also to be to him a sign and seal of the covenant of grace, of his engrafting into Christ, of regeneration, of remission of sins, and of his giving up unto God, through Jesus Christ, to walk in newness of life."

The Larger Catechism: "Baptism is...a sign and seal of engrafting into Christ, of remission of sins by his blood and regeneration by his Spirit."

METHODIST:

Wesley's Commentary on the New Testament, pg. 350: "Baptism administered to penitents is both a means and a seal of pardon. Nor did God ordinarily in the primitive church, bestow this upon any unless through this means."

WESLEYAN/CHURCH OF NAZARENE:

Church Constitution, **Articles XIII:** "We believe that Christian baptism is a sacrament signifying acceptance of the benefits of the atonement of Jesus Christ, to be administered to believers." [24]

God, I really do love you. You know that. I've lived my whole life for you. And I don't like people telling me what to do. I've made up my mind.

I Love You, But....

When we love someone, we don't try to see how much we can get by with NOT doing that they ask. When we love someone, we do everything we can that they ask. The only exception is if we think the request is unfair. Do we think God bringing up baptism in the New Testament is unfair?

When we love someone, sometimes jealous outsiders try to break us up by various means, usually telling what one did or said that the other wouldn't like. When we truly love someone and we know it is right, we don't care what other people do to break us up. Our love will endure all outside attacks.

Yet there are pamphlets, books, sermons, websites, and articles too numerous to even begin to count explaining why we are justified in REFUSING to be baptized. What is it about baptism that turns so many people off? This is the only thing that the early Christians did to be saved that many of us bristle about and say, "Never!"

Why? Even though some people love the idea, why do some people hate it so?

Confession is only mentioned 26 times in the New Testament. But we don't refuse to confess. Repentance is only mentioned 57 times in the New Testament. But we don't refuse to repent. Baptism is mentioned 98 times in the New Testament. But we refuse to be baptized. Why? Why don't we hate confession and refuse to do that? Why don't we hate repentance and refuse to do that? Why is it we pick on baptism and refuse to do that?

The "sinner's prayer" is expounded by many as the only thing people need to do to be saved. But where in the Bible is the sinner's prayer or an example of it in order to be saved?

Many people, when the subject of baptism is brought up, brag that they have never been baptized. Shouldn't this be embarrassing for them to admit? After all, Jesus was baptized. Are they wanting us to use them as our standard or Jesus?

I have known men go to church for forty years before becoming humble enough to be baptized. I have never known of women doing this. Baptism seems to be especially hard for men. Men perhaps need to feel in control more than women do. Do we not realize that once we submit to Jesus, he makes us spiritual warriors; but it doesn't happen until we are Christians?

Some time ago there were two men who had been ministers of the gospel for many years who finally decided they needed to be baptized as part of their salvation. Of course, being ministers and used to leading things, they maintained part of that dignity by calling together all their friends to where they were going to be baptized. They preached long sermons about baptism. Then they were baptized.

Justification. That's a good word if used regarding God's use of it. When God justifies us, he takes us as the sinners we are, and makes us just in his sight. But when the word is used regarding man's use of it, it is wrong. When we justify, we take something we do that is unjust, and try to make it sound just. God has the right to do this. We do not.

How do we know when we are justifying? It is hard for us to identify our own sins. Probably the best way is if we make a statement, then go into long discussions as to why we had to do it. "I had to take the money under the table because...." "I had to lie to them because...." "I had to pretend I wasn't home because...."

Applying this to biblical principles, we are justifying if we take a scripture and go into a long explanation as to why it doesn't really mean what it says. Usually this explanation ends up giving the scripture a symbolic rather than literal meaning.

For instance, some people say the water mentioned in connection with New Testament baptisms was the symbolic water of life or the water of the Word.

In that case, John baptized people by a symbolic Jordan River where there was much symbolic water (John 3:23). It was also in the symbolic Jordan River that Jesus was baptized and came up out of (Matthew 3:6, 15-16).

In that case, the Ethiopian, after being taught by Philip, rode along in his chariot until he could find some symbolic water. Then "both Philip and the eunuch went down into" the symbolic water "and Philip baptized him" (Acts 8:37-39).

In that case, it was symbolic water that saved Noah when he passed through it with symbolic floods below and symbolic rains above (1 Peter 3:21-22).

Other people justify themselves for not being baptized by saying that water cannot save us. Of course the power is not in the water any more than the power was in the wooden cross Jesus was nailed to. It is the blood of Jesus that made it possible for us to be saved. But that wooden cross was necessary. Why? Because there was some magic in wood? No. Because that's what God chose (for reasons he does not choose to tell us).

Also water is necessary. Why? Because there is some magic

in the water? No. Because that's what God chose (for reasons he does not choose to tell us.) If God had told us we had to be buried for one second under earth in imitation of Jesus' death, burial and resurrection, would we be willing to do it? Earth could have been God's choice, but instead he chose water. Who are we to question God and twist around the symbols he has chosen?

To claim that people who are baptized are claiming there is something magic in the water is just as bad as claiming that the bread and wine of the Lord's supper is magically turned into the actual body and blood of Jesus. You can't have one without the other, for these are the only two Christian rituals.

Still other people say that baptism is a work and we are not saved by works. True, we are not saved by works, but what are works? They are activities that benefit another person. We are not being baptized to help another person.

Salvation is free, but we do have to do something to receive our free gift. God does not force it on us. What if you went to work and told each person you work with that if they'd walk over to your desk at 6:00, you'd give them $50? What is likely to happen? Probably no one will come. Why? Because they don't believe you. That is one of the reasons people do not receive salvation. They do not believe God.

What if the next day you told everyone again that if they'd walk over to your desk at 6:00, you'd give them $50? The second time they probably wouldn't believe you either. Therefore, no one would come.

But what if you did this for a week and finally someone came to your desk at 6:00 to collect their $50? Would they have worked for it? No, it would be your free gift. Certainly their making the trip over to your desk would not be considered work. But that was the stipulation you laid out for them to receive their free gift of the $50.

Please, God. I've told so many people they don't need to be baptized. Why did you have to include it in the Bible?

Will Worship

God warned us of religious practices and attitudes which "have indeed a show of wisdom in will worship" (Colossians 2:23). Do we worship God according to our will or his?

Do we take the scriptures at face value or expend entire books trying to "spiritualize" and "symbolize" and explain them away? Why can't we take scriptures at face value? Why do we have to justify ourselves? Why can we not see our own arrogance?

Refusing to yield our bodies to the humiliation of baptism demonstrates that we are antagonistic to complete surrender to the example and command of Jesus Christ whom we claim to be our Lord. BAPTISM IS A TEST FOR STUBBORN HEARTS.

Despite all the mentions of baptism in the New Testament, some people will still say, "But it only takes faith to be saved." In that case, we need to eliminate hearing the gospel and confession.

Others say, "It only takes the blood of Christ to be saved." In that case, we need to eliminate hearing, faith and confession.

Isn't it ridiculous the extremes we will go to in order to justify our own actions? Our arguing among each other over the obvious is tearing us apart.

The exact split second in time, doesn't matter. Why not just do it ALL? Once we've done it all, we know we are saved. The exact moment of salvation is known to God. As long as we do it ALL, we can have no doubts.

When we are walking or driving near the edge of a steep dropoff, do we try to see how far from safety and close to the edge we can go? Of course not. We do as much as we can to stay away from that edge. Why tempt our prospects for survival?

Besides, when we leave off one of the things to do to be saved, we are going "....after the commandments and doctrines of men....have indeed a shew of wisdom in will worship...." (Colossians 2:22-23, KJV).

Whose will do we worship? Our own or God's? Why do we

bother to worship God? Do we not want to be confused by the facts? Why do we bother to go to church at all?

Are we going to church for the social interaction only? If so, we don't care what the Bible says. We're going to do what we want.

Are we going to church to put in our time so God will feel guilty if he doesn't take us to heaven when we die? If so, we don't care what the Bible says. We make our own rules.

Are we going to church so we can perform or hear the performances? If so, we don't care what the Bible says. It has nothing to do with anything.

Are we going to church because we love ourselves? If so, we don't care what the Bible says. We're not interested in loving the Author.

The Bible is not just a book of stories about Abraham, Moses, David, and Jesus. There are rules in it. The audacity of God telling us what to do! But we must remember that God is our creator and loves us so very much, just like any other parent who gives rules to a child.

Sins are things that we do that will ultimately hurt us. God does not randomly list things for us to stay away from or things for us to do just to give us a hard time. As our creator, he knows what will hurt and help us. He doesn't want any of us to be hurt.

When the apostles were arrested and taken before the ruling body of the Jewish religion, "Peter and the other apostles replied: 'We must obey God rather than man!' " (Acts 5:29).

There are many church leaders who have been educated in the Bible and yet tell us we do not need to be baptized and that some uncaring people are just pressuring us to do that. After all, they were never baptized, so why should anyone else?

I personally know many people who went to their ministers requesting that he baptize them, and the minister refused, adamantly telling them they didn't need to be baptized. Could it be that, if they did, they would be telling others that everyone needed to be, including themselves?

On a call-in religious program just this week, a woman called in to ask about baptism. The man told her that "those people" believed water saved them instead of Jesus' blood (something "those people" do not believe). He said that "those people" who believe baptism saves them are lost and she should stay away from them because they were dangerous.

Extreme caution must be given when listening to a person who (1) tells you what other people believe, as though they can climb into their heads and know; and (2) refuses to tell you just what they believe a religious act is for. We must give ourselves more credit for reading and understanding the Bible for ourselves, and less to getting seminary-trained religious leaders' opinions and calling it gospel.

First, putting all the educated church leaders end to end around the globe will only give us a multitude of opinions. Many church leaders do not take the Bible literally. Many do not believe in the miracles of the Bible. Many believe that the god of the Buddhists is just as true. Many believe that the church is more infallible than the Bible.

Second, will these educated church leaders judge us at the end of our life? No. They, too, will be judged by the same God you and I will be. We must read the Bible for ourselves. That is what we will be judged by.

Some will say that their deceased relatives went to church all the time and were never baptized. Others will say that people in remote parts of the world never had a Bible or never learned to read, so never even knew about Jesus. In both of these instances we must remember that God knows whether they would have been baptized had they known to.

Jesus said, "If anyone loves me, he will obey my teachings....He who does not love me will not obey my teaching....You are my friends if you do what I command" (John 14:23-24; 15:14).

WHAT ARE WE WILLING TO DO TO BE SAVED?

Do we only pay lip service to Jesus? Do we draw the line as to how far we will go? If God said we must climb cathedral steps one hundred times on our knees to be saved from hell, would we? If God said we must go without food for twenty days to be saved from hell, would we? If God said we had to cut off our hand to be saved from hell, would we? How far are we willing to go for an eternity with the God who loves us?

Is it hard to go against our friends? You bet it is. For, as soon as we are baptized, if they are still used to following man's word instead of God's word, they will feel threatened by you and will possibly persecute you.

Look at the persecution of thousands of Christians through the ages for insisting on following the Bible. Get a copy of the other book in this series, *Worship Changes Since the First Century*, and read the detailed descriptions of torturous deaths endured for the sake of following God and not man.

Even more than that, look at the persecution Jesus went through for you and me....

God, I never saw things this way before. But I can't go back now. It's too late for me. I just can't. Could you forgive me, God? Just this one thing?

Jesus, I Didn't Understand

Oh, Jesus, I didn't understand. Your flesh. It was torn for me. I was the one who should have received the lashing that turned Your back into meat. And the thorny slivers on the cross. The slivers that went into Your already shredded back to create gangrene. The lashing and thorns were supposed to be for me, not You. And the nails too, Jesus. The nails too. How could You go through that in my place?

Oh, Jesus, I didn't understand. Your nakedness. They stripped You instead of me. I was the one who's nakedness should have been exposed, and put on display for the whole world to gawk at and ridicule. I was the one who was supposed to have been subjected to exposure, enduring both the heat of the day and the cold of that strange noon-time darkness. How could you have endured this for me?

Oh, Jesus, I didn't understand. Your blood. It was shed for me. If I had been the only sinner in the world, You still would have had to die to free me from hell. That was my blood that was supposed to be falling off the cross that day, not Yours. How could

You love me that much?

Oh, Jesus, I didn't understand. Your every breath. Taken away from You a gasp at a time as You hung there by merciless nails tearing away at Your life, rendering Your lungs almost paralyzed, piercing Your soul. Each time You chose to ignore the screaming blood vessels in Your back and the unbearable spasms in Your arms and legs just so You could get just one more taste of breath, that should have been me. How could You volunteer Your own body to be tortured like that in my place?

Oh, Jesus, I didn't understand. In the flames of Your fever and the darkness of my sins, You descended to a horrible place where God does not go. Completely forsaken by Your God. Completely deserted by Love. Not because You simply bore my sins, but You actually became my sins. How could You, who struggled a lifetime to make sure You never sinned, become exactly what You hated for me?

Oh, Jesus, I did not understand. All my little lies, little things I took home accidentally and kept, the strangers I never encouraged, the friends I never shared my love for You with, my arrogance in not following you. Oh, Jesus, I am so ashamed. How can I ever make it up to You? How can I tell You how sorry I am? I want to see You face to face and tell You how much I love You. How can I convince You to let me do that?

Jesus personally replies, "I am the resurrection and the life. He who believes in Me will live, even though he dies" (John 11:25). Oh, Jesus, say no more! I do believe that You are the Son of God! I do believe!

Jesus personally replies, "Unless you repent, you too will all perish" (Luke 13:3). I'm so glad You said that, Jesus! I truly am sorry for all those sins I have committed that caused You to die!

Jesus personally replies, "Whoever disowns Me before men, I will disown him before My Father in heaven" (Matthew 10:31f). Well, isn't it enough that I believe? Do I have to get my friends involved? If I told them I believed in You, they'd kill my reputation. Are You sure, Jesus?

Jesus personally replies, "Whoever believes and is baptized will be saved" (Mark 16:15). "Jesus came...to be baptized....'It is proper for us to do this to fulfill all righteousness' " (Matthew 3:13-15). Oh, Jesus, I wish you hadn't been baptized and said I needed to be also. My friends and pastor tell me I don't need to be. I know they didn't die for me, but surely they wouldn't steer me wrong. Please, Jesus, not that! Please....

Would it be okay, Jesus, if I just do the first two—believe and repent? Everyone says that's all I have to do to please You. I'll even throw in the third one and tell a few of my friends what You've done for me because I believe in You. But the last one. I know You Yourself said to, but I just couldn't! Please, spare me that! Please, Jesus! It would kill me....

Punishment or Privilege?

How many people have you met over the years who said they thought they were saved? But later in their lives they decided they hadn't been, but now they knew for sure they were saved? Then later in their lives they decided they hadn't really been saved then either, but now they knew for certain they were saved? What uncertainty must torture their soul!

I have talked with several wives who have said they were astonished when their husbands said they'd like to become a Christian. These husbands had been going to church with their wives sometimes as long as 25 years. "I always thought he was a Christian," the wives would tell me.

R. L. Coleman day after day mourned for his sins at church in hopes of receiving that assurance of salvation he had been taught to expect. He knew he was willing to be saved, but he had no assurance that he was saved, and remained unable to give any reason why he did not enjoy this assurance. After a couple of years, he quit going to church completely. Still uncomfortable and unhappy, he remained at home to read the Bible and pray.

Finally he went to hear a visiting preacher who quoted from the Bible scriptures about baptism. As soon as Mr. Coleman was baptized, he felt completely released from his old sense of guilt. He realized that his sins had been washed away in the blood of Christ, and that of this he had received, in baptism, the assurance he had so long sought in vain. From that moment his former anxieties and fears forever disappeared. [25]

John Rogers had earnestly sought for some time that "religious experience" which was supposed to be conversion, and which apparently had been obtained by some of his friends. Not feeling assured, his friends exhorted him to pray on, which he did, still hoping for some inexplicable, palpable or sensible manifestation by which he would "know his sins forgiven." Finally he read about baptism in the Bible, and not a religious experience or a sinner's prayer. Once baptized, he never doubted his salvation again. [26]

Walter Scott explained that he had been "tossed on the waves of uncertainty, laboring, praying and striving to obtain saving faith—sometimes desponding and almost despairing of ever getting it." After a long struggle, he at length obtained peace of mind alone in a wooded area with his Bible.

Then he decided to become a minister. "About this time my mind was continually tossed on the waves....Clashing, controversial theories were urged by the different sects with much zeal and bad feeling. No surer sign of the low state of true religion.

"From this state of perplexity I was relieved by the precious word of God." He spent time reading about baptism and decided that is what he had to do. Immediately after his baptism he experience a happy relief from the elusive hopes and fears based on frames and feelings, which for several years had been all he had been taught regarding assurance of salvation. [27]

Another man, a Dr. Wayland, explained, "I had marked out for myself a plan of conversion in accordance with the prevailing theological notions. First, I must have agonizing convictions, then deep and overwhelming repentance, then a view of Christ as my Saviour, which should fill me with transports, and from all this would proceed a new and holy life. Until this was done, I could perform no work pleasing to God and all that I could do was abomination in his sight. For these emotions, then, I prayed, but received nothing in answer which corresponded to my theory of conversion."

Then, upon concentrating on what baptism does for sinners as explained in the Bible, he was baptized and received that elusive knowledge (not feeling, but knowledge) of relief. [28]

Why do we continue to dodge the outward sign God provided for us so that we and everyone around us can know assuredly that we made a conscientious decision to become a Christian? It is not only hard on us; it is hard on our families.

What a wretched life!

Living in a nation with Christians does not automatically make us a Christian, any more than living in a nation with Boy Scouts automatically makes us a Boy Scout.

Living in a family with Christians does not automatically make us a Christian, any more than living in a family with Boy Scouts automatically makes us a Boy Scout.

Owning a Bible does not automatically make us a Christian, any more than owning a Boy Scout handbook automatically makes us a Boy Scout.

Showing up at church services once a week does not automatically make us a Christian, any more than showing up at Boy Scout meetings once a week automatically makes us a Boy Scout.

It is not automatic. It is not by osmosis.

There is a way to know for sure! Just as we have to contact the headquarters of the Boy Scouts to do what it tells us to do to become a Boy Scout, we have to contact the headquarters of Christians to do what it tells us to do to become a Christian.

Where is the headquarters for Christians? It is not on earth. It is in heaven.

Jesus said, "All authority in heaven and on earth has been given to me. Therefore go and make disciples of all nations, baptizing them in the name of the Father and of the Son and of the Holy Spirit, AND teaching them to obey everything I have COMMANDED you. And surely I am with you always, to the very end of the age" (Matthew 28:18-20).

Why be baptized? So we don't have to guess when we became a Christian. Some will surely say it doesn't matter when we become a Christian. It apparently does to Jesus. Whose opinion do we prefer—man's or Jesus'?

The apostle Peter said "even so does baptism now save us, not putting away the filth of the flesh, but an answer of a good conscience toward God (I Peter 3:21).

Dear reader, if you still do not believe a person needs to be baptized, then WHAT IS BAPTISM FOR? Stop right now and answer that question. And WHY IS IT IN THE BIBLE? Stop right now and answer that question also.

Let us view baptism for what it is. Baptism is the HONOR AND PRIVILEGE OF IMITATING WHAT JESUS DID FOR US!

God describes it beautifully through his apostle Paul: "Or don't you know that all of us who were baptized into Christ Jesus were baptized into his death? We were therefore buried WITH HIM through baptism into death in order that, just as Christ was raised from the dead through the glory of the Father, WE TOO MAY LIVE A NEW LIFE" (Romans 6:3-4).

If we consider baptism a punishment by God and too humiliating to go through, then we are still one step away from admitting that we are the ones who deserved to die and be buried—not Jesus. God said that if we recognize that fact, then symbolically we can die with Jesus. We can be with Jesus up on that cross. How do we die? We die to our sinful nature (Romans 6:6-7), that part of us that sins and doesn't care.

Then, just as Jesus was buried, we have the honor and privilege of being buried with him symbolically in the water.

Finally, just as Jesus was raised to live forever the Savior, we are raised to live forever the Saved Ones.

What a privilege! How can we even think of holding back? This is when our souls can become one with Jesus!

So, as the Apostle Paul was told at his own conversion, "And now what are you waiting for? Get up, be baptized and wash your sins away, calling on his name" (Acts 22:16).

Oh God, I think in the back of my mind I was always curious about baptism, but my family would have disowned me if I'd brought it up. My church too. How could they have been wrong? They loved you so.

Act of Worship

I have seen numerous baptisms through the years, and heard of many others. I've seen them in public and private. I've seen them in lakes, rivers, swimming pools, baptismal fonts. I've heard of people being baptized in wells, water troughs, barrels, saunas, bathtubs and lined beds of pickup trucks. I have seen people baptized by being laid back in the water by the baptizer, and I have heard of people baptized by stooping and being gently pushed on their head until they were immersed.

I've seen baptisms surrounded by fear, excitement, tears, laughter. I've seen people come up out of the water laughing. I've seen people come up out of the water crying. But no one ever came up out of the water with a ho-hum attitude.

I recall one young lady who decided she wanted to be baptized, but was deathly afraid of water. She even showered instead of bathing, she was so afraid of water. So we, her close friends, promised to stand close to her and pull her out of the water ourselves if she was held under too long. We even offered to get in the water with her. She said that was too dangerous; she'd prefer we stay on firm footing. So we stood on the floor in front of the baptistery, our arms outstretched to her.

When she came up out of the water two seconds later, she was overjoyed. She was willing to go through something so fearful that she thought she might die, just to be baptized.

I personally know people who have been baptized into Christ behind locked doors because they live in countries where being baptized is a crime punishable by imprisonment and/or death. The fear they had, the rest of us can only imagine. The courage they mustered up to go through with it! But they wanted to please God and be part of God's family so much, they locked their doors and did it. Afterward, though they knew they could be arrested, they'd all say, "I'm free! I'm free!"

I recall a young man who decided he wanted to be baptized

where the church was meeting in a school. So a vat was rushed out on rollers. It was filled with water. The young man got in, and someone guided him with his immersion.

When he came up out of the water, he raised both hands in triumph and the entire congregation stood and let out a shout of victory that would have dwarfed the roars of the crowd at the most exciting football or soccer game ever. You couldn't stop them from clapping and shouting. It went on and on. It was a victory! One more victory over Satan! One more spiritually dead, then raised to live forever! One more for God!

Victory above all victories!

Where you worship, why not offer an invitation toward the end of your service to the worshippers to become Christians? Why couldn't someone stand up and read about the baptism of one of the first century Christians? Or read about the many explanations of baptism given in the New Testament? Then tell people in your crowd, "What are you waiting for? Arise and be baptized and wash away your sins!" just like the Apostle Paul was told (Acts 22:16).

Perhaps your congregation can then stand and begin singing a song of encouragement for people to walk forward. Or sit in silence with your eyes closed, allowing time for people to think and make their decision, praying as you wait for them. Or even turn to the person to your left or right and say, "Have you been baptized? Would you like to be?"

Early Christians were baptized every day of the week and under every circumstance. So, whenever your congregation meets, ask people, "Would you like to be baptized right now? Why wait?"

Don't have one certain Sunday of the year or month set aside for baptisms. Allow each person the opportunity to be baptized immediately. As Paul was told, "What are you waiting for?"

I have known many people decide to be baptized after a private study in their home. In that case, it is the same question, "What are you waiting for?" They were baptized within the hour all times of day and night.

On the first day of the church's existence when 3000 people were baptized, they were all baptized the same day. "Those who accepted his message were baptized, and about three thousand were added to their number [the church] THAT DAY" (Acts 2:41).

When Philip taught the Ethiopian eunuch riding along in a chariot, "as they traveled along the road, they came to some water and the eunuch said, "Look, here is water. Why shouldn't I be baptized? And he gave orders to stop the chariot. Then both Philip and the eunuch went down into the water and Philip baptized him" (Acts 8:36-38).

When the future Apostle Paul was taught by a simple Christian named Ananias (he didn't even have a title in the church), Ananias healed Paul of his blindness. But Paul still had something else he had to do and wouldn't even eat until he did it. "Immediately, something like scales fell from Saul's [Paul's] eyes, and he could see again. He got up and was baptized, and after taking some food, he regained his strength" (Acts 9:18-19).

When Peter went to another town to teach Cornelius, "the following day he arrived in Caesarea. Cornelius was expecting them and had called together his relatives and close friends....So he ordered they be baptized in the name of Jesus Christ. Then they asked Peter to stay with them for a few days" (Acts 10:24, 48).

When Paul taught Lydia and her household, "we sat down and began to speak to the women who had gathered there [riverside]....When she and the members of her household were baptized, she invited us to her home" (Acts 16:13-15). They did not go home until they were baptized.

When Paul and Silas taught their jailer, they said, "Believe in the Lord Jesus, and you will be saved — you and your household. Then they spoke the word [so they'd know what to believe] of the Lord to him and to all the others in his house. At that hour of the night the jailer took them and washed their wounds; then immediately he and all his family were baptized" (Acts 16:31-33).

Never postpone anyone's baptism. Once they know what to do and have thought about their sins and really asked God to forgive them, let them be baptized immediately.

Do they have to be baptized by an ordained minister? If so, the Apostle Paul did not practice what he preached. The Apostle Paul was baptized by a man who was identified only as "a disciple" (Acts 9:10). Besides, if we did insist on being baptized by an ordained minister, what if we found out later that minister was committing some terrible sins and was about to leave the church, or that minister believed Buddhist was just as holy as Jesus? In that case, our baptism would be invalid. How many of us truly know the heart of another person?

Our baptism does not depend on who baptizes us. It depends on the fact that we were baptized.

So, in the case of people who are baptized privately, when they arrive at worship the first time, it should be announced and people should be given an opportunity right then to go to him/her and give them a hug or shake their hand and congratulate them. Special prayers should be offered on their behalf.

Further, their address should be shared unless they insist it not be, so the members can follow up with notes, cards, letters of encouragement.

Baptism should be a special celebration. It should be a day each person never, ever forgets. After all, it is our sinful death and burial with Jesus, an rising to never die spiritually again. A long time ago, I heard of a tombstone that read something like this: John Doe. Born: August 21, 1939. Reborn: April 27, 1978. Died: He didn't.

Oh, Jesus, I fall at your feet. Forgive me. I didn't understand. I want to be baptized. I want to follow your example. If it meant enough for you do it, I want to also. Forgive my putting it off all this time. Forgive my arrogance.

Second-Generation Church Accounts

Ignatius wrote about 90 AD in his Epistle to Polycarp, v. 6: "Let your baptism abide with you as your shield; your faith as your helmet; your love as your spear; your patience as your body armour. Let your works be your deposits, that ye may receive your assets due to you." [29]

A collection of miscellaneous writings called **Didache 9, written about 100 AD**, says, "No one is to eat or drink of your eucharist except those who have been baptized in the name of the Lord. For also concerning this the Lord has said, 'Do not give that which is holy to the dogs.' " [30]

Justin Martyr wrote in his Apology I, 65 about 150 AD, "After we thus wash [baptize] him who has been persuaded and agreed entirely with our teachings, we take him to the place where the brethren have gathered together to make fervent prayers in common on behalf of themselves and of the one who has been illuminated in baptism and of all others everywhere. We pray that we who have learned the truth may be counted worthy and may be found good citizens through our works and keepers of his commandments so that we may receive the eternal salvation. When we cease from our prayers, we salute one another with a kiss. [31]

Addendum I: Baptism of Infants

Some people, in their enthusiasm for baptism, have decided to baptize their babies. It certainly does not hurt a baby to be baptized since the baby has no idea what is going on.

Some people do it as a way of dedicating their baby to God. Others do it for the baby's salvation. The clergy knows that when these babies grow up, they tend to feel affiliated with their particular denomination they were baptized into. The baptism is a kind of down payment toward having that person in adulthood also.

Because baptism does not really hurt or help a baby, this topic is not part of the main chapter. But for those interested in investigating it, some food for thought follows. The reasoning given by church leaders for baptizing infants is that it is a Christian substitute for Jewish circumcision.

To be consistent, babies must be baptized on the eighth day and can only be boys. And, everyone who works for that family must also have their baby boys circumcised or be fired. (See Genesis 17:12,13).

The only time baptism is mentioned in connection with circumcision is this [capitals mine]: "In him you were also circumcised, in the putting off of the sinful nature, NOT with a circumcision done BY THE HANDS OF MEN but with the circumcision done by Christ, having been BURIED WITH HIM IN BAPTISM and raised with him through YOUR FAITH in the power of God, who raised him from the dead.

"When you were dead in your sins and in the uncircumcision of your sinful nature, God made you alive with Christ. He forgave us all our sins, having canceled the written code

[Old Testament] with its regulations, that was against us and that stood opposed to us; he took it away, nailing it to the cross" (Colossians 2:11-14).

This scripture refers to someone with faith and a form of circumcision not performed by men, which would eliminate babies and baptism which is performed by men.

Further, whenever the apostles argued with Jewish Christians not to circumcise their babies as a religious rite, never did he tell them to baptize their babies instead (Acts 15:1-21; 1st Corinthians 7:17-20; Galatians 2:3-5; 5:1-12; 6:12-16).

Never in the scriptures is there a story saying directly that a baby was baptized. None. Preachers who practice this will say it is inferred when entire households were baptized. But if you investigate these, you will find those entire households also believed. Can infants believe?

The scripture most cited for infant baptism is in the Old Testament where David said in Psalm 51:5, "Surely I was sinful at birth, sinful from the time my mother conceived me."

David had just had to admit he had committed adultery and she was now pregnant. It nearly killed him. And while he was at it, he referred to the adulterous situation under which his lineage was born, as though "It has happened again."

Why? Because Deuteronomy 23:2, part of the Law of Moses David lived under, says, "No one born of a forbidden marriage nor any of his descendants may enter the assembly of the Lord, even down to the tenth generation." What was a forbidden marriage? Among others, it was one between a father and daughter-in-law (Leviticus 18:15).

Genesis 38 says that Judah's son married Tamar and then died. But for various reasons, his brothers refused to carry on their deceased brother's name as commanded in Deuteronomy 24:5-10. So she dressed up like a prostitute, and when Judah, newly widowed, saw her, he went to bed with her. As a result, she had an illegitimate son named Perez, David's ancestor.

Matthew 1:3-6 gives the lineage of David. Counting the generations between Perez and David reveals it to be ten generations. (Remember Deuteronomy 23:2 explaining he couldn't enter the assembly?) In this sense, David was conceived in sin. (And, by the way, it was his son, Solomon of the 11th generation who built the temple.)

All babies and little children are as saved as adult Christians. Hebrews 1:14 says, "Are not all angels ministering spirits sent to serve those who will inherit salvation?" And Jesus himself said in Matthew 18:10, " 'See that you do not look down on one of these little ones. For I tell you that their angels in heaven always see the face of my Father in heaven.' " Did he say only baptized children? Never.

Further, Jesus said in Matthew 19:14, "Let the little children come to me, and do not hinder them, for the kingdom of heaven belongs to such as these." He did not say, for the kingdom of heaven belongs to children after they are baptized. He said the kingdom of heaven right now belongs to them.

Never did David believe a baby was doomed to hell. This psalm was written when he found out Bathsheba was pregnant by him outside of wedlock. The account of that event is in 2 Samuel 11 and 12. After the baby was born, he got sick and died seven days later, too early to be scripturally circumcised. Did David believe his uncircumcised baby went to hell? No. He said, "'Can I bring him back again? I will go to him, but he will not return to me' " (2nd Samuel 12:23).

About Book I:
WORSHIP CHANGES SINCE
THE FIRST CENTURY

Trace the exact date changes were made in church worship since the first century. These changes were mostly led by popes who had bought their office, led armies against people rejecting them, and had questionable relationships.

Trace the protesters since the second century and the persecution they endured, often being burned at the stake.

Discover the hymns we sing still today written by the protesters, sometimes just hours before their torturous death.

Then be challenged to go forward! Back to the Bible. Be challenged to get rid of denominationalism and unite only in Christ with our only headquarters being in heaven.

Can it be done? Christian unity? Read this, and make the challenge your own.

Thank You

Thank you for reading my book! I'm so honored that you chose to spend your precious time with my research. You are appreciated. I'm an independent author who relies on my readers to help spread the word about stories you enjoy. Would you take a few minutes to let your friends know on Facebook, Pinterest... wherever you go online?

Also, each honest review at online retailers means a lot to me and helps other readers know if this is a book they might enjoy,

I welcome contact from readers. At my website (below), you can do so. You can also sign up for my newsletter (below) to be notified of half-price books and new releases

Buy Your Next Book Now

Connect With The Author

Website: **https://inspirationsbykatheryn.com**

Facebook: **bit.ly/FacebooksKatherynMaddoxHaddad**

Linkedin: **http://bit.ly/KatherynLinkedin**

Twitter: **https://twitter.com/KatherynHaddad**

Pinterest: **https://www.pinterest.com/haddad1940/**

Goodreads:
https://www.goodreads.com/katherynmaddoxhaddad

Get A Free Book
Sign up for Katheryn's monthly newsletter with half-price books for the whole family and insider tips on what's coming next.
http://bit.ly/katheryn

Join My Dream Team
Members get the first peek at my newest book and have fun offering me advice sometimes. I have a point system of rewards for helping me get the word out. Check it out here: **http://bit.ly/KatherynsDreamTeam**

ENDNOTES

ENDNOTES FOR CH. 1 ~
DARE-TO-CARE WORSHIP

1. *Wikipedia,* "Weekly church Attendance Statistics"

2. *Social Liberty,* "Life in England in the 16th and 17th century"

3. *The Literary Digest,* 1929, "Male church Attendance Dropped in the Twenties: Religious Faith Wanes in the Age of Disillusion"

4. *Click Magazine,* "World War Two Brought the Americans Back to church", December 1942, pg. 20

5. *Los Angeles Times,* "Keeping the Faithful" special to the times by David Silver.

6. *US Catholic,* "Returning Vets: Nobody Knows the Trouble I've Seen", October 2012

7. *Cornel Chronicle,* Cornel University, "No Atheists In Foxholes: WW II Vets Remain Religious", May 2013

8. *Christian Century,* "Why Do Men Stay Away?", October 2011

9. *Aspen Education,* "Entitlement: Narcissistic and Entitled to Everything! Does Gen Y Have Too Much Self-Esteem?"

10. The Blaze online publication for Glenn Beck's radio and television series, January 16, 2013, "Beck Takes On the Entitlement Generation"

11. Suzan Myhre, M.S.S.W., LICSW, LPC, Practical Family Living: Entitlement, Money and Families, Winter 2009, Vol. 16, Issue 1.

12. Roof, Wade Clark, *A Generation of Seekers: Spiritual Journeys of the Baby Boom Generation,"* Harper San Francisco, 1993.

13. Twenge, Jean M. and W. Keith Campbell, *The Narcissism Epidemic: Living in the Age of Entitlement,* 2009, http://www.narcissmepidemic.com/aboutbook.html

14. Myhre, Suzan, op cit.

15. Wolfe, Thomas, *Look Homeward Angel,* Simon and Schuster, 1977.

16. Llewellyn, Richard, *How Green Was My Valley,* Simon and Schuster, 1997 (reprint).

17. McAdams, Dan, *Intimacy: The Need to be Close,* Doubleday, 1989.

18. Rosen, Margaret, "All Alone," *Ladies Home Journal,* June 1991.

19. Kraft, Vickie, *The Influential Woman,* Word Publishing, 1992.

20. Patterson, James and Peter Kim, *The Day America Told the Truth,* Plume, 1992.

21. Bubna, Donald L. and Sarah Ricketts, *Building People Through a Caring Sharing Fellowship,* Tyndale House Publishers, Inc., 1983, p.9.

22. Thompson, James, *Our Life Together,* Journey Books, 1997, pg. 8.

23. Thompson, James, *Our Life Together,* pg. 16-17.

24. *The Holy Bible, New International Version,* International Bible Society, 1973 [and all future Bible references unless otherwise specified].

25. Thompson, James, *Our Life Together,* pg. 134.

26. Flach, Frederic F., M.D., *The Secret Strength of Depression,* J. B. Lippincott company, 1974, pg. 128-129.

27. Kim, Peter, *The Day America Told the Truth,* pg. 71, 76.

28. Flach, Frederic, *The Secret Strength of Depression*, pg. 182.

29. Patterson, James, *The Day America Told the Truth*, pg. 133.

30. Flach, Frederic, *The Secret Strength of Depression*, pg. 27.

31. Flach, Frederic, *The Secret Strength of Depression*, pg. 36.

32. Tippens, Darryl, "Rediscovering Christian Worship," *21st Century Christian Magazine*, December 1991, pg. 19.

33. Kahoe, R.D. & Dunn, R.F., "The Fear of Death and Religious Attitudes and Behavior", Journal for the Scientific Study of Religion, 1976, 14 (4), pg. 379-382.

34 . Wink, P., "Who Is "Afraid of Death? Religiousness, Spirituality, and Death Anxiety in Late Adulthood", Journal of Religion, Spirituality, & Aging, 2006, 18 (2), pg. 93-110.

35. Clifton, Jim, Gallup Chairman and CEO, and Deepak Chopra, M.D., "The Fear Factor: How Scared Are People", May 15, 2013.

363636. "Letter of the Smyrnaeans," Lightfoot, J. B., Translator and Editor, *The Apostolic Fathers*, Baker Book House, 1965, pg. 109-110.

37. *The Apostolic Fathers*, "To the Corinthians" by Clement of Rome, pg. 39.

38. *Apostolic Fathers*, "An Ancient Homily by an Unknown Author," pg. 49.

39. *Apostolic Fathers*, "The Epistle to Diognetus," pg. 251-257.

ENDNOTES FOR FOR CH. 2 ~ THE BAFFLING BIBLE

[1].. Harris, Stephen R. Harris [Lt Cmdr] with James C. Hefley, *My Anchor Held,* Old Tappan, NJ: Revell, 1970.

[2].. *Voice of the Martyrs*, http://www.persecution.net/af-2011-04-14.htm, April 14, 2011

[3].. Myrvold, Kristina (2010). *The Death of Sacred Texts: Ritual Disposal and Renovation of Texts in World.* Farnham Surrey England: Ashgate Publishing. pp. 31–57.

[4].. Disposing of the sheets of Quran, ourdialogue.com, reprint from Our Dialogue Q&A series, Adil Salahi, *Arab News*, Jeddah

[5].. *The Holy Quran*, translated by Abdullah Ysuf Ali, Goodword Books, New Delhi, India, 2003[6].. "Six Christians killed in Pakistan over Koran 'insult' ", Persecutionbd.org, August 2009, webpage: Persec-insult

[7].. McDonald, William J., Editor in Chief, New Catholic Encyclopedia, 1966, McGraw-Hill Book Company, pg. 514.

[8].. *Catholic Cyclopedia*, 1960, Vol. 2, pg. 250 and 261

[9].. Forbush, William B., Editor, *Fox's Book of Martyrs*, Zondervan Publishing House, Grand Rapids, MI., 1968, pp. 135-139.

[10].. *New Catholic Encyclopedia*, pg. 514.

[11].. *New Catholic Encyclopedi*a, pg. 451

[12].. *Fox's Book of Martyrs*, pg. 144-146

[13].. *Fox's Book of Martyrs*, pg. 190-191

[14].. *Fox's Book of Martyrs*, pg. 191

[15].. *Fox's Book of Martyrs*, p. 193-194

[16].. *Fox's Book of Martyrs*, pg. 195

[17].. *Fox's Book of Martyrs*, pg. 94

[18].. *Fox's Book of Martyrs*, pg. 46

[19].. *Fox's Book of Martyrs*, pg. 102-103
[20].. *Fox's Book of Martyrs*, pg. 166-168
[21].. *Fox's Book of Martyrs*, pg. 199-200
[22].. *Fox's Book of Martyrs*, pg. 209-210
[23].. *Fox's Book of Martyrs*, pg. 210-211
[24].. *Fox's Book of Martyrs*, pg. 230
[25].. *Fox's Book of Martyrs*, pg. 240-249
[26].. *Fox's Book of Martyrs*, pg. 261-262
[27].. *Fox's Book of Martyrs*, pg. 275-279
[28].. *Fox's Book of Martyrs*, pg. 172-173
[29].. *Fox's Book of Martyrs*, pg. 64-67
[30].. *Fox's Book of Martyrs*, pg. 173
[31].. *Fox's Book of Martyrs*, pg. 174-475
[32].. *Fox's Book of Martyrs*, pg. 174-175
[33].. *Fox's Book of Martyrs*, pg. 263
[34].. *Fox's Book of Martyrs*, pg. 94-100
[35].. *Fox's Book of Martyrs*, pg. 108-110
[36].. Campbell, Alexander, Editor, *Millennial Harbinger*, 1833, *Confessions of a Regular Baptist,* by Thomas [No Last Name], December 1833, pg. 588-589
[37].. Halley, Henry H., *Pocket Bible Handbook*, Henry Halley Pub., Chicago, 1952, p. 714
[38].. *Pocket Bible Handbook*, pg. 738
[39].. Barna, George, *What Americans Believe*, Regal Books, Ventura, Ca., 1991, pg. 210
[40].. Barna, pg. 206
[41].. Rutledge, Howard and Phyllis, *In the Presence of Mine Enemies 1965-1973: A Prisoner of War*, Fleming Revel, New Jersey, 1973, pg. 34-37
[42].. Ferguson, Everett, *Early Christians Speak: Faith and Life in the First Three Centuries*, "The Christian Assemblies," Sweet Publishing, Austin, 1981, p. 67-68
[43].. Ferguson, p. 82
[44].... *Ibid*

ENDNOTES FOR CH. 3 — PLAY-BY-PLAY PRAYER

[1]. Barna, George, *What Americans Believe*, Regal Books, Calif., 1991, pg. 207
[2]. Barna, p. 213
[3] Matthew 7:7
[4]. Parker, Dr. William and Elaine St. Johns, *Prayer Can Change Your Life*, Prentice-Hall, N.J., 1968, pg. xv.
[5]. Parker, pg. 20-21
[6]. Parker, pg. 34
[7]. Lightfoot, J. B., Editor, *The Apostolic Fathers*, "The Letter of the Smyrnaeans on the

Martyrdom of S. Polycarp," v. 9-14, Baker Book House, Grand Rapids, 1965, pg. 112-114

[8]. *The Windsor Star*, "Cuban Youth Renewing Their Ties to the church," by Anita Snow, January 10, 1998, Windsor, Ontario, Canada.

[9]. Barna, pg. 234

[10]. Ferguson, Everett, *Early Christian Speak: Faith and Life in the First Three Centuries*, Sweet Publishing, Austin, 1971, pg. 81

[11]. Ferguson, p. 82

[12]. Ibid.

ENDNOTES FOR CH. 4 – THOSE BORING ANNOUNCEMENTS

[1]. Barna, George, *What Americans Believe*, Regal Books, Calif., 1991, pg. 182

[2]. Barna, pg. 185

[3]. Barna, pg. 234-235

[4]. Barna, pg. 257

[5]. Barna, pg. 277-279

[6]. Roof, Wade Clark, *A Generation of Seekers: The Spiritual Journeys of the Baby Boom Generation*, HarperSanFrancisco, 1993, pg. 78

[7]. Roof, pg. 81

[8]. Roof, pg. 91

[9]. Roof, pg. 157-160

[10]. Roof, p. 183

[11]. Roof, pg. 187

[12]. Roof, pg. 193

[13]. Roof, pg. 204

[14]. Roof, pg. 235-236

[15]. Roof, pg. 246

[16]. *Collected Verse of Edgar A. Guest*, Contemporary Books, Inc., Chicago, 1934 (Publishing company no longer exists).

[17]. Jones, E. Stanley, *The Christ of the Indian Road*, Abingdon Press, Nashville, 1925, p. 122

[18]. Ferguson, Everett, *Early Christians Speak*, Sweet Publishing, Austin, 1971, p. 208

[19]. Ferguson, p. 207

[20]. *Ibid.*

[21]. Ferguson, p. 208

[22]. Ferguson, pg. 208-209

[23]. Ferguson, pg. 81-82

[24]. Ferguson, p. 69

[25]. Ferguson, p. 210

ENDNOTES FOR CH. 5 —
LAST SUPPER OR LOST SUPPER?

[1]. Campbell, Alexander, *The Millennial Harbinger,*"Extra on the Breaking of the Loaf," pg. 74-82

[2]. Sine, Tom, *The Mustard Seed Conspiracy*, Word Books, Waco, 1981, p. 167

[3]. *THE BIBLE*, ISAIAH 53:4; 2 THESALONIANS 1:8-9 — Yet it was our grief he bore, our sorrows that weighed him down. And we thought his troubles were a punishment from God, for his own sins!....Those who refuse to know God and refuse to obey the Message [what
Jesus did for them] will pay for what they've done. Eternal exile from the presence of [God] and his splendid power is their sentence.

[4]. *THE BIBLE*, MATTHEW 8:12 [NIV] — But the subject of the kingdom will be thrown outside into the darkness where there will be weeping and gnashing of teeth.

[5]. *THE BIBLE*, LUKE 23:33-34 — When they got to the place called Skull Hill, they crucified him, along with the criminals, one on his right, the other on his left. Jesus prayed, "Father, forgive them; they don't know what they're doing."

[6]. *THE BIBLE*, MATTHEW 26:41b; 2 CORINTHIANS 12:10; 13:4 [NIV] -The spirit is willing, but the body is weak. That is why, for Christ's sake, I delight in weaknesses...For when I am weak, then I am strong....He was crucified in weakness, yet he lives by God's power.

[7]. *THE BIBLE*, JOHN 12:46 — I am Light that has come into the world so that all who believe in me won't have to stay any longer in the dark.

[8]. *THE BIBLE*, HEBREWS 5:8 — Though he was God's Son, he learned trusting obedience by what he suffered, just as we do.

[9]. *THE BIBLE*, JOHN 10:30 — I and the Father are one heart and mind.

[10]. *THE BIBLE*, MATTHEW 4:1-11 (Jesus' temptation after his baptism at the beginning of his three years of preaching.)

[11]. *THE BIBLE*, REVELATION 1:18 — Don't fear: I am First, I am Last, I'm Alive, I died, but I came to life, and my life is now forever. See these keys in my hand? They open and lock Death's doors, they open and lock Hell's gates.

[12]. Ferguson, Everett, *Early Christians Speak*, Sweet Publishing, Austin, 1971, p. 94

[13]. Ferguson, p. 93-94

[14]. Ferguson, p. 67

[15]. Ferguson, p. 94

[16]. Forbush, William B., Editor, *Fox's Book of Martyrs*, Zondervan Publishing House, Grand Rapids, 1968, p. 275-276

[17]. *Fox's Book of Martyrs*, p. 74-75

[18]. *Fox's Book of Martyrs*, p. 113-114

[19] Ferguson, p. 196

ENDNOTES FOR CH. 6 ~
UNEXPLOITED GIVERS

[1]. Gallup, George Jr., and Jim Castelli, *The People's Religion: American Faith in the '90s*, McMillan, New York, 1989, pg. 137-138.
[2]. Barna, George, *Never On a Sunday*, Barna Research Group, 1990, Glendale, Calif., p. 3-4.
[3]. Patterson, James and Peter Kim, *The Day America Told the Truth*, Plume, 1992, pg. 143.
[4]. Strobel, Lee, *Inside the Mind of Unchurched Harry and Mary*, Zondervan Publishing House, Grand Rapids, MI., 1993, pg. 206.
[5]. *The Holy Bible*, New International Version, Zondervan Bible Publishers, Grand Rapids, MI, 1988. [All quotations of the Bible except otherwise indicated]
[6]. Miller, Timothy, *How to Want What You Have*, Henry Holt, 1995, pg. 39.
[7]. Taylor, Kenneth, translator *The Living Bible*, Tyndale House Publishers, Inc., Wheaton, IL, 1962.
[8]. *The Living Bible*, ibid.
[9]. Ferguson, Everett, *Early Christians Speak*, Sweet Publishing Company, Austin, 1971, pg. 67.
[10]. Ferguson, *Early Christians Speak*, pg. 195.
[11]. Ferguson, *Early Christians Speak*, pg. 82.
[12]. Cruse, Christian Frederick, Translator, *The Ecclesiastical History of Eusebius Pamphilus, Bishop of Caesarea in Palestine*, Baker Book House, Grand Rapids, MI., 1971, pg. 160.
[13]. Ferguson, Everett, *Early Christians Speak*, pg. 209.
[14]. Ferguson, Everett, *Early Christians Speak*, pg. 209.

ENDNOTES FOR CH. 7 ~ SPIRITUALITY OR RELIGIOUS FIX?

[1]. *Vancouver Sun* reprinted in *The Windsor Star*, Todd, Douglas, "The Rapture of Islam's Sufis," August 23, 1997.
[2]. Shadid, Anthony, *The Windsor Star*, "Islam's Changing Face," The Associated Press, January 25, 1997.
[3]. Prabhavananda, Swami and Frederick Manchester, editors, *The Upanishads: Breath of the Eternal*, The New American Library, The Mentor Religious Classics, New York, 1960, pg. 40
[4]. Burtt, E. A., Editor, *The Teachings of the Compassionate Buddha*, The New American Library, Mentor Religious Classics, New York, 1958, pg. 106
[5]. *Encyclopedia Britannica*, "Tongues, Gift of," Vol. 22, William Benton Publisher, Chicago, pg. 288.
[6]. Cruse, Christian Frederick, *The Ecclesiastical History of Eusebius Pamphilus*, Baker Book House, Grand Rapids, 1971, pg. 196-197
[7]. *Ibid*, pg. 199
[8]. Ironside, H. A., Holiness: *The False and the Truth*, Loizeaux Brothers, Neptune, New Jersey, 1964
[8]. Ferguson, Everett, *Early Christians Speak*, Sweet Publishing Co., Austin, pg. 193
[9]. *Ibid*, p. 194
[10]. *Ibid*, p. 24

ENDNOTES FOR CH. 8 ~
MUSIC AND THE MASK

[1]. Clark, Adam, Commentary

[2]. Hadas, Moses, *Great Ages of Man: Imperial Rome*, Time Inc., New York, 1965, pg. 51

[3]. *Ibid*, pg. 103

[4]. *Ibid*, pg. 134

[5]. *Ibid*, pg. 58-59

[6]. McDonald, William J., *New Catholic Encyclopedia*, "Choir," pg. 621, "Music, Sacred," pg. 129-131

[7]. D'Aubigne, J. H. Merle, *History of the Reformation of the Sixteenth Century*, The Religious Tract Society, London, pg. 376-377

[8]. Spurgeon, Charles H., *The Metropolitan Tabernacle Pulpit During the Year 1881*, Vol. XXVII, Pilgrim Publications, Pasadena, 1973, pg. 483

[9]. Halley, Henry H., *Pocket Bible Handbook*, Henry H. Halley Publisher, Chicago, 1952, pg. 740-741

[10]. Wells, H. G. *The Outline of History*, Garden City Books, NY, Book 6, Ch.28, Pg.448

[11]. McDonald, William J., *New Catholic Encyclopedia*, McGraw-Hill, Chicago, 1962, pg. 129-131, 746

[12]. Ferguson, Everett, *Early Christians Speak*, Sweet Publishing Co., Austin, 1971, pg. 161

[14]. George, David L., *The Family Book of Best Loved Poems*, Hanover House, Garden City, NY, 1952, pg. 465-466

[15]. Ferguson, pg. 81

[16]. *Ibid*, pg. 82

[17]. *Ibid*.

[18]. Roberts, Alexander, Ed, *Ante-Nicean Fathers*, Vol. II, Hendrickson Publishers, 1994.

[19]. Carrol, Dave, *All the Lonely People: A Concert is Rarely What it Seems to Be*, September 14, 2012, http://bigearcreations.blogspot.ca/2012/09

ENDNOTES FOR CH. 9 ~
BAPTISM: WHAT IN THE WORLD FOR?

[1]. Campbell, Alexander, *Millinneal Harbinger*, Extra on Baptism, October 10, 1831, pg. 44

[2]. Campbell, Alexander, *Millineal Harbinger*, Extra on Baptism, October 10, 1831, pg. 45

[3]. Campbell, Alexander, *Millinneal Harbinger*, Extra on Baptism, 1830

[4]. Ibid.

[5]. Thayer, Joseph H., *Thayer's Greek-English Lexicon of the New Testament*, Zondervan Publishing House, Grand Rapids, 1974, pg. 94

[6]. *Catholic Encyclopedia*, Vol. II, 1967, pg. 261-262

[7]. Ferguson, Everett, *Early Christians Speak*, Sweet Publishing, Austin, 1971, pg. 50

[8]. *Encyclopedia Britannica*, Vol. III, William Benton, Publisher, Chicago, pg. 139

[9]. *Ibid*, Vol. IX, pg. 529

[10]. Ferguson, pg. 33
[11]. *Ibid.*
[12]. *Ibid,* pg. 34
[13]. *Ibid,* pg. 34-35
[14]. *Ibid,* pg. 35
[15]. *Ibid.* pg. 36
[16]. *Ibid,* pg. 45
[17]. *Ibid.*
[18]. *Ibid.*
[19]. *Ibid.,* pg. 46
[20]. *Ibid.*
[21]. *Ibid.,* pg. 34
[22]. *Ibid.,* pg. 46
[23]. *Ibid.*
[24] Campbell, Alexander, *Millennial Harbinger,* "Extra on Baptism," Published by Editor, 1830, pg. 47-50
[25]. Richardson, Robert, *Memoirs of Alexander Campbell,* Vol. II, pg. 314-316
[26]. Richardson, Vol. II, pg. 374-376
[27]. Richardson, Vol. II, pg. 206-220
[28]. Richardson, Vol. II, pg. 113-115
[29]. Ferguson,
[30]. Ferguson, pg. 93
[31]. *Ibid.,* pg. 94